From silent screen to multi-screen

A history of cinema exhibition
in Britain since 1896

STUART HANSON

Manchester University Press
Manchester and New York

distributed exclusively in the USA by Palgrave

Published by Manchester University Press
Oxford Road, Manchester M13 9NR, UK
and Room 400, 175 Fifth Avenue, New York, NY 10010, USA
www.manchesteruniversitypress.co.uk

Distributed exclusively in the USA by
Palgrave, 175 Fifth Avenue, New York,
NY 10010, USA

Distributed exclusively in Canada by
UBC Press, University of British Columbia, 2029 West Mall,
Vancouver, BC, Canada V6T 1Z2

British Library Cataloguing-in-Publication Data
A catalogue record for this book is available from the British Library

Library of Congress Cataloging-in-Publication Data applied for

ISBN   978 0 7190 6944 4 *hardback*
ISBN   978 0 7190 6945 1 *paperback*

First published 2007

16 15 14 13 12 11 10 09 08 07   10 9 8 7 6 5 4 3 2 1

Edited and typeset by
Frances Hackeson Freelance Publishing Services, Brinscall, Lancs
Printed in Great Britain by
Biddles Ltd, King's Lynn

STUDIES IN
POPULAR
CULTURE

There has in recent years been an explosion of interest in culture and cultural studies. The impetus has come from two directions and out of two different traditions. On the one hand, cultural history has grown out of social history to become a distinct and identifiable school of historical investigation. On the other hand, cultural studies has grown out of English literature and has concerned itself to a large extent with contemporary issues. Nevertheless, there is a shared project, its aim, to elucidate the meanings and values implicit and explicit in the art, literature, learning, institutions and everyday behaviour within a given society. Both the cultural historian and the cultural studies scholar seek to explore the ways in which a culture is imagined, represented and received, how it interacts with social processes, how it contributes to individual and collective identities and world views, to stability and change, to social, political and economic activities and programmes. This series aims to provide an arena for the cross-fertilisation of the discipline, so that the work of the cultural historian can take advantage of the most useful and illuminating of the theoretical developments and the cultural studies scholars can extend the purely historical underpinnings of their investigations. The ultimate objective of the series is to provide a range of books which will explain in a readable and accessible way where we are now socially and culturally and how we got to where we are. This should enable people to be better informed, promote an interdisciplinary approach to cultural issues and encourage deeper thought about the issues, attitudes and institutions of popular culture.

Jeffrey Richards

For Lois, James, Fraser and Cameron – I hope that you all have the
opportunity to enjoy the thrill of the big screen.
And Linda with love

Contents

The show is over and we creep into the dull
Blaze of mid-afternoon sunshine, the hollow dole
Of the real descends on everything and we can know
That we have been in some place wholly elsewhere, a night
At noonday, not without dreams, whose portals shine
(Not ivory, not horn in ever-changing shapes)

John Hollander, *Movie-Going*

General editor's foreword

Today more people than ever before are watching films. But they are not always watching them in cinemas. The experience of cinema-going is unique and that experience is the subject of this excellent book. The exhibition of films has developed from a lowly fairground attraction in the 1890s to the multi-million pound industry of today. That process of evolution is carefully charted by Stuart Hanson from the establishment of cinema-going as an essential leisure experience by the time of the First World War through the growth of cinema chains in the 1920s, the impact of the arrival of sound in the 1930s, the heyday of cinema-going in the 1940s (with 1946 as the all-time peak year of British cinema attendance), the steady decline of cinema-going in the 1950s, the acceleration of that decline in the 1960s to the dramatic revival of cinema-going in the 1980s with the rise of the multiplex. Every phase of this history is examined, analysed and explained.

But this book is far more than just a chronological account of the cinema exhibition industry, valuable though that is in itself. It is a broad-based social and cultural examination of the whole phenomenon of cinema-going. One of the critics cited by Hanson compares the building of the picture palaces in the twentieth century to the creation of the Gothic cathedrals in the Middle Ages, both building types allowing the masses a glimpse of heaven. To explain this, Hanson investigates the role of cinema-going in everyday life, exploring issues of gender, age and class in the mass audience. He looks at cinema design, changes in technology, marketing strategies, government regulation, the role of cinema in the dissemination of propaganda, censorship and moral panics, American competition to the British film industry and the debate about the Americanisation of society. Thoroughly researched, immensely readable, a model of intelligent and insightful analysis, this is a comprehensive and valuable study of a vital aspect of British popular culture.

Jeffrey Richards

Acknowledgements

I am indebted to many people who have helped me in the course of writing this book; first and foremost to Miranda Robinson and Mark Erickson who both read through drafts and whose incisive comments and suggestions were an enormous help.

I would also like to thank my former colleagues at the Department of Cultural Studies and Sociology at The University of Birmingham, especially Jan Campbell, Beth Edginton, Ann Gray, Michael Green, Nuala Killeen, Jorge Larrain, David Parker, Frank Webster and Helen Wood, all of whom helped provide the supportive academic atmosphere in which this book was nurtured. It is therefore tragic that the University of Birmingham chose to close the department in 2002; apparently unable or unwilling to see the value of both its staff and students.

Most of this study was completed while I was a lecturer at the University of Wolverhampton, where I enjoyed the support of a great many colleagues. In particular I would like to thank Alan Apperley, with whom I have enjoyed a working relationship of immense satisfaction and Lisa Taylor, who listened patiently to my excuses for having not written anything 'for a while'.

Professor Jeffrey Richards deserves very special thanks for his constant support and encouragement, along with the editorial staff of Manchester University Press.

My lifetime interest in the cinema was engendered by my parents; Barrie and Hilda who let me go off as a child to the cinemas of Birmingham on Saturday and Sundays. The films have faded from memory but the cinemas have not: the Plaza, Stockland Green; the Beaufort, Ward End; the Palace, Erdington; the Odeon, New Street and especially the Gaumont, Steelhouse Lane.

Finally, I must thank my wife Linda without whose love and support I would not have considered starting this book let alone finishing it.

Tables

Introduction

This book charts the development of cinema exhibition and cinema-going in Britain from the first public film screening – the Lumière Brothers' showing of their Cinématographe show at London's Regent Street Polytechnic in February 1896 – through to the opening of 30-screen 'megaplexes' such as Birmingham's Star City. In 1896 there were no permanent buildings dedicated to the showing of moving pictures in Britain: by the start of the Second World War there were approximately 4,800 cinemas. As the Second World War ended there were 1.6 billion admissions annually as over three-quarters of the population attended the cinema at least once a year, and one-third once a week or more. By 1984, however, cinema attendance stood at 54 million admissions per year, having fallen every year from 1946, as three-quarters of the adult population did *not* attend the cinema at all. It was at this point, which would be the nadir of cinema-going as a public entertainment that the downward spiral of cinema attendance was reversed with the introduction of the first multiplex cinema in 1985.

In part the existence of cinema is the result of an array of technological developments going back arguably to the sixteenth century with the camera obscura and encompassing the development of celluloid film and its projection to a large audience. It is also the result of the efforts to create spaces for the public exhibition of moving images; grand spaces which have embraced and reflected the great modernist project of the twentieth century. Hansen argues that cinema was integral to the notion of 'modern life' with all of its upheavals and sensuous pleasures:

> In this context the cinema figures as part of the violent restructuring of human perception and interaction effected by industrial-capitalist modes of production and exchange; by modern technologies such as trains, photography, electric lighting, telegraph, and telephone; and by the large-scale construction of metropolitan streets populated with anonymous crowds, prostitutes, and not-quite-so anonymous flâneurs.[1]

Nevertheless, this study is not, it is hoped, *just* about technology or *just* about cinemas. Such a story would be over-deterministic. On the contrary it seeks to place the development of cinema in a broad social, economic, cultural and political context. For as Belton observes: '[t]he identity of the cinema as an institution remains bound up with the sociocultural conditions in which it was conceived and developed by the growing film industry and in which it was experienced and consumed by an emerging society of habitual moviegoers'.[2]

To this end the book adopts a chronological structure. Chapter 1 recounts the beginnings of cinema and in particular its rapid development, by the eve of the Great War, as the pre-eminent mass entertainment. By the second decade of the twentieth century the cinema began to establish itself as an independent entertainment, occupying initially any building that could be found and later, from around 1910 onwards, purpose-built premises. This chapter considers these developments, examining the positioning of cinemas within the burgeoning metropolitan spaces, the associated search for artistic respectability and a large-scale audience.

The period from 1913 to 1930, considered in Chapter 2, was one in which the cinema industry underwent dramatic restructuring as cinemas grew in size and sophistication and new chains emerged. The late 1920s also witnessed perhaps the most momentous technological development since the development of moving pictures: that of synchronised sound or what quickly became known as the 'talkies'. It was also a time when Hollywood substantially increased its presence in British cinemas, despite various attempts to bolster British film production and exhibition such as the efforts to establish quotas for British films. With this perceived domination of Hollywood came an increasing cultural and ideological alarm about US films. This was itself part of a wider concern surrounding the commercialisation of culture and the function of the cinema as a leisure activity.

Chapter 3 examines the period from 1930 until immediately after the Second World War, which has been represented by many observers as a 'Golden Age' for the British cinema industry. In the period between the two world wars cinema-going became what A. J. P. Taylor called 'the essential social habit of the age',[3] when the dream palaces that became synonymous with cinema were built. An American anthropologist Hortense Powdermaker coined the phrase 'dream factory' when describing the new Hollywood studios and the notion of a symbiotic relationship between dreams and cinema was firmly embedded in popular thought by the end of the 1930s.[4] Ben Hall spoke of 'an acre of seats in a garden of dreams'[5] while the poet Cecil Day Lewis wrote of entering the 'dream-house'.[6] By the beginning of the Second World War cinema-going had become the most popular form of indoor recreation. Moreover, although overwhelmingly a working-class leisure form the cinema had broadened its appeal and respectability. Here cinema-going will be critically analysed in the context of two powerful myths; the 'Golden Age' and the 'universal audience'. Cinema-going in this period was heavily biased towards certain age and social groups.[7]

Chapter 4 will consider the state of cinema exhibition in Britain in the aftermath of the Second World War and on into the 1950s. From 1946, some fifty years after its invention, cinema-going began to decline, becoming increasingly less important in the lives of people than other forms of leisure. Structural problems, precipitated by war and a subsequent lack of investment, would be compounded by social and cultural change on a vast scale. As Pavesi argues, the 1950s to 1960s was a time of crisis for the cinema, which needs to be 'applied to socio-cultural processes and phenomena which go far beyond the specifics of one industry'.[8] Chief amongst these socio-cultural processes was the demographic change amongst Britain's traditional cinema audience: the urban working class. This decline in audiences is discussed in the context of *both* a transformation in the make-up of post-war society, and the development of television. The widely perceived causal relationship between the growth of television and the decline of cinema-going will be evaluated critically, highlighting the ways in which this is open to challenge. What is less contested are the contemporary anxieties expressed about television, especially how it was perceived as undermining the public consumption of images in favour of a more privatised consumption. These contemporary fears, expressed by those both within the cinema industry and outside, around television and its challenge to the collectivity of the cinema, will be examined.

Chapter 5 considers what appeared to be the terminal decline of cinema-going from the 1960s until 1984 (the eve of the first multiplex opening). In doing so we will need to examine the extent to which a shifting population, allied to changes in the nature of the family, undermined a cinema industry that would become more obsessed with television and less concerned to adapt to its audience and their expectations. The impact of television and associated domestic viewing technologies such as video cassette recorders (VCRs) on the cinema is both complex and contested. Their effect on cinema was by no means a case of one technological visual medium triumphing over another, which was certainly the perception of much of the cinema industry. Moreover, as this study will show, the development of television and the move beyond state monopoly to encompass independent broadcasting, was a source of deep unease for many contemporary intellectuals and cultural commentators. These debates are important because they set the scene for the remarkable resurgence in cinema-going as a direct result of the development of the multiplex.

Chapter 5 also looks at the development of the multiplex in the United States from the 1960s and examines the importance of the shopping mall and the suburb as the main focus for these cinema developments. From these starting points the new multiplex companies consolidated their interests and looked increasingly to other countries in the 1980s, especially Britain. By the mid-1980s the dominance of Hollywood was more or less complete in many world markets and US-based companies felt that along with US films audiences might be drawn to US-style multiplexes.

Chapter 6 examines the development of the multiplex in Britain from the opening of the first purpose-built multiplex cinema, The Point, in Milton Keynes, in 1985. Multiplexes are a new kind of cinema; new in the sense of being conceived and built since the mid-1980s, and new in that they represent a radical divergence from the ways cinema-going has been seen within the social and cultural sphere.[9] The development of the multiplex has run in tandem with a year-on-year increase in cinema admissions.

Chapter 6 also analyses the extent to which the multiplex 'experience' accounts for the increase in overall attendance and questions whether we are seeing a broadening of the cinema-going demographic, as people return to the cinema in greater numbers. In order to encourage the regular cinema-goer keep coming, the irregular cinema-goer to come more often and the people who 'never' go to the cinema to come at all, multiplexes have had to market cinema going as an 'event' and themselves as the best cinema in which to watch a film. To this end one must also consider the location, design and operation of the multiplex cinema.

Cinemas exist to exhibit feature films and, therefore, implicit in the consideration of how cinemas have sought to present themselves are the films that they have to show. Chapter 7, therefore, examines how developments in the marketing of films have run in tandem with developments in the cinema. Though there is still some diversity in the kinds of films exhibited in Britain and independent cinemas still play an important role in maintaining this diversity, it is the Hollywood film which maintains hegemony in cinema distribution and exhibition in Britain. Moreover, though still a minority form in the totality of the cinema infrastructure, the multiplex exerts a disproportionate power in terms of box-office revenues and cinema admissions. The distribution and exhibition of films, and the selection offered by multiplexes reflect a pattern of domination by US multinational film companies that is actually restricting 'choice': the oft-trumpeted primary attraction of the multiplex. The study ends with a consideration of the new developments in digital cinema, particularly digital projection, and with a discussion of the future directions that cinema may take in Britain.

Notes

1   M. B. Hansen, 'America, Paris, the Alps: Kracauer (and Benjamin) on Cinema and Modernity', in L. Charney and V. R. Schwartz (eds), *Cinema and the Invention of Modern Life* (Berkeley, CA: University of California Press, 1995), pp. 362–3.

2   J. Belton, *American Cinema/American Culture*, second edition (New York: McGraw-Hill, 2004), p. 6.

3   A. J. P. Taylor, *English History 1914-1945* (Harmondsworth: Penguin, 1976), p. 392.

4   H. Powdermaker, *Hollywood, the Dream Factory: An Anthropologist Studies the Movie Makers* (Boston, MA: Little, Brown and Company, 1950).

5   B. M. Hall, *The Best Remaining Streets* (New York: Crown, 1975) reprinted in part in I. R. Hark (ed.), *Exhibition: The Film Reader* (London: Routledge, 2002).

6   Cecil Day-Lewis 'Newsreel' (1938).

7   See D. Docherty, D. Morrison and M. Tracey, *The Last Picture Show: Britain's Changing Film Audience* (London: British Film Institute, 1987).

8   P. Pavesi, *European Cinema Yearbook, 1997 edition*, MEDIA Salles, 1997, www.mediasalles.it (accessed September 1998).

9   In order to bring about some unity in the use of the term multiplex, the General Assembly of the Union Internationale des Cinémas (UNIC), the federation of European exhibitors' associations, decided in 1998 unanimously that a cinema has to have eight screens or more to be called a multiplex.

From the fairground to the picture palace: 1896–1913

Film history is not the history of a medium, it is the story of how that medium was transformed by the intervention of a mass audience with its own desires and demands. (Nicholas Hiley)[1]

The chronological and geographical starting point for this book and the story to be told about cinema-going in Britain is the Grand Café on the Boulevard des Capucines in Paris. For it was here on 28 December 1895 that two brothers, Auguste and Louis Lumière, utilising their new invention the Cinématographe, projected a series of photographic images on a roll of celluloid film in rapid succession, onto a screen for a fee-paying audience.[2] The films that were shown included *L'Arrivée d'un train en gare de la Ciotat* (*The arrival of a train in a country station*) which, it is recounted anecdotally, caused the audience to panic and flee as the train approached. As George Reyes observed, 'Suddenly a train appeared. Women cried out with terror. Men threw themselves to one side to avoid being run over. It was panic. And triumph.'[3] What is remarkable about the development of the Cinématographe is the realisation on the part of those first cinema audiences that what they were seeing was a representation of their own world. As Bottomore observed, '[t]he cinema enabled a person to "stand outside himself" and see again an event he had already experienced – an extraordinary idea in the nineteenth century'.[4] It was as if 'this new machine made the real more real than the real itself'.[5]

The popularity of the Cinématographe in Paris and its potential as a new form of public entertainment saw it brought to London in 1896 by a friend of the Lumière brothers called Félicien Trewey. He had appeared in several of their films and was himself a performer familiar to music hall audiences in Britain as an exponent of the shadowgraph. The venue for the first performance was the Great Hall of the Polytechnic Institution, Regent Street, London, which took place on 20 February 1896, for invited members of the press. On the following day Britain's first fee-paying audience, numbering fifty-four people, paid 1s to see the seventeen-minute programme, which included an accompanying lecture. The programme which that first audience saw consisted of a range of French titles, including *L'Arrivée d'un train en gare de la Ciotat*, though later the portability of the Lumière's camera was aptly demonstrated by the shooting of a range of London scenes.[6]

The reaction of many who attended the press screening was extremely favourable. Barnes cites a review by Anna de Bremont in the *St Paul's Magazine* entitled 'Living Photography':

> Of all the marvels that have recently been brought to light in the way of photography the Cinématographe, which reproduces photographs of actual scenes and persons from life – moving, breathing, in fact, living pictures – is the most startling and sensational … It is the most perfect illusion that has heretofore been attempted in photography. Without the aid of any of the usual paraphernalia of the photographer, pictures are thrown on a screen through the medium of the Cinématographe with a realism that baffles description. People move about, enter and disappear, gesticulate, laugh, smoke, eat, drink and perform the most ordinary actions with a fidelity to life that leads one to doubt the evidence of one's senses.[7]

One of the first and most prestigious subjects of the cinematograph (as it was known in Britain) was Queen Victoria, who had been filmed by the Royal Photographer William Downey at Balmoral Castle in October 1896. After a private exhibition of the film for the Queen at Windsor Castle in November 1897, shown on one of Robert Paul's Theatrograph projectors, Victoria herself noted in her diary that it was 'a wonderful process, representing people, their movements and actions, as if they were alive'.[8] Having received the royal seal of approval the medium had come of age as a legitimate form of public entertainment.

However, one must be careful not to isolate the cinema from previous developments in visual entertainments and in particular a series of developments in the public exhibition of images that had a direct influence on the cinema. In her study of cinema and magic lantern culture, Rossell argues that in the nineteenth century audiences would have been familiar with the projected image via magic lanterns, and that it would constitute a 'shared experience' across both this and cinema culture.[9] Thus, the magic lantern was 'not so much a "precursor" of the cinema, as it was the environment into which the cinema was born, the *milieu* which nursed it through its extended period of invention to about 1903, the institution which provided its early business practices'.[10]

Pre-cinema: technological developments

When did cinema *begin?* It is a simple question: yet less simple to answer. Audiences have been viewing projected images as part of public entertainments since the sixteenth century. In 1558 Giambattista della Porta detailed the application of the camera obscura (Latin for 'dark room') in his book *Magiae naturalis*. Samuel Pepys described in his diary for 1666 a demonstration of a device called a 'lanthorn' which made 'strange things appear on a wall'.[11] This forerunner of the magic lantern would be joined in subsequent years by an ever widening range of technological devices and amusements – phantasmagoria, panoramas and dioramas amongst others – that would eventually encompass the development of photography in the 1830s and begin to change peoples' perception of the world. As these technologies developed the illusion of physical movement advanced closer, culminating in the 'moving pictures' of Edison's Kinetoscope in 1893.

All of the devices that presented optical and/or projected images for a viewing public prior to cinema can be seen as pre-cursors in that they were qualitatively different from other forms of visual media. As Herbert points out, they can be considered: '"time-based" visual media: that is the viewer experienced a changing or moving image or scene over a certain time, such as the period needed by the storyteller to narrate his peepshow images or lantern slide set, or the time taken for a visitor to the panorama to walk around the viewing gallery examining the entire scenic canvas'.[12]

Their description as 'pre-cinema' suggests that they introduced technologies, contexts, experiences and sensations that were later incorporated into film and cinema. Although many of the technologies encompassed were subsequently developed in tandem to cinema, conventional history tells us that it was but a short step to the unveiling, literally, of the world's first projected moving image by Auguste and Louis Lumière in 1895.

As Rossell and others suggest, the origins of the cinema are linked to the magic lantern, as devised by the Dutch physicist Christian Huygens in around 1659 and demonstrated in a number of European cities by another Dutch physicist Tomas Rasmussen Walgenstein in around 1662.[13] Christened the 'magic lantern' by Walgenstein its true potential was realised in the latter part of the eighteenth century. The lantern itself was a box that contained a light source and two convex lenses in front of which painted glass plates were placed. The light sources, which got more sophisticated as time progressed, were initially generated by candles. The lantern was itself born out of a contemporary fascination with lenses and was initially felt to have only scientific applications. Lanterns were taken up by a range of itinerant showmen who toured the country putting on shows in a range of venues. Initially, the images were static, though they must have seemed magical to contemporary audiences. Within a short time projectionists were incorporating a second glass side, overlaid onto the first, which could be moved and manipulated, in order to simulate movement.

The developing sophistication and imaginations of the showmen led to the incorporation of the magic lantern into a dramatic form of public entertainment called the phantasmagoria. It was a Belgian showman called Ètienne-Gaspard Robertson who is most associated with the perfection of this entertainment. He exhibited his *Fantasmagorie* in Paris in 1798, though as Heard points out, Robertson was himself inspired by the magic lantern shows of a mysterious German showman called Paul Philidor in around 1790.[14] Much is recorded of Robertson's first shows, which took place in an exhibition room that seems a model for subsequent cinemas. A text entitled *The Wonder of Optics* (1868) by F. Marion described the exhibition room as sixty to eighty feet long and twenty feet wide and blacked out completely.[15] The screen was made of calico and soaked in starch and gum arabic in order that it would become translucent, and stretched out to approximately twenty feet wide. A projector was placed behind the screen so that it would not be visible to the audience, who were thus watching a back projection.

This separating of the projector from audience both allowed the audience an unimpeded view of the screen and rendered the technology invisible. This allowed Robertson to invest the proceedings with considerable mysticism and drama, which he did by utilising a range of other presentation techniques such as a pseudo-scientific lecture-style introduction, the ability to move the projector backwards and forwards in order to make images increase or decrease in size and the use of smoke. Succeeding showmen, depending on their skills, would utilise electricity, pyrotechnics and masks, and even real actors were projected, hidden behind a screen. The subject of Robertson's and others' phantasmagoria ('gathering of ghosts') were stories and images of the supernatural, which Robertson had himself developed in smaller public 'séances' held in a Paris apartment.[16]

As Robertson's reputation grew he moved to a new and larger site in Paris, appropriately located behind a deserted church and graveyard. His presentations got more sophisticated – he claimed he could 'bring the dead back to life' – but it became clear that he was not the sole exponent of this new form of public entertainment. Despite efforts to patent the apparatus, which were ultimately unsuccessful, the phantasmagoria spread and its popularity was prolific. The first phantasmagoria in London was held in the Lyceum Theatre in October 1801 and was presented by Paul de Philipsthal (Paul Philidor using his real name). Heard recounts that the instant success of Philipsthal's show (the number of shows per day was increased) set in train a rapid development in venues and the dissemination out to provincial cities that can be compared with the development of cinema a century or so later.[17]

The phantasmagoria utilised existing rooms and spaces that allowed for large audiences viewing projected images; other developments such as the Panorama and Diorama required specialist buildings. The Panorama required a circular room, later called a rotunda, onto the walls of which were painted linked scenes, with the audience standing at the centre of the room. The Panorama in Edinburgh's Haymarket, painted by Robert Barker in 1789, consisted of a continuous view of Edinburgh as seen from Carlton Hill. It was a great success with spectators and in 1793 he opened a new building in London's Leicester Square, which consisted of three separate viewing rooms. The Panorama was superseded by the Diorama, which utilised the painting but added other effects including magic lanterns and translucent colours.

The Diorama was developed by the Frenchman Louis Daguerre, who subsequently would be most associated with the development of photography, and opened in 1822 in Paris. Unlike the Panorama, which was static and invited the spectator to turn 360 degrees in order to take in the scene, the early Dioramas had the audience revolve around the scenery, which was seen through a proscenium opening. Daguerre opened his first Diorama in Britain in 1823, choosing as its location London's fashionable Regent's Park. Located amidst Nash's Georgian square the great rotunda was designed by the architect Augustus Charles Pugin. In the year of the Great Exhibition of 1851 the most ambitious Diorama was constructed in Leicester Square by one Mr Wylde. Christened the 'Great Globe', Wylde's building incorporated a globe that was sixty feet in diameter along with four exhibition rooms.

McGrath points out that the move from phantasmagoria to the Diorama was a move from the irrational to the rational, with the Diorama's emphasis on the topological and the architectural.[18] In describing the Kineorama, which was a combination of the Panorama's expansiveness and the Diorama's sense of illusion, McGrath sees these new technologies as meaning a 'new and heightened sense of three-dimensionality and visual tangibility'.[19] It would be the Kinetoscope, whose invention is credited to Thomas Alva Edison but now accepted as primarily due to the efforts of his assistant William Kennedy Laurie Dickson that would finally realise the illusion of physical movement in 1893.[20] However, as Crangle argues, the subsequent development of 'moving pictures' did not signal the end of the magic lantern, rather, it signalled a change in the nature of the magic lantern and the context for its utilisation, particularly with the development of the 'slide projector'.[21]

Utilising roll film, brought to the market in 1888, Dickson experimented in an effort to develop moving pictures, based upon the principle of photographing successive phases of motion so as to create the illusion of movement. The camera for photographing the action was called the Kinetograph and the machine for displaying or exhibiting it was called the Kinetoscope. The development of the Kinetoscope in particular was a significant moment in the story of cinema. As Barnes argues 'it is from the Kinetoscope that all subsequent motion picture invention is derived, including the work of the brothers A. and L. Lumière in France'.[22] While the Kinetoscope embodied the principles of moving pictures it did not project images. Rather it was a wooden cabinet containing the mechanism that utilised transmitted light and a lens, viewed through an eyepiece located on top of the cabinet. The machine allowed only one spectator at a time to view the images.

The commercialisation of the Kinetoscope took off with the placing of machines in the Holland Brothers' amusement arcade on New York's Broadway in April 1894. They would be subsequently known as 'Kinetoscope parlours' or 'peep-show parlours'. Initially, patrons paid the proprietor who started up each machine individually. Subsequently they were equipped with slots into which a nickel was placed in order to start up the machine for a fixed period of time. Britain's first peepshow parlour was opened in October 1894 at 70 Oxford Street, London and showed about forty films, each lasting approximately one minute. Though the Kinetograph was the only machine able to make the films for the Kinetoscope and was thus carefully protected by patent, Edison had neglected to patent the Kinetoscope in Britain and Europe. This meant that almost immediately engineers like Robert William Paul set to work making replicas in order to satisfy the demand for the machines. More problematic was the fact that the films made in Edison's studio were carefully copyrighted and supplied only to owners of original Edison machines. Harnessing his experience in making replicas, Paul began to consider how he might make a camera that could produce film strips that were able to be shown on Kinetoscopes. This Paul did and was undertaking trials of his camera at around the same time as the Lumière Brothers were patenting their Cinématographe.[23] Peep-show parlours proliferated in London and in some provincial cities and though initially popular with audiences the enthusiasm for the Kinetoscope lasted for only two years or so.

The legacy and importance of the Kinetoscope's unveiling was that almost immediately inventors from both Europe and the USA began to consider how the peep-show could be developed into an apparatus for projecting images so they could be viewed by an audience. Again, Robert Paul was one of a number of inventors who successfully projected an image, along with two brothers called Skladanowsky who projected a series of 'intermittent photographs' in Berlin's Winter Gardens using their double projector in November 1895.[24] However, the history of cinema as told recognises that moment in Paris in December 1895 when the Lumière Brothers showed a train entering a country station, as the point from which all subsequent developments began.[25]

Spaces and sites of cinema

> If celluloid had been only a fraction more expensive to produce, or just a little more fragile, it would have been impossible for travelling showmen and entertainers to adopt the new moving pictures. The film camera would have remained a scientific instrument, and there would have been no impulse to develop dramatic narrative or to appeal to a mass audience. There would have been film, but not film history as we understand it … It is not the history of the medium of film, but rather the story of how that medium was adapted to the needs of a paying audience.[26]

Edison himself had also recognised the possibilities of adapting his Kinetoscope to project images and on 4 April 1896 he displayed his Vitascope at Koster and Bial's Music Hall on New York's Broadway. The Vitascope used the same rolls of films but projected them onto a canvas screen. The films were introduced to paying customers on 23 April 1896 as part of a variety programme, with the first 'picture parlour' being opened in 1897 in Los Angeles. Projected films were but one part of the attraction as the parlours also included peep-shows. Thomas Tally, the proprietor subsequently opened what is acknowledged to be the world's first purpose-built building dedicated to the provision of moving pictures in 1902. Like his first parlour it was located in Los Angeles and called the 'Electric Theatre' and it became the model for a simple form of cinema called the Nickelodeon, named after the admission fee. They rapidly proliferated across the USA.[27]

In Britain, Robert Paul's rival system called the Theatrograph (later called the Animatograph) which was a projector based on Edison's Kinetoscope, was also a success. It played at London's Olympia before Paul was offered the opportunity to display his moving pictures at the Alhambra Theatre in London's Leicester Square in March 1896. Paul's original booking was for two weeks but the shows were so successful that they ran for four years. In the same month the Lumière Brothers' Cinématographe show transferred from the Regent Street Polytechnic to the old Empire Music Hall in London's Leicester Square, thus establishing the cinema (the enduring abbreviation of 'cinematograph theatre') in what would subsequently become the centre of British film industry.

It was, therefore, the legitimate theatre, and music hall in particular, which became one of the earliest sites of public exhibition of moving pictures and it is no surprise that they became one of the most important models for subsequent cinema developments some ten years later. There is no doubt that theatre and music hall played a key role in introducing moving pictures to a large and regular audience, indeed Low and Manvell argued that the 'music hall was the commercial cinema's first home'.[28] Those early film pioneers like Robert Paul were engaged by theatre and music hall owners who, even if they considered moving pictures to be a passing fad, saw their potential as public entertainment.

Music halls were an established part of the urban fabric of popular entertainment by the time moving pictures appeared, having emerged in the mid-nineteenth century in Britain probably with the opening of the Canterbury in Lambeth in 1852 by Charles Morton.[29] The origins of the music hall lay in the 1830s and a variety of public entertainments that took place in a variety of venues, including the backrooms and cellars of public houses and fairs. The late eighteenth century saw the emergence of the Pleasure Garden, in which a variety of public entertainments, concerts and amusements took place. Music halls appealed primarily, though not exclusively, to working-class audiences through a combination of differentiated seat prices and a variety format which saw bills include operettas, comics, popular music, conjurers and magicians.[30]

The period after Morton's innovation saw a great deal of music hall development, with halls opening in towns and cities across Britain, in a precursor of cinema's development some sixty years later. The social composition of the audience depended on where a hall was located, although of course parts of the music hall itself attracted different social classes because of the varying seat prices. As cinema proprietors would do much later, music hall owners looked at working-class areas of cities in order to attract the poorer patrons, suburban areas in order to attract the aspiring upper working and lower middle classes and the city centres in order to attract the tourists and a more prosperous clientele. It would be the urban working class and the suburban petit bourgeois that would later form the 'ready audience' for the cinema.[31]

Music halls played an important role in helping to establish cinema. There is no doubt that grand structures like the Empire and Alhambra theatres and others in Britain's provincial cities projected considerable glamour. The story of cinema's move from parlour novelty to the widespread establishment of purpose-built cinemas after 1910 must acknowledge the wide range of venues in which audiences engaged with the new moving pictures. Increasingly, films were shown in any premises that could be converted through the erection of a simple screen and the provision of simple wooden benches. In urban areas such venues and premises were common but the cinema was also established as an enduring entertainment across the country through the efforts of itinerant showmen who provided impermanent structures. In his analysis of the role of showmen in early cinema, Stead observed that a new and vigorous breed of showmen 'knew that film could be shown anywhere, in any old storeroom or vacant shop, and even away from the cities in booths and makeshift structures in fairgrounds, on wasteland, and in fact anywhere crowds were likely to gather'.[32]

For a period after the decline of the music hall as a prime venue the cinema relied upon other more temporary homes, especially the fairground.[33] The fairground would be a more important and enduring site of spectatorship, driven by a group of entrepreneurial and imaginative showmen. Cinema's ultimate success was to a large extent the result of these showmen. As Low and Manvell argue:

> It is to the fairground showmen that the cinema owes its ultimate success. The new toy, a passing fancy in the music-halls, became a firmly established feature of the fairgrounds. It was they who bridged the gap between the music hall days and the later, more respectable picture palaces, and they disappeared only with the First World War – long after the coming of regular cinema.[34]

Rossell distinguishes between two broadly defined categories of early cinema: that of travelling exhibitors and exhibitions in fixed theatres.[35] Fairground venues had been established by proprietors soon after the first exhibition of moving pictures, many building on their presentation of peep shows, while others, like Walter Haggar, also produced their own films. Randall Williams is believed to have been the first of the itinerant showmen, presenting his cinematograph in a portable booth from 1897 onwards, having exhibited at the Royal Agricultural Hall in Islington in 1896. Little evidence or record survives of these early fairs, though Barnes lists a series that took place across the country in 1897, including a fair at Great Gorton in Bradford in which Williams entertained patrons with his 'living photography'.[36] While many of these booths were rudimentary in form – some little more than tents with hand-cranked projectors – some were extremely elaborate in their construction and decoration. These bioscopes, as they were largely known, were often big enough to accommodate hundreds of spectators, with Mrs Holland's Palace of Light able to sit 600 with 400 standing at the rear. Sharp details a travelling show built by Savages of King's Lynn in 1897:

> It was a canvas-covered arena sixty feet by forty feet with a boarded floor and an elaborately carved front. It could seat forty customers on folding seats and could also cater for prestige clientele with twelve plush front-row seats with arms. The relatively bare interior had a small stage. The paybox and front were gilded and decorated with life-size carved statues and the whole frontage was lit at night by giant electric lamps. Added to this attraction was a large steam organ that boomed out its tune at the start of each performance.[37]

Barnes suggests that the 'fairground bioscope marks the transitional stage between the music hall and the cinema theatre'.[38] The influence of the fairground showmen, Rossell argues, on subsequent film practices, institutions and technologies, and in particular the projection apparatus is significant.[39] The practices of showmanship and the importance of presentation that was so crucial to the development of the showground bioscope were also refined later by cinema owners.

The period from 1897 until the outbreak of the First World War was the heyday of the fairground show. The demise of the fairground bioscope was brought about not by a waning of interest in moving pictures but a growth in the popularity of more permanent cinemas. Further, the outbreak of war saw many men, including the showmen and other fairground labour, conscripted and the materials required to make film stock – nitrate and celluloid – were increasingly required for the manufacture of explosives.

With regard to the development of exhibition in fixed theatres, in many of Britain's towns and cities showmen also took advantage of empty buildings and spaces, most notably shop fronts, in order to set up temporary cinemas. The term 'penny gaff' (named after the cost of entry) has been attributed to these shows, though Burrows points out that this was a pejorative term which recalled the disreputable music halls and theatres of the Victorian era.[40] In an era when regulation of building and their uses was practically non-existent, the penny shows, or 'shop-shows', were often crude and rather inhospitable places, not least because many of the proprietors of these establishments were out to make as much money as possible with the minimum of investment. While the penny cinemas were undoubtedly part of the development of cinema their significance lies in the ways some of them became more permanent structures, heralding the establishment of Britain's first buildings dedicated to the presentation of moving images.

In 1904 A. C. Bromhead, one of Britain's first cinema entrepreneurs, opened the 'Daily Bioscope' on Bishopgate Street, London, which was converted from a row of shop fronts. This was followed by a series of similarly converted shop shows, and although these crude cinemas were significant in their influence on later construction they were singularly less prolific than others as sites of exhibition. A promoter from the United States called George Washington Grant went one better than a simple conversion when he opened the Bioscope in Wilton Road, Victoria, London in March 1905. Grant utilised an existing shop front as a foyer but built a new hall behind. There is some debate as to whether this constitutes Britain's earliest purpose-built cinema (see Duckworth's Central Hall below), however the popularity of the penny shows did encourage some speculative investment. Apart from the possibilities afforded by conversion of existing penny cinemas other promoters continued to look to the theatre. This was not through the continuance of mixed bills in which film was placed alongside live performers, but rather to the conversion of the buildings themselves as cinemas, or their long-term renting. In 1907 the Balham Empire was reopened as a film-only venue by the British Cinema Company (although it had been preceded by the Theatre Royal in Sheffield in 1904). What is certain is that in the first seven years of the twentieth century the majority of film shows were taking place in music halls and other halls that were temporarily hired for the purpose.

That cinema ever moved into purpose-built, single-use premises is largely down to the vision of entrepreneurs and showmen like Bromhead, Joshua Duckworth and Montague Pyke and their preparedness to invest not inconsiderable sums of their own money or, in the case of Pyke, their ability to capitalise on a growing interest by speculative investors in the cinema. In 1907 at a time when many still felt that cinema was a passing fad Duckworth, a magic lantern showman, built the Central Hall in Colne, Lancashire for the sum of £2,000, exclusively for the showing of moving pictures. Despite reservations about the possible viability of purpose-built cinemas of contemporary observers and others involved in the industry, there was a growth in cinema building and in the giving over of existing theatres to 'all-picture shows'. At the time of Duckworth's endeavour many speculators were reluctant to invest in 'a thing liable to run out in two years'.[41]

At this time Britain was undergoing a craze for another form of popular entertainment that required specialised premises – roller skating. The 'Rinking' boom, as it became known, was absorbing the kind of speculative investment in new forms of public entertainments that might perhaps have come cinema's way. An Anglo-United States company such as the American Roller Rink Company opened rinks in Newcastle, Liverpool and at London's Olympia, and the high point of early 1910 saw 300 companies registered.[42] Such was the desire of speculators to invest that many looked, with encouragement from both scrupulous and unscrupulous promoters, at the potential for cinemas. Herein lay the initial impetus for the penny cinema conversions, with promoters like Montague Pyke establishing companies such as Recreations Limited which then looked for suitable properties for conversion. During the Rinking boom of 1908–09, seventy-eight cinema companies were established with many able to capitalise on the subsequent collapse of the boom in early 1910 by occupying the rinks and converting them to cinemas, and taking their ready-made audiences.[43]

The events surrounding the Rinking boom and its sudden collapse can be seen as stimulating the cinema insofar as investment was concerned. However, it was the form of this investment that would engender significant changes in the way cinemas were funded in subsequent years. Prior to 1909 it is possible to see individual investors as the prime source of capital, especially the showmen characteristic of the penny show and the fairground. After 1909 the majority of investment was characterised by the private limited company, and what Hiley described as the 'disinterested investors and professional managers … hoping to make a quick profit from moving pictures without any commitment to their future development'.[44]

Nevertheless, the money that came in funded a rapid growth in cinema building as evidenced by a company such as Electric Theatres (1908) Ltd which had opened twelve new cinemas by 1909 and ran twenty-three by July 1923.[45] Similarly, Biograph Theatres Ltd, also formed in 1908, operated five cinemas by 1909 with plans for seven more. Both companies initially paid out handsome dividends to shareholders but fell victim to fierce competition and the necessity of diverting profits into maintenance and upgrading. More successful and a precursor for the cinema chains that would emerge in the 1920s and 1930s was Provincial Cinematograph Theatres Ltd (PCT), which was formed in 1909 with capital of some £100,000. The company's strategy was to build larger and more prestigious cinemas in some of Britain's more densely populated cities and towns and use its size to promote economies of scale in areas like film booking and technical developments.[46] PCT was the most durable and better capitalised of all the early chains and would go on to form the basis of the British-Gaumont Picture Corporation in the 1920s.

New companies were formed and cinemas began to spring up across the country, though the focus was inevitably on London and major cities like Birmingham, Manchester, Glasgow, Leeds and Liverpool. As they flourished the traditional venues that had nurtured cinema declined. Accurate figures for the total number of cinemas operating in Britain in the period up until 1914 are difficult to ascertain, though drawing upon contemporary trade papers Low estimates that in 1915 there were some 3,500,[47] while Hiley estimates that in 1913 there were 3,800 purpose-built cinemas in Britain.[48]

The growth in cinemas was common across the country, though there were regional variations. For instance, in 1914 Manchester had 111 cinemas, Birmingham had 48, Glasgow had 42, Sheffield had 34, Liverpool had 33 and Leeds had 56.[49] All of these cities had a great variety of types and sizes of cinema, though by 1914 they had substantial proportions (30 per cent in the case of Sheffield) of buildings with 1,000 seats or more.

Inevitably, the new cinemas were more attractive, not least in the relative sophistication of the accommodation and projection technology, though there was also one other significant factor in the decline of older venues: the Cinematograph Act 1909 (the '1909 Act'). The 1909 Act, which had been proposed by Herbert Gladstone, the Home Secretary, was the first major legislation relating to moving pictures and came into force on 1 January 1910. It explicitly sought 'to make better provision for cinematograph and other exhibitions'.[50] Its purpose was to lay down a set of safety regulations, which would be enforced by local authorities through annual inspection and the provision of licences.

The impetus for regulation was the potential volatility of the film stock itself which had a cellulose-nitrate base and could ignite and burst into flames with explosive force. There was some danger from the projector as a result of the heat from the light source; the storage of film stock had to be done with the utmost care since in particular conditions it could spontaneously combust, especially when stored in poor conditions and in a state of decomposition. The risks were particularly acute in the fairground Bioscopes, which were often canvas tents. The penny cinemas were often little better, especially since few, if any had fire exits. Some promoters and showmen kept buckets of sand nearby but fires were a constant risk, and the public perception of these risks was exacerbated by press coverage of a few incidents. In September 1907 a fire broke out in Newmarket Town Hall and although it resulted in the death of one patron, newspaper reports exaggerated the number of fatalities.[51] The fire had in fact been caused by members of the departing audience upsetting the projector and igniting the hydrogen gas cylinder, causing a panic.

There had been various attempts to mitigate the risk of fires through the fitting of safety condensers – a glass globe full of water – to projectors or the encasing of projectors in an iron projection booth. The 1909 Act made the provision of fireproof projection booths compulsory and, as Atwell points out, this often acted as an incentive for owners to build new cinemas that could be marketed as complying with the new regulations.[52] The 1909 Act was specific and detailed concerning the projection room, which had to have a close-fitting and fireproof door and automatically controlled screens to contain any blaze. Moreover, the auditorium was to have a specified number of entrance doors of specified widths and the provision of fire appliances was compulsory, while the building had to have toilets for both staff and patrons.[53] The 1909 Act was also extended to itinerant showmen since the provisions covered 'booth, tent or structure'.

Prior to the introduction of the 1909 Act, the scope for regulation on the grounds of safety existed in a few areas. The London County Council (LCC) utilised regulations for public safety on licensed premises that had been introduced in 1898 and refined in subsequent years. They stated that no cinematograph performances could take place 'involving the use of a lengthy combustible film' on premises licensed by the council unless 'all reasonable precautions had been taken against accident and danger to the public'.[54] The requirement to enclose the apparatus in a fireproof room and regulations around lighting and exits were a precursor to those of the 1909 Act.

According to those lobbying for government intervention, many performances were taking place in unlicensed halls in which the only recourse for councils like the LCC was to the *Disorderly Houses Act of 1751*. In this instance the act covered only the playing of live music, which in theory could be applied to the accompanying piano at film showings. Exhibitors were urged to support legislation as a way of differentiating themselves from the more unscrupulous companies and operators in the industry. The inevitable financial cost to the industry, it was further argued, would discourage the proprietors of the 'penny gaffs', and help establish the cinema exhibition industry as a legitimate and responsible one. Walter Reynolds, of the LCC and an advocate of legislation, told a trade paper in 1909 that it was 'not the desire of the London County Council to harm the legitimate business of the 'living picture man', but it was their desire to protect the public from danger.'[55]

The 1909 Act worked, according to Hiley, to the 'advantage of the wealthy company or private owner, and seems to have played a significant part in the transformation of exhibition'.[56] In 1908 there were only three exhibition companies registered in Britain, but by 1914 there were 1,833.[57] The 1909 Act changed the landscape of cinema exhibition, ushering in a new era of purpose-built cinemas and ever grander designs and it is no coincidence that 1910 has come to be called 'the moment of cinema'.

Distribution and industrial organisation

We know that in the few years immediately before and after the Lumière brothers' invention in 1895, critics, journalists and the pioneer cinematographers disagreed considerably among themselves as to the *social function* that they attributed to, or predicted for, the new machine … That, over all these possibilities the cinema could evolve into a machine for telling stories had never been really considered … The merging of the cinema and of narrativity was a great fact, which was by no means predestined – nor was it strictly fortuitous.[58]

The structuring of the film industry into the levels of producer, distributor and exhibitor took some fifteen years to emerge in Britain, while the division of labour characteristic of film production was largely absent. Initially, most films were manufactured like any other commodity and simply sold to anyone in a position to exhibit them. As Chanan observes, the early film manufacturers were largely interested in the production of equipment – cameras and projectors – and thus, 'did not make equipment in order to sell films; they made films in order to sell equipment: their own'.[59]

Manufacture of films, especially in the period from 1896 to 1906, was essentially a cottage industry in Britain and was characteristically a one-man operation. Low and Manvell detail a series of these producers including Walter Haggar, whose company Haggar and Sons made their own films with their own camera for exhibition in their travelling fairground bioscopes and by other showmen.[60] What was significant about Haggar was that he struck a deal with the Gaumont Company who agreed to cover the developing and printing costs in return for the rights to show the films, except in places Haggar was touring. Cecil Hepworth's studio at Walton-on-Thames, established in 1899, was producing approximately 200 films by 1906, while R. W. Paul, in addition to being instrumental in the first public screenings of moving pictures in Britain, was a short-lived but influential producer.

The films these and others produced in the first years of cinema were largely short 'actualities' in which 'movement, without topical or dramatic interest, provided the necessary thrill to bring the first audiences together'.[61] The thrill was also generated by the novelty of the cinema and in what Gunning called a 'cinema of attractions'.[62] In the period prior to 1906–07 narrative cinema was not the dominating impulse as audiences went to see the machines demonstrated – the technologies – rather than the films. The 'cinema of attractions', Gunning argues, 'directly solicits spectator attention, inciting visual curiosity, and supplying pleasure through an exciting spectacle – a unique event, whether fictional or documentary, that of interest in itself'.[63]

Films were often comprised of a single 'scene', photographed from one angle with a static camera, and included scenes of trains rushing past, a street scene or people undertaking routine tasks or particular physical activities. Travelling showmen, like Walter Haggar, would often incorporate local scenes into their shows. In all these instances the attraction to those early audiences was the reproduction of the familiar.[64] These earliest of films were not exclusively 'actualities' since there was a parallel development in what might be called 'topicals' in which an event is photographed that might have a news value (they were the forerunner of the newsreel).[65] Most famous of these early topical films was R. W. Paul's filming of the Derby horse race in 1896, while Hepworth filmed the Coronation of Edward VII in 1902.

In all cases the length of films was relatively short with the earliest films comprising fifty feet of film with a running time of less than a minute and dictated by factors such as the cost of raw film stock and the speed at which the film passed through the shutter. In the days before sound the film was shot and projected at around sixteen frames per second, with the length of film determined in feet – sixteen frames per foot of film meant one foot of film per second. Exhibitors paid the manufacturers for the films per foot, which by the end of the nineteenth century had become a standard 6d. Programmes of short films would be run almost continuously, usually until they wore out, since the smaller audiences at the penny shows and fairground bioscopes meant that films took longer to make their money back for the exhibitor. The price was determined to a large extent by the cost of the film stock as a raw product, but unlike many other products a film can be used more than once.

Thus, one of the main impetuses for the development of the distribution sector came from the burgeoning second-hand trade in films and the possibility of exchanging and renting out films, particularly as many showmen and other exhibitors often accumulated large stocks. Initially, as we have seen, the selling of a film by a manufacturer direct to an exhibitor meant that the film became the property of that exhibitor, who could show it as much as he liked. However, as Chanan points out, the nascent distributors realised that 'the film need not pass physically into the hands of the consumer for its exchange value to be realized, nor need it pass into the ownership of the exhibitor, since the exhibitor can rent it instead'.[66] Though there were (and still are) considerable risks in distribution, since the distributor had to both purchase the films and print additional copies, the potential was for all sectors of the industry to profit. Exhibitors could afford to change their programmes more regularly, which led to a greater demand from producers who also found that a distributor might purchase several titles. According to Bachlin, 'the birth of the branch of distribution accelerated the development of the film industry: the reduction in the price of films, their diffusion and more rapid distribution led to an increase in the number of cinemas'.[67]

As the film industry became more stratified around production, distribution and exhibition the various sectors began to organise themselves into interest groups, trade unions and trade bodies that reflected the separation. In 1906 the Kinematograph Manufacturers Association (KMA) was formed, representing the smallest sector of the industry. In the same year the National Association of Cinematograph Operators (NACO), the industry's first trade union, was formed as a branch of the Association of Theatrical Employees. The KMA sought early on to try to control the circulation of films, so as to keep prices higher for producers and curtail abuse of copyright, but without the cooperation of the distributors this proved difficult. When the distributors themselves formed a secretive trade organisation, the Incorporated Association of Film Renters (IAFR) in 1910, the KMA sought and gained an agreement to fix prices and control the market for films. The years before the start of the First World War were characterised by arguments and protests from other interest groups, and in particular the exhibitors, who were the last group to organise when they formed the Cinematograph Exhibitors Association (CEA) in 1912.

By 1906 producers were making films of 800 feet in length (the limit for a 35 mm reel) with running times of approximately ten minutes, which became known as 'single reelers'. The gradual lengthening of films over the remaining period before the First World War reveals a complex relationship between audience, exhibitor and producer that was structured increasingly around the narrative fiction feature film. The early 'actualities' and 'topicals', though the dominant aesthetic in the first years of cinema, underwent a transformation into a narrative cinema. Abel talks of a transitional period in which the 'cinema of attractions' shared elements with later narrative cinema and describes it thus:

> Initially, what was involved was a change in spatial coherence: the autonomous tableau gave way to a synthetic space constructed out of interrelated, discrete shots. Correlated with this was a change in temporality, with greater attention given to issues of succession, simultaneity and internally generated causality.[68]

The emergence of narrative cinema is integral to the development of longer films, which themselves led to the first 'feature films', utilising multiple reels of film. For audiences the narrativisation of cinema led to the necessity of watching the film from the beginning, but also, as Musser argues, exhibitors often had to help the audience understand the film.[69] This was done in a number of ways, though the most popular were lectures and/or sound effects. Foreknowledge and familiarity were also important, especially with the early adaptations of literary material. As simple stories gave way to more complex narratives, the addition of intertitles (pioneered in 1903 by Pathé) by the film producers and a developing appreciation for the new grammar of the film meant that audiences accepted a greater responsibility for 'making meaning'.[70] The audience was increasingly engaged in a form of individualisation in relation to the narrative, which, according to Gunning was more in line with the traditions of bourgeois representation.[71] This was important since, as we shall see, the desire for respectability on the part of producers, distributors and particularly exhibitors for the cinema meant acknowledging that although the cinema aimed for a mass audience, attracting a middle-class audience meant changing not only the space of cinema but what was shown on the screen.

The cinema and the city

Philip Corrigan argues that the history of cinema-going needs to be related to social histories of particular periods. This entails a consideration of what '"going to the pictures" means or could mean for large audiences'.[72] Thus, the period from the 'birth' of cinema until the outbreak of the First World War was characterised by the embracing of cinema by the urban working class. This relationship between the cinema, its largely working-class audience and the metropolitan space is central to an understanding of the establishment of cinema-going as the pre-eminent mass public leisure activity of the first half of the twentieth century. It was, according to Stead, the city itself that was a key determinant of the nature of the cinema and especially the extent to which 'cultural patterns in the modern era were determined within the context of the late nineteenth-century city'.[73] Of course, cities were not a new geographical phenomenon; what *was* qualitatively new was the industrialised metropolis that developed in the wake of the industrial revolution. The rate of population growth was truly phenomenal. For instance, in 1801 Manchester's population was approximately 75,000 though by 1901 it had grown to over 645,000; in Inner London (the former London County and not including the outer boroughs) the population of 959,000 in 1801 had grown to a staggering 4.5 million by 1901.

The physical adjustments required in order for these new metropolitan areas to work were significant, not least given the grim realities of such population densities. However, it was, as Stead points out, the 'social adjustments that needed to be made to accommodate the new masses' that characterised the development of what became known as a 'popular culture'.[74] Thus the city became the context for the development of modern life and urban life came to define modernity. Metropolitan urban culture led to new forms of entertainment and leisure and the expression of a new consumerism in which all manner of products, experiences, spectacles and goods were offered to the city's inhabitants.[75] In 1903 French sociologist Georg Simmel characterised the modern city as 'the rapid crowding of changing images, the sharp discontinuity in the grasp of a single glance, and the unexpectedness of onrushing impressions'.[76]

For Charney and Schwartz, Simmel's conception of the city could describe cinema itself, 'since the experience of the city set the terms for the experience of the other elements of modernity'.[77] Indeed, one of the consequences of the modern urban space was, according to Simmel, a craving for excitement and 'extreme impressions'.[78] Frisby highlights how contemporary urban dwellers were thirsty for stimulation and amusement, partly as a response to the stresses inherent in the close physical proximity to so many others with its consequent desire to escape; but also as a consequence of the rapidly developing money economy in which all manner of things could be acquired through the market.[79]

In this context Betts argues that the cinema developed in the late nineteenth century because the means existed to satisfy the social needs of the time, particularly amongst the urban working class for whom there was 'little amusement'.[80] In his detailed study of domestic life amongst all Edwardian social classes Laski highlighted the lack of evening pleasures in the home for the poor, which resulted in many seeking solace in public houses and through alcohol.[81] Laski calculated that Edwardian working-class families spent six shillings a week on intoxicants but with homes that 'could provide no pleasure or relaxation there was little else for the poor to do'.[82] By 1912, the notion of 'secondary poverty' as detailed in Rowntree's famous York study, was developed by Snowden in his book entitled *The Living Wage* (1912), whereupon he listed a series of new expenses as necessities. They included newspapers, tramways and books but also music hall and the picture palace. Snowden argued that to be deprived of these new luxuries 'intended specifically for your kind, is penury indeed'.[83]

The cinema was not alone amongst public entertainments that attracted the working classes, since the music hall had already established itself as the pre-eminent form. As Stead cautions, however, it is difficult to gauge just how genuinely popular the music hall was or what its relationship was to the development of cinema-going.[84] Nevertheless, the importance of music hall and subsequently cinema-going is that they symbolise what Hall and Whannel identified as the move from a traditional folk culture to a more commercialised form of 'mass culture' characteristic of the twentieth century.[85] In this sense music hall has some connections to an earlier 'folk' culture – its cultural references, sense of shared experience and social milieu are rooted in the lives of its audiences – but Hall and Whannel saw music hall as a 'transitional form – in a transitional society'.[86]

The context for the first developments of the cinema was a unique coalescence of several key social, cultural and economic factors, which included industrialisation, urban living and the commodification of culture. Williams argues that film found its place in an 'already dense, complex and changing popular culture'.[87] He goes on to argue that:

> The 'popular culture' of a predominantly urban and industrial society comprises a radically different set of phenomena from preindustrial popular, or 'folk', culture. The latter is relatively traditional in form and content, and its contrast is with 'court' or 'aristocratic' – or 'polite' ('liberal', 'learned') – culture. Modern popular culture however is not only a response to predominantly urban and industrial living. It is also in its central processes, (1) largely urban-based, (2) an application of new industrial processes to a broad range of old and new cultural processes and forms, and thus (3) predominantly mobile and innovative, but with very complex relations to older and still persistent conditions and forms. Film arrived at the end of a century of such developments.[88]

The emergence of more industrialised and commercialised forms of 'mass culture' is perhaps best exemplified by the development of a large-scale popular press, epitomised by the introduction of the *Daily Mail* in 1896, the *Daily Express* in 1900 and the *Daily Mirror* in 1903.

Like the subsequent developments in cinema exhibition, particularly after 1910, the commercialisation of the press can be seen as best symbolising the commodification of culture and what many felt was its subsequent debasement. In *Dialectic of Enlightenment* Adorno and Horkheimer talked of the 'culture industry', though Adorno himself acknowledged that in their drafts they spoke of 'mass culture'.[89] What Adorno and Horkheimer were seeking to do was to reject the notion that culture arose out of the masses themselves in favour of the thesis that the 'culture industry' tailors its 'products' for consumption *by* the masses.[90] Put simply, the 'culture industry intentionally integrates its consumers from above'.[91] However, this view, while acknowledging the industrialisation of cultural production in the early to middle part of the twentieth century, is itself contested, not least by those who see the commercialisation of culture as not necessarily a function of commodification. In relation to the burgeoning press at the turn of the twentieth century Curran and Seaton saw the 'debasement of culture' argument not as a function of commercialisation itself but rather as a 'system of controls institutionalized by the industrialization of the Victorian press'.[92] In other words, it is the abilities of certain groups and individuals to assume ownership and control of large-scale cultural production over others that was the seminal issue.

In the light of Adorno and Horkheimer's work the argument runs that though popular *with* the masses the emergence of cinema is an activity that does not in any way *belong* to the masses. For many commentators, particularly those described broadly as on the left, the exploitation of working-class spectators during the first twenty years of cinema's development characterises the 'expropriation and packaging of what had previously been popular forms by middle-class organisations and in most cases by businessmen and entrepreneurs'.[93]

From the penny show to the picture palace

In her definitive history of early film in Britain Low characterises the early cinema audience's avowed working-class complexion, and its roots in the music hall tradition that preceded it.[94] 'Consequently,' Low argued, 'it was no cause for surprise that the audience for the two types of show was substantially the same. Cheapness and accessibility made the film the drama of the masses.'[95] Nevertheless, the cinema's very popularity fuelled a belief on the part of many contemporary commentators that it lacked respectability, which was shared amongst many cinema proprietors. The industry's attempts to make the cinema more respectable would see a focus upon a range of aspects of the presentation of films, including the buildings and subsequently the films themselves. In doing so it is clear to many scholars that the impetus for 'reform' originated with various groups within both society – particularly middle-class pressure groups and moral reformers – and the 'establishment', most notably via regulation and legislation.

Williams argues cogently that although cinema ultimately became the central art form of the twentieth century its development was slow, particularly amongst some classes.[96] That it assumed such a prominent position in the context of popular culture was largely down to its form of artistic production. Here Williams is referring, in part, to the industrial nature of cinema's production and circulation and to its growing pre-eminence as a narrative medium and entertainment. Though it would redefine what popular culture was, in the first instance cinema had to 'move towards respectability within the terms of the established culture.'[97]

The purpose-built cinema, which began to appear in greater numbers from 1910 onwards, after the introduction of the 1909 Act, was the first serious attempt to establish cinema as a prominent and permanent entertainment. Low argues that the period from 1908–14 saw the transformation of the industry and a boom in investment in exhibition, while the 'penny gaff was to give way to the Bijou Palace'.[98] Though there was a significant increase in cinema building after 1910, and the 1909 Act did result in many penny shows being closed due to the introduction of licensing, Burrows argues that this did not see the end of the penny show; indeed the numbers obtaining licences, in London at least, increased after 1910.[99] Nevertheless, in seeking to differentiate the new cinemas from those which preceded them proprietors took their aesthetic and architectural inspiration from the most prominent public entertainment of the time: the prestigious metropolitan theatre.

Simplicity had characterised the first cinemas, particularly the penny cinemas and shop shows with their plain, rectangular halls – sometimes only corrugated iron – and wooden benches. Not unlike the modern multiplex, which is largely a steel and concrete 'box', these earliest cinemas were often fronted with a more elaborate façade, designed to attract the passer-by. With the construction of single-use or purpose-built cinemas, or 'fixed shows' as they were sometimes called, exhibitors looked to establish a new image, which drew its inspiration from a range of sources, not least the live theatre and in particular the Baroque style of architecture, which itself gave way to a form of Neo-classicism just before the First World War.[100]

For those exhibitors erecting new buildings, the need to differentiate their cinemas from the penny shows and fairground bioscopes lay in impressing the cinema-goer from the entrance right through to the auditorium itself. The desire was to establish an air of elegance and good taste, which it was supposed would both moderate the rowdier aspects of audience behaviour and, importantly, widen the audience for cinema socially. Increasingly the accent was on 'good taste' in the form of more elaborate decoration, plusher materials including upholstered seating, electric lighting and carpeting. Of increasing importance was the entrance foyer, as the first part of the building encountered by the audience and which sought to project the values of the new cinema. Extensive use was made of mirrors, which Low observed were necessary in order to make it a 'high-class rendezvous'.[101] On the exterior the fashion was often for highly decorated glazed terracotta, or faience tiling, which suggested both modernity and also cleanliness. Although the early cinemas were often called 'Electric Theatres' or increasingly 'Picture Houses' exhibitors drew upon a rich new lexicon of names in order to signal the grandeur and glamour of the cinema: the Palace, Coliseum, Adelphi, Scala, Majestic, Globe, Regal, Mayfair, Ritz, Empress, Savoy and Empire.

The spread of the picture palace is attested by an article in the weekly news magazine *The Sphere*, published in April 1913:

> The rise of the 'picture palace' is one of the most astonishing features of modern life. A year or two ago and the thing was not. Now every little town has its whitewashed frontage with Empire decorations lit with a couple of assertive arc lights. The bigger towns and cities have more pretentious halls, and London itself is being provided with cinema 'palaces' which are really well-appointed theatres adapted to their special use.[102]

Cinemas like the Electric on London's Portobello Road (which is possibly the oldest surviving purpose-built cinema in the UK, having opened in 1910), were typical of the earlier and still rather straightforward constructions, often with a barrel-vaulted roof and a screen placed on an end wall. The building seated some 600 people all on one level, though cinemas accommodating up to 2,000 people were also a feature of the time. Balconies were uncommon in the first cinemas, though there was a tendency to incorporate plasterwork decoration and gilding in the auditorium.

In his history of cinema architecture Gray describes London's West End Cinema Theatre of 1913, designed to reflect the luxury playhouses on the Shaftsbury Road, in which patrons entered through 'an elegant Louis XVI foyer' located above a basement restaurant, into an auditorium 'adorned with pavilion "loges", terminating the ends of the balcony'.[103] Other cinemas designed and built at around the same time, immediately prior to the First World War, variously embodied Rococo, Jacobean country house and Ionic styling.

Two significant outcomes have been attributed to the new purpose-built cinemas: firstly, that they encouraged more regular attendance and secondly, that they changed the pattern of attendance by encouraging cinema-goers to stay for longer in the cinema. In the days of early cinema the film programmes encouraged people to come in and out of the theatre throughout, especially since the films were short and the narratives not yet complex enough that audiences need see the film from the beginning. By 1914 audiences were much more likely to encounter cinema programmes that would last between one-and-a-half and two hours and while the continuous screening of a range of films was still a feature in many cinemas, a growing number of cinemas would run their programme two or three times a day. Since the new cinemas seated anything from 500–1,000 people exhibitors could make profits from a smaller number of screenings.

The goal of the exhibition industry in the first years in which cinema developed permanent sites was for the habitual audience. As programmes got longer and cinemas were both more affordable and more comfortable, the regular cinema-goer began to emerge who might go several times a week. Figures for attendance in the period prior to 1914 are unreliable, however Low reports that contemporary figures for weekly cinema attendance in 1914 were 7–8 million.[104] An indication of the greater frequency of cinema-going is suggested by Hiley's analysis of the relationship between the output of British studios and cinema construction.[105] More regular attendance meant more frequent change of programmes which fed into a greater demand for films. Robinson found that the same trend was true of the cinema in the USA where the more often the programme changed, the more often the audience returned.[106]

One of the undoubted reasons why the cinema habit became so established amongst pre-war audiences was that the new cinemas attracted family groups and increasingly children. In part this was a function of the cinema space itself, since for poorer families attendance at the cinema meant not having to light a fire in a cramped and cold dwelling. In addition the cinema was a public entertainment unlike the public house and the music hall in that it was less antithetical to children. The emerging and increasingly institutionalised cinema industry was conscious of the need to broaden out the audience as part of their unrelenting quest for respectability. As Stead argues the cinema recognised that its audience was significant in numbers but that it would be 'permanently restricted if the industry remained at the edge of society proper ... The way to greater profitability, then, lay in the direction of bringing in better sorts of people and, to ensure that, a careful eye had to be kept on what was actually shown in the cinemas.'[107]

Cinema owners sought to broaden the audience not just in terms of social class, but in terms of gender too. Despite contemporary anxieties about the presence of women, and young women in particular, in cinemas Shapiro Sanders highlights the ways in which women were 'incorporated into the ideology of respectability'.[108] There were constant tensions between critics of cinemas as sites of immorality, particularly for the 'lower-classes', and the exhibitors anxious to make the cinema more respectable. However, they found some common ground in relation to the more durable and historical anxieties around drunkardness, since the attendance of more men, and particular those accompanied by their families, suggested an alternative to the public house. In 1912 a cinema owner could remark that it was the pub that he was competing with, observing that the 'two coal-heavers' in with their two children would have normally spent their Saturday nights in the public house.[109]

Almost from the moment when moving pictures were introduced they were the source of concern to many social commentators. Shapiro Sanders cites a letter to *The Times* from Samuel Smith MP in 1899 warning against the 'new source of evil' that was the Kinetoscope: 'It is hardly possible to exaggerate the corruption of the young that comes from exhibiting, under a strong light, nude female figures represented as living and moving, going in and out of baths, sitting as artists' models &c.'[110]

Though Smith is referring to the peepshow parlours many extended their anxieties to the exhibition of films in more public venues, such as the 'penny gaffs' and early dedicated cinemas. With the music hall in mind, observers of the earliest cinemas recorded their shock at the perceived lewd behaviour of many audience members, largely since the cinema, like music hall, was one of the few places in which men and women could indulge in courting rituals and other forms of sexual activity. Though inevitably subject to exaggeration on the part of moral campaigners, the fears about the behaviour of cinema audiences were influential, particularly amongst cinema proprietors. The desire to broaden the audience to include women led exhibitors to consider a range of initiatives in order to counter the critics, not least the focus on the darkened space itself.

Notes

1 N. Hiley, "At the Picture Palace': The British Cinema Audience, 1895–1920', in J. Fullerton (ed.), *Celebrating 1895: The Centenary of Cinema* (Sydney: John Libbey and the National Museum of Photography, Film and Television, Bradford, UK, 1998), p. 102.

2 The first person to patent a device to capture moving images in Britain (on 10 January 1888) was Louis Aimé Augustin Le Prince, the son of a French army officer who moved to Leeds in the late 1860s. The device, which used paper negatives, was used to record images in his father-in-law's garden in Roundhay and of traffic on Leeds Bridge in 1888, some seven years before the Lumière brothers. He was unable to successfully project the images publicly and the images now exist only as photographic copies. He disappeared mysteriously in 1890 while travelling on a train from Dijon to Paris. For more information on Le Prince see S. Herbert and L. McKernan (eds), *Who's Who of Victorian Cinema: A Worldwide Survey* (London: British Film Institute, 1996) and C. Rawlence, *The Missing Reel: The Untold Story of*

the Lost Inventor of Moving Pictures (London: Collins, 1990).

3 Cited in S. Bottomore, 'The Panicking Audience?: Early Cinema and the "Train Effect"', *Historical Journal of Film, Radio and Television*, 19:2 (1999), 177–210, p. 177.

4 Bottomore, 'The Panicking Audience?', p. 179.

5 N. Denzin, *The Cinematic Society: The Voyeur's Gaze* (London, Thousand Oaks, CA and New Delhi: Sage, 1995), p. 16.

6 See J. Hunningher, 'Première on Regent Street', in C. Williams (ed.), *Cinema: The Beginnings and the Future* (London: University of Westminster Press, 1996).

7 J. Barnes, *The Beginnings of the Cinema in England 1894–1901, Volume One: 1894–1896*, revised and enlarged edition, ed. R. Maltby (Exeter: University of Exeter Press, 1998), p. 94.

8 Cited in C. Harding and S. Popple, *In the Kingdom of Shadows: A Companion to Early Cinema* (London: Cygnus Arts, 1996), p. 137.

9 D. Rossell, 'Double Think: The Cinema and Magic Lantern Culture', in Fullerton (ed.), *Celebrating 1895*, p. 30.

10 *Ibid.*, pp. 29–30.

11 Cited in M. Heard, 'The Magic Lantern's Wild Years', in Williams (ed.), *Cinema: the Beginnings and the Future*, p. 25.

12 S. Herbert, *A History of Pre-Cinema: Volume 1* (London: Routledge, 2000), p. xi.

13 Rossell, 'Double Think'; see also D. Atwell, *Cathedrals of the Movies: A History of British Cinemas* (London: Architectural Press, 1981); Heard, 'The Magic Lantern's Wild Years'; D. Sharp, *The Picture Palace and other Buildings of the Movies* (London: Hugh Evelyn, 1969); and D. B. Thomas, *The Origins of the Motion Picture* (London: Science Museum/HMSO, 1964).

14 Heard, 'The Magic Lantern's Wild Years'.

15 Cited in Sharp, *The Picture Palace and other Buildings of the Movies*, p. 12.

16 See T. Gunning, "Animated Pictures': Tales of Cinema's Forgotten Future, after 100 Years of Films', in C. Gledhill and L. Williams (eds), *Reinventing Film Studies* (London: Arnold, 2000).

17 Heard, 'The Magic Lantern's Wild Years'. See also L. Mannoni, *The Great Art of Light and Shadow: Archaeology of the Cinema*, trans. and ed. R. Crangle, (Exeter: University of Exeter Press, 2000) for other examples.

18 R. McGrath, 'Natural Magic and Science Fiction: Instruction, Amusement and the Popular Show 1795–1895', in Williams (ed.), *Cinema: The Beginnings and the Future*.

19 *Ibid.*, p. 14.

20 The US patent for the Kinetograph and the Kinetoscope was filed in August 1891 and the first public demonstration took place at the Brooklyn Institute of Arts and Sciences on 9 May 1893. For a detailed chronology of developments in early cinema see D. Rossell, 'A Chronology of Cinema 1889–1896', *Film History*, 7:2 (1995), 115–236.

21 R. Crangle, 'What do those Old Slides Mean? Or why the Magic Lantern is not an Important Part of Cinema History', in S. Popple and V. Toulmin (eds), *Visual*

Delights: Essays on the Popular and Projected Image in the 19th Century (Trowbridge: Flicks Books, 2000).

22 Barnes, *The Beginnings of the Cinema in England 1894–1901, Volume One: 1894–1896*, p. 1.

23 See *ibid.*

24 Sharp, *The Picture Palace and other Buildings of the Movies*, p. 26.

25 Brian Winston takes up Bazin's question of why the cinema began in 1895 when no innovation appeared that year that was technically relevant, and argues that it was the 'invention' of the modern audience which constituted the critical context for cinema's development' adding that 'by 1895, the broad mass of the audience, addicted to naturalistic illusion and narrative, was sitting in the darkened seats of the auditorium watching highly professional entertainments created by logistically complex, capital-intensive, if somewhat risky, industry'. See B. Winston, *Technologies of Seeing: Photography, Cinematography and Television* (London: British Film Institute, 1996), p. 31.

26 Hiley, 'At the Picture Palace', p. 96.

27 For an overview of early cinema developments in the USA see R. Sklar, *Movie-Made America: A Cultural History of American Movies*, revised and updated edition (New York: Vintage, 1994) and T. Balio, *The American Film Industry*, revised edition (Madison, WI: The University of Wisconsin Press, 1985).

28 R. Low and R. Manvell, *The History of British Film 1896–1906* (London: George Allen & Unwin, [1948] 1973). See also A. Medhurst, 'Music Hall and British Cinema', in C. Barr (ed.), *All Our Yesterdays: 90 Years of British Cinema* (London: British Film Institute, 1986).

29 Low and Manvell, *The History of British Film 1896–1906*.

30 See P. Bailey (ed.), *Music Hall: The Business of Pleasure* (Milton Keynes: Open University Press, 1986).

31 M. Chanan, *The Dream that Kicks: The Prehistory and Early Years of Cinema in Britain*, second edition (London: Routledge, 1996), p. 148.

32 P. Stead, *Film and the Working Class: The Feature Film in British and American Society* (London: Routledge, 1989), p. 11.

33 The National Fairground Archive (NFA), based at the University of Sheffield, contains a wealth of historical information and material on travelling show people including the development of cinema on the fairground. See the NFA website: www.shef.ac.uk/nfa/index.php.

34 Low and Manvell, *The History of British Film 1896–1906*, p. 37.

35 D. Rossell, 'A Slippery Job: Travelling Exhibitors in Early Cinema', in Popple and Toulmin (eds), *Visual Delights*.

36 J. Barnes, *The Rise of Cinema in Great Britain, Volume Two: Jubilee Year 1897* (London: Bishopgate Press, 1983).

37 Sharp, *The Picture Palace and other Buildings of the Movies*, p. 42.

38 Barnes, *The Beginnings of the Cinema in England 1894–1901, Volume One: 1894–1896*, p. 177. See also Low and Manvell, *The History of British Film 1896–1906*.

39 Rossell, 'A Slippery Job: Travelling Exhibitors in Early Cinema'.

40 J. Burrows, 'Penny Pleasures: Film Exhibition in London during the Nickelodeon Era, 1906–1914', *Film History*, 16 (2004), 60–91.

41 N. Hiley, 'Nothing More than a 'Craze'', in A. Higson, *Young and Innocent?: The Cinema in Britain 1896–1930* (Exeter: University of Exeter Press, 2002), p. 113.

42 *Ibid.*

43 *Ibid.*, p. 115.

44 *Ibid.*, p. 118.

45 R. Low, *The History of the British Film 1906–1914* (London: George Allen & Unwin, [1949] 1973).

46 *Ibid.*

47 Low, *The History of the British Film 1906–1914*, pp. 22–23. See also R. Gray, *Cinemas in Britain: 100 Years of Cinema Architecture* (London: Cinema Theatre Association/British Film Institute, 1996) and S. Street, *British National Cinema* (London: Routledge, 1997).

48 Hiley, 'Nothing More than a 'Craze'', p. 120.

49 Low, *The History of the British Film 1906–1914*, p. 50.

50 The Cinematograph Act 1909, 9 Edw.7 c.30.

51 See D. Williams, 'The Cinematograph Act of 1909: An Introduction to the Impetus behind the Legislation and some Early Effects', *Film History*, 9 (1997), 341–50.

52 Atwell, *Cathedrals of the Movies*, p. 54.

53 See Sharp, *The Picture Palace and other Buildings of the Movies* and Williams, 'The Cinematograph Act of 1909'.

54 Williams, 'The Cinematograph Act of 1909', pp. 342–3.

55 Cited in *ibid.*, p. 346.

56 Hiley, 'Nothing More than a 'Craze'', p. 120.

57 PEP (Political and Economic Planning), *The British Film Industry* (London: Political and Economic Planning Office, 1952).

58 C. Metz, *Film Language: A Semiotics of Cinema*, trans M. Taylor (New York: Oxford University Press, 1974), p. 93.

59 M. Chanan, 'The Emergence of an Industry', in J. Curran and V. Porter (eds), *British Cinema History* (London: Weidenfeld and Nicolson, 1983), p. 45.

60 Low and Manvell, *The History of British Film 1896–1906*.

61 *Ibid.*, p. 51.

62 T. Gunning, 'The Cinema of Attractions: Early Film, its Spectator and the Avant-Garde', in T. Elsaesser (ed.), *Early Cinema: Space, Frame, Narrative* (London: British Film Institute, 1990), first published in *Wide Angle*, 8:3/4 (1986), 63–70.

63 *Ibid.*, p. 58. For a critique of Gunning's position see Winston, *Technologies of Seeing*.

64 In the late 1990s approximately 800 rolls of nitrate film were discovered in a shop in Blackburn, Lancashire. They constituted a series of actuality films shot around the north of England at the turn of the twentieth century by the partnership of Mitchell and Kenyon, who ran a film company together. The films were stored for decades until 'discovered'. They are now in the process of being restored by the British Film Institute. See V. Toulmin, S. Popple and P. Russell (eds), *The Lost World of Mitchell & Kenyon: Edwardian Britain on Film* (London: British Film Institute, 2004).

65 See Low and Manvell, *The History of British Film 1896–1906*.

66 Chanan, 'The Emergence of an Industry', p. 48.

67 P. Bachlin, *Histoire Economique du Cinéma*, new edition (Paris, 1947), cited in Chanan, *The Dream that Kicks*, p. 189.

68 R. Abel, 'Early Cinema: After Brighton', in P. Cook and M. Bernink (eds), *The Cinema Book*, second edition (London: British Film Institute, 1999), p. 95.

69 C. Musser, 'The Nickelodeon Era Begins: Establishing the Framework for Hollywood's Mode of Representation', in Elsaesser (ed.), *Early Cinema: Space, Frame, Narrative*, originally published in *Framework*, Autumn 1984.

70 Abel, 'Early Cinema: After Brighton', p. 95.

71 T. Gunning, 'Weaving a Narrative: Style and Economic Background in Griffith's Biograph Films', in Elsaesser (ed.), *Early Cinema: Space, Frame, Narrative*, first published in *Quarterly Review of Film Studies*, Winter 1981, 11–26.

72 P. Corrigan, 'Film Entertainment as Ideology and Pleasure: A Preliminary Approach to a History of Audiences', in Curran and Porter (eds), *British Cinema History*, p. 26.

73 Stead, *Film and the Working Class*, p. 1.

74 *Ibid.*

75 See L. Charney and V. R. Schwartz (eds), *Cinema and the Invention of Modern Life* (Berkeley, CA: University of California Press, 1995).

76 G. Simmel, 'The Metropolis and Mental Life', in K. Wolff (ed.), *Sociology of Georg Simmel* (New York: Free Press, [1903] 1950), p. 410.

77 Charney and Schwartz (eds), *Cinema and the Invention of Modern Life*, p. 3.

78 G. Simmel, *The Philosophy of Money*, trans. T. Bottomore and D. Frisby (London: Routledge, [1907] 1978).

79 D. Frisby, *Fragments of Modernity: Theories of Modernity in the Work of Simmel, Kracauer and Benjamin* (London: Polity Press, 1985), p. 75.

80 E. Betts, *The Film Business: A History of British Cinema 1896–1972* (London: George Allen & Unwin, 1973), p. 25.

81 M. Laski, 'Domestic Life', in S. Nowell-Smith (ed.), *Edwardian England* (Oxford: Oxford University Press, 1964).

82 *Ibid.*, pp. 192–3.

83 Cited in Laski, 'Domestic Life', p. 174.

84 Stead, *Film and the Working Class*.

85 S. Hall and P. Whannel, *The Popular Arts* (London: Hutchinson Educational, 1964).

86 *Ibid.*, p. 56.

87 R. Williams, 'British Film History: New Perspectives', in Curran and Porter (eds), *British Cinema History*, p. 14.

88 *Ibid.*, p. 15.

89 T. Adorno and M. Horkheimer, *Dialectic of Enlightenment* (London: Verso, 1979) and T. Adorno, 'Cultural Industry Reconsidered', in J. M. Bernstein (ed.), *The Culture Industry: Selected Essays on Mass Culture* (London: Routledge, 1991).

90 Adorno and Horkheimer, *Dialectic of Enlightenment*.

91 Adorno, 'Cultural Industry Reconsidered', p. 85.

92 J. Curran and J. Seaton, *Power Without Responsibility: The Press and Broadcasting in*

Britain, third edition (London: Routledge 1988), p. 33.

93 Stead, *Film and the Working Class,* pp. 2–3.

94 Low, *The History of the British Film 1906–1914.*

95 *Ibid.,* p. 25.

96 Williams, 'British Film History: New Perspectives'.

97 *Ibid.,* p. 17.

98 Low, *The History of the British Film 1906–1914,* p. 15.

99 Burrows, 'Penny Pleasures'.

100 Gray, *Cinemas in Britain.*

101 Low, *The History of the British Film 1906–1914,* p. 16.

102 Cited in C. Harding and S. Popple, *In the Kingdom of Shadows: A Companion to Early Cinema* (London: Cygnus Arts, 1996), p. 207.

103 Gray, *Cinemas in Britain,* p. 30.

104 Low, *The History of the British Film 1906–1914,* p. 25.

105 Hiley, 'At the Picture Palace'.

106 D. Robinson, *From Peep Show to Palace: The Birth of American Film* (New York: Columbia University Press, 1996).

107 Stead, *Film and the Working Class,* p. 14.

108 L. Shapiro Sanders, '"Indecent Incentives to Vice": Regulating Films and Audience Behaviour from the 1890s to the 1910s', in A. Higson (ed.), *Young and Innocent? The Cinema in Britain 1896–1930* (Exeter: University of Exeter Press, 2002), p. 99.

109 See Hiley, 'At the Picture Palace', p. 101. In 1912 an anonymous author published *How to Run a Picture Theatre: A Handbook for Proprietors, Managers and Exhibitors,* which offers an illuminating insight into the contemporary efforts to establish the cinema as a respectable public entertainment (see Harding and Popple, *In the Kingdom of Shadows,* pp. 226–31).

110 Shapiro Sanders, 'Indecent Incentives to Vice', p. 101.

2

Post-war consolidation, the coming of sound and Hollywood: 1913–30

Our taverns and our metropolitan streets, our offices and our furnished rooms, our railroad stations and our factories appeared to have us locked up hopelessly. Then came the film and burst this prison-world asunder by the dynamite of the tenth of a second, so that now, in the midst of its far-flung ruins and debris, we calmly and adventurously go travelling. (Walter Benjamin)[1]

All the adventure, all the romance, all the excitement you lack in your daily life are in – Pictures. (Paramount Studios advertisement, 1925)

The period after 1913, in particular that of the late 1920s was a time of dramatic developments and the establishment of several features of the British cinema industry that resonate to this day. In 1913 the cinema industry established the British Board of Film Censors in response to concerted criticism of the cinema's influence on public taste. The First World War and the associated conflicts in Europe saw the hegemony of US films established and consolidated in the post-war period through the establishment of the vertically integrated Hollywood studio, with its eventual duplication in Britain. Despite the beginnings of what would become a significant film production and exhibition duopoly in Britain, the 1920s saw a corresponding decline in the numbers of British films showing in cinemas, resulting in the first of a series of interventions by government in the British film industry in the shape of the *Cinematograph Films Act 1927*. The 1920s ended with a momentous technological advance in the shape of the 'talkies' in 1929 – the development of synchronised sound.

The British Board of Film Censors and cinema regulation

In the period after 1910 there had been a concerted attempt to regulate the behaviour of cinema audiences, not only by middle-class pressure groups and organisations, but also by the clergy and local authorities. Concern was expressed about both the physical environment and the content of the films. Of particular concern were representations of sexuality, 'lewdness' and violence. In 1910 certain distributors had begun importing 'continental films', particularly from Germany which were considered at the time to be 'daring', most notably a film called *Sündige Liebe* (*Fools of Society*) (1911) which was about an adulterous affair.[2]

The industry was profoundly suspicious of any outside regulation. There was an awareness that the Cinematograph Act 1909, ostensibly designed to guarantee the safety of audiences, allowed county councils to stipulate other conditions before issuing a licence, to the extent that censorship was potentially possible.[3] Sunday opening became a significant issue. Much opposition to cinema was articulated in particular by the clergy. Many, though not all, local authorities and councils (for example the London County Council) had made Sunday closing an important condition of the granting of a licence.[4] By 1914 and the start of war many cities and towns had relented in the face of pressure from electors and industry and allowed Sunday opening. Nevertheless, the issue would not finally be resolved until the passing of The Sunday Entertainments Act in 1932.

Such was the agitation for control of censorship that the industry itself, largely via the Kinematograph Manufacturers Association (KMA), which had been created in 1906 in order to regulate the price of films to exhibitors, established the British Board of Film Censors (BBFC) in 1912 (renamed the British Board of Film Classification in 1984).[5] The Board was in effect a form of self-regulation, though one that was designed, according to Low, to 'help the trade by ridding it of its own worst elements'.[6] In order to broaden the industry support for the BBFC representatives of the Cinematograph Exhibitors Association (which had been formed out of the defunct Cinematograph Defence League and represented cinema owners) were invited to sit on the controlling committee. The BBFC was itself modelled on a US body called the National Board of Censorship of Motion Pictures, which had been established in 1909 by the People's Institute of New York and Dr Charles Sprague Smith.[7]

When it formally began operations on 1 January 1913, under its first Chairman George Redford, the BBFC's declared duty was 'to induce confidence in the minds of the licensing authorities, and of those who have in their charge the moral welfare of the community generally'.[8] Crucially, the BBFC would be funded by charging a levy on each foot of film submitted for censorship, which along with general funding from the industry meant that it was self-financing. What was less clear however, in those early years, was the relationship between the BBFC as arbiter of taste and decency and that of local authorities who retained formal powers of censorship via the police and magistrates. It had been hoped that the BBFC's decisions would be adopted across the country by all licensing authorities; however, many films passed by the BBFC were subsequently banned by some local authorities. As Lewis argues, local authorities' independence and their relationship with the BBFC 'was a defining characteristic of the formative years of film censorship, and often jealously guarded'.[9] The fact that there were more than several hundred authorities empowered to grant licences to cinemas meant, according to Robertson, that the 'BBFC was far from established after three years of operations.'[10]

The relationship between local authorities and the BBFC was complicated by the fact that the exercising of local censorship was anything but standardised, so that responsibility might rest in some areas with borough councils and in others with county councils. Many licensing authorities established Watch Committees or Local Vigilance Committees to examine and oversee censorship, others delegated powers to an individual 'whose character was considered beyond reproach'.[11] The lack of standardisation resulted in many local authorities taking a more relaxed attitude to censorship. Nevertheless, both the BBFC and indeed, many local authorities were subject to considerable pressure for increased censorship.

The debate about censorship in the wake of the BBFC's establishment took place in the context of a realisation that, during the First World War in particular, cinema would become the major form of mass communication. As Richards observed, 'the cinema was *the* mass medium, regularly patronised by the working classes, and the potential of films for influencing, even inflaming, this huge audience was fully appreciated by the Establishment' (original emphasis).[12] For the film industry the creation of the BBFC was in many ways a political move intended to pacify middle-class pressure groups, local authorities and central government which, it was feared in the case of the latter, would impose state censorship.

Much of the agitation for greater censorship and regulation of the cinema came from a plethora of moral and religious pressure groups, drawing their constituents largely from amongst the middle and upper classes, such as the National Council of Public Morals and the London Public Morality Council.[13] In 1917, at the request of the Cinematograph Trade Council, the National Council of Public Morals (an unofficial committee of religious, scientific, and cultural leaders) instituted a Commission of Enquiry into the cinema and its perceived reputation. The Commission's brief was to 'institute an enquiry into the physical, social, moral and educational influence of the cinema, with special reference to young people'.[14] It led to the publication of a report entitled *The Cinema: Its Present Position and Future Possibilities.* The BBFC's second President and Liberal MP, T. P. O'Connor, was a member of the Commission and was able to announce the creation of forty-three rules, which would determine whether a film was cut or banned.

The forty-three rules became known as 'O'Connor's 43'. Working with these the BBFC sought to limit and ban the depiction of many scenes of a sexual nature, swearing, crime, vulgarity in dress or manner and drugs.[15] O'Connor's role on the Commission and the implementation of his rules led, according to Low, to a report that was 'generally favourable' in its tone, and indeed recommended the sweeping away of the 'virtual censorship' of local authorities.[16] Its recommendations were, however, never implemented. The cinema might have been an overwhelmingly working-class pastime and increasingly organised along corporate lines, but for many moral and religious campaigners their groups' influence and power was out of all proportion to their composition. Increasingly, while in the minority as cinema-goers, the middle class could compensate by influencing censorship, criticism and most importantly, 'the social ambitions and cultural values of film-makers themselves'.[17] Though ostensibly adopting an openly moralistic stance, as enshrined in 'O'Connor's 43', the BBFC also revealed a political stance. Within this broader debate about the supposed necessity of censorship the key is perhaps the extent to which, according to Corrigan, censorship 'has long been wrongly construed as being concerned with morality'.[18] As MacKenzie argued, 'many of the regulations which may seem at first sight to be based on grounds of morality are in fact on closer examination political in purpose'.[19] Therefore, in addition to morality the BBFC was also concerned with cinematic representations that challenged the political status quo. Filmmakers were thus prevented from including 'References to controversial politics', 'Relations of Capital and Labour', 'scenes tending to disparage public characters and institutions' and 'bringing into disrepute British prestige in the Empire'.[20]

The development of the BBFC took place on the eve of the First World War and while the potential for cinema to play a role in the maintenance of morale would be realised, along with the adaptation to a new status quo; when the war began there was little sense of the role that cinema might play in the purveyance of propaganda.

The cinema in wartime

The Boer War of 1899–1902 was one of the first to be recorded on film and both actuality films and reconstructions (often presented as actuality but faked) were shown extensively in cinemas.[21] In 1900 the Boxer Rebellion in China generated much interest, momentarily overshadowing the Boer War, and was also the subject of several films, including Williamson's *Attack on a China Mission – Bluejackets to the Rescue* (1900), which played in cinemas with great success.[22] Many of the films shown drew upon dominant colonial discourses especially that of 'east' and 'west', 'civilisation' and 'barbarism' while racial stereotyping was often employed. Nevertheless, there was little sense in which the various films and images were the result of state intervention or state sanction. On the contrary the scale of the First World War prompted the Liberal government to instigate a series of ministerial and governmental organisations whose role it was in the first years of the war to produce propaganda targeted at those outside the country, particularly elites in countries of the Empire. Increasingly, however, as the conduct of the war progressed the focus became the domestic sphere and this saw the development of the Department of Information in 1917 and its replacement the Ministry of Information in 1918.

The role that cinema could play in the dissemination of propaganda only began to be considered as the war progressed. As Reeves observed, for many in the political establishment the cinema was seen as 'at best trivial, at worst a pernicious means of filling the leisure time of those who knew no better, and the idea that it might make some contribution to the serious business of winning the war was both incomprehensible and distasteful'.[23] When agreement was reached on the role cinema might play it was on the understanding that the films shown must be factual, though it was also clear that the cooperation of the commercial film industry was vital in the dissemination of propaganda films. This was a deal that suited the government since the commercial cinema sector was where the mass audience was, while the film industry, particularly the exhibition sector, anticipated significant financial reward.

During the ensuing conflict the cinema became an important focus for official propaganda, though initially the difficulties and obstacles to filming at the battlefront meant that what was presented as war footage invariably lacked any scenes of combat or excitement. In 1916, in the aftermath of the Somme offensive a film version entitled *The Battle of the Somme* was released.[24] At seventy-seven minutes long the film was a major commercial success and was followed by *The Battle of Ancre and the Advance of the Tanks* (1917). The popularity of these two films was not to be emulated by the third film in the series, *The German Retreat and the Battle of Arras* (1917), which was less successful critically, and signalled the end of the feature-length battlefield film.[25]

Whether the cinema was an effective propaganda tool is a moot point, with Reeves in particular less certain.[26] The government's interest in cinema during the First World War was far clearer in relation to its potential as a source of tax revenue. In 1915 the 'McKenna Duties' were introduced, which imposed taxes on a series of imported luxury goods including films and raw film stock. More significant was the wartime Entertainments Duty which sought to raise revenue from admissions not just to the cinema but to theatres, football matches and horse racing as well. The duty was graduated but the scale of the increases fell disproportionately on the cheapest cinema seats (1d on seats priced 2d to 6d), rather than the more expensive seats, bought by those who might be expected to be able to pay more. The duty had a profound impact upon the exhibition industry since the cinemas with the cheaper seats, attracting an overwhelmingly working-class audience, were the ones more likely to be owned by smaller chains or independent operators. As Low observed, these small exhibitors were the least able to absorb a drop in receipts.[27]

The exhibition industry was convinced of the grave threat posed by the duty, especially as attendances began to decline after its imposition. In 1918 attendances had dropped to fifteen million a week and they continued to fall after the end of hostilities with weekly attendances in 1921 estimated to be only nine million a week.[28] Despite some concessions by the government in 1917 in relation to the duty on cheaper seats, cinema closures were a significant feature of the war years.[29] *Bioscope* reported that in 1918 700 cinemas had closed since the imposition of the duty, though this was disputed by the government.[30] This number, if accurate, was a significant proportion of those cinemas in operation during the war years, which were estimated variously at anything between 4,000 and 6,000.[31] The estimate that is considered most reliable however is that of 4,500 advanced by the National Council of Public Morals in 1917.[32]

Cinema building and the development of the large circuits

At the start of the First World War in 1914 there were 109 cinema circuits in Britain, accounting for 20 per cent of cinemas. Only three of these circuits had twenty cinemas or more.[33] Small independent companies dominated the British film industry and the exhibition sector, but this was beginning to change. The first major catalyst for change had been The Cinematograph Act 1909 (see Chapter 1) and the beginnings of chains like Provincial Cinematograph Theatres Ltd (PCT).[34]

With restrictions on building there was little cinema construction during the war or immediately after, indeed, according to Atwell the period from 1914–21 saw no development in cinema in Britain at all.[35] The *Kinematograph Year Book*, an annual digest of statistical data for the industry, estimated that there were 4,000 cinemas in Britain in 1921. Though numbers attending the cinema had declined from the wartime high of 1917 the exhibition industry was of the view that the predominant form of cinemas – smaller buildings seating between 300 to 600 people on a single floor – needed to be partly replaced or at least augmented by larger and more prestigious cinemas. In part this was out of a concern to create a new market for cinema, but also a recognition that pre-war audiences had begun to demand better cinemas and more lavish surroundings. Furthermore, there was the realisation that the demand for cinema was predicated on the popularity of US films and the control that was increasingly being exercised over distribution by US companies.[36]

The war had disrupted the supply of both French and Italian films and it was hoped that British film production would expand to fill the gap, particularly since it singularly had failed to capitalise on the boom in demand for films before the war. In the event, the lack of support for the British film industry by both the government and City finance capital, as well as the conscription of many of the industry's key personnel, meant that Hollywood seized the initiative. During the war exhibitors came increasingly to rely on US films as domestic film production declined to less than 10 per cent.[37] By 1918 some 80 per cent of films shown in British cinemas were from the USA, while the prospect of increasing the numbers of British films was limited by the introduction of practices such as 'block booking'. This required cinemas to take a number of lesser films in order to be able to show prestige films. There was also 'blind booking', which was based upon a similar principle but this time involved taking films that may not even have been made yet.[38] There seemed no space on Britain's existing screens for British films. Of course, the exhibition industry was largely content with this since audience demand for US films meant expansion. As Ryall suggests, this established a familiar shape to the British film industry, with its imbalance in profitability between exhibition and production, the former being in the service of Hollywood.[39]

Cinema construction recommenced in earnest in 1921 and so began the transformation of the hitherto small, single-floored and simple buildings into the prototypes of the 'super cinemas' of the 1930s. One of the first cinemas built after the lifting of building restrictions in 1919 was the Dalston Picture Theatre, in North London, which was described by *Kinematograph Weekly* as a 'super cinema' – one of the first uses of this description.[40] When an announcement was made that the Tivoli cinema was to be built on the site of the old music hall in London's West End, *Pictures and Picturegoer* described the proposal similarly, as the 'first of the New Super-Cinemas'.[41] Brighton's Regent Cinema, designed by Robert Atkinson and opened in 1921 by PCT Ltd, is popularly claimed to be the first notable cinema of the post-war period, especially in relation to its functionality, modernity and decoration. Atkinson took his inspiration partly from theatre design but also from the United States, which he had visited in 1919 and where he had studied the latest cinema developments. The Regent cost £400,000 and seated 2,200 people in an auditorium bathed in 'warm shades of orange and vermilion, with figurative paintings for decoration'.[42]

The demand for larger and grander cinemas was satisfied increasingly, as in the case of the Regent, by larger circuits which were in a position to raise the necessary capital, especially from institutional investors. The rise of the larger national circuits and strongly capitalised regional circuits was based upon economies of scale both in terms of building costs and in renting films. PCT Ltd, formed in 1909, was the first major national circuit, which expanded by opening new cinemas and through the takeover of smaller circuits. In 1920 it operated sixty-eight cinemas. It sought further expansion by issuing new shares, using the capital raised to purchase further sites. Consequently, by 1927 the company was operating eighty-five cinemas.[43] The ability of cinema owners to open new and larger venues was not necessarily a result of burgeoning attendances; on the contrary the numbers of people going to the cinema had declined towards the end of the First World War and continued to do so after 1918. The expansion was largely the result of the ability of larger cinemas to remain profitable even as films and film programmes got longer, since fewer showings could be compensated by larger numbers of seats. Moreover, for the larger national and local circuits the ability to bargain with distributors meant that the cost of film rental could be reduced.[44] This did not necessarily mean that all large cinemas came into the orbit of major cinema circuits, since as Murphy explains the role of the entrepreneur was still important and most of the newest cinemas built in the early 1920s were invariably part of smaller, local circuits.[45]

Nevertheless, as the 1920s progressed the trend was towards national circuit building. The arrival of larger institutional investors in the late 1920s was inevitably directed towards more organised and, crucially, publicly quoted companies. In 1927 it was estimated that some £30–50m was invested in fifty-three public companies involved in exhibition.[46] This investment was funding new and bigger cinemas, particularly those seating 1,000 people or more, with the latter part of the 1920s seeing a shift to larger venues seating 1,000 to 2,000 people. In part the increase in investment in the cinema industry was due to the relaxing of the Entertainment Duty in 1924 (after concerted lobbying from the Cinematograph Exhibitors' Association) whereupon the duty was removed on tickets priced 6d or under. The correlation between ticket price and attendance, especially given that the cinema audience was predominantly working class, was seemingly confirmed as weekly admissions rose to some twenty million in 1925.[47]

Gaumont British Picture Corporation, which emerged from the 1920s as the largest film company in Britain, was a major beneficiary of the growth in institutional investment. In 1906 the British Gaumont company was formed as a subsidiary of the French company Société Léon Gaumont, which took over the production company run by A. C. Bromhead (see Chapter 1), though he stayed on as one of the directors. In the aftermath of the First World War the French parent company was in severe financial trouble and in 1922 sold the British Gaumont company to Bromhead and his brother. The deal was financed by the Ostrer Brothers' merchant bank of which the older brother Isidore would exercise considerable power and influence over British Gaumont. The significance of British Gaumont is that under the Ostrer brothers the company was the first to invest in the three branches of the film industry – production, distribution and exhibition (so-called 'vertical integration'). In 1926 it was renamed the Gaumont British Picture Corporation (GBPC). Having acquired several cinema chains, Gainsborough studios and two major distribution companies, GBPC (henceforth Gaumont) bought out the Bromheads and began building up the exhibition arm of the company in particular. This culminated in the purchase in 1929 of PCT Ltd, whereupon Gaumont controlled some 287 cinemas.

The example set by the Ostrer brothers was followed by John Maxwell, whose British International Pictures (BIP), a moderately successful producer of films including Alfred Hitchcock's *Blackmail* (made in 1929 and Britain's first sound film), formed a subsidiary called Associated British Cinemas (ABC) in 1928. Maxwell himself bid unsuccessfully for PCT Ltd. Nevertheless, by the end of the 1920s BIP (renamed Associated British Picture Corporation in 1933) controlled ninety cinemas through its ABC subsidiary and engaged in vigorous expansion from then on. As the decade ended the exhibition industry would increasingly be identified with the activities of both ABC and Gaumont, at least until the arrival of Oscar Deutsch's Odeon chain in 1933.

The coming of sound

Since the cinema had begun in 1895 audiences had rarely viewed films in silence, with gramophone records or more popularly pianists accompanying screenings. By 1919 distributors would often supply cue sheets for musical accompaniment with suggestions on what styles of music to adopt at particular moments of the film. However, in 1927 Warner Bros. studios released *The Jazz Singer*, starring Al Jolson, which was the first film to utilise synchronised dialogue, using technology developed by the Vitaphone Corporation of America.[48] Although the film was largely silent, with the sound element a brief sequence, it was an enormous commercial success, premiering in Britain in September 1928, and heralding the arrival of what would become known as the 'talkies'.

The introduction of the Vitaphone system was one of a series of attempts to develop synchronised sound, or 'sound films', from inventors in several countries. Vitaphone's system utilised a phonographic record made simultaneously with the film and then played back on a machine linked to the projector which turned the sound into electrical voltage. In Britain in 1926 De Forest Phonofilms, a subsidiary of a US parent company, premiered a system where the soundtrack was contained on the side of the film print. In the same year British Acoustic, a subsidiary of Gaumont, developed a two-strip system which had the sound on another strip of film.[49] The exhibition industry in Britain noted the developments but remained sceptical as late as 1928 with the Cinematograph Exhibitors' Association seemingly unable to see a time when sound might be a technical possibility.[50] However, the British premiere and commercial success of another Jolson film, *The Singing Fool* (1928) in 1929 dispelled the scepticism and set in motion the widespread installation of sound equipment.

Cinema owners looking to install sound were presented with a range of technologies and systems, including those developed in Britain and marketed as cheaper though often inferior alternatives to US systems. Increasingly, the market was dominated by two US-based companies; Western Electric, with its Vitaphone sound on record system and Radio Corporation of America (RCA), with its Photophone sound on film system. Initially both Western Electric and RCA refused to allow 'interchangeability', insisting that only their own films could be played on their sound equipment. Views as to the superiority of the relative systems differed, but both companies quickly produced comparable equipment. The preparedness on the part of exhibitors to equip their cinemas with sound apparatus was initially restricted to the larger cinemas seating audiences of over 1,000 so that by 1930 approximately 2,000 cinemas were suitably equipped.[51] For smaller cinemas the cost of installation, estimated at between £2,000 and £4,000, was a significant restriction. Added to this was the increased rental charges levied by the distributors for the first sound films. Many limped along showing silent films before duly closing down.[52] Nevertheless, by the end of 1931 the number of cinemas equipped to show talkies reached 3,750, notwithstanding that the vigorous shakeout of the exhibition industry in 1933–34 saw many cinemas close.[53] Hiley's analysis of the period concludes that the coming of sound did not result in a significant increase in attendance but it did have an effect on the size of cinemas.[54]

The demands of sound meant a significant re-evaluation of the design of cinemas, with an increased emphasis on the acoustic qualities of the auditorium. In a sense cinemas needed to become 'acoustic boxes' in which the sound of the film was to be kept and presented as clearly as possible, and external sound was to be kept out.[55] It was the advent of sound, Sharp posits, that 'proved the most fundamental change in cinema design since the industry began'.[56]

Government regulation and intervention – responding to Hollywood

The relationship between the cinema and the state in Britain finds expression in two main areas. The first is economic, and mainly concerns attempts to protect the British film industry from the worst effects of American competition. The second is, broadly speaking, ideological, and has to do with censorship.[57]

The proportion of screen time allotted to British films had been declining year-on-year since 1914 and although, as we have seen, it was of less concern to the exhibition industry it had began to vex other sections of the British film industry and the government. In 1923 only 10 per cent of the films shown in Britain's cinemas were British and this declined still further until it reached only 5 per cent by 1925.[58] British films available for exhibition in 1925 numbered only thirty, which was down from around a hundred in the period immediately after the First World War.[59] Things looked very bad for film production in Britain and as a result the government sought to intervene directly. As Miles and Smith pointed out, the film industry in Britain was not the only industry suffering through heightened competition, therefore the government's decision to intervene indicates the anxiety felt about the situation.[60] This anxiety was in small part about the economic well-being of the industry itself but more significantly it was about the supposed power of US films, or what had increasingly come to be known collectively as 'Hollywood'. The promotion of British film was highly charged culturally and politically and, as Ryall observed, 'had as much to do with resisting Americanization as [it] had to do with supporting a distinctive cultural dimension of English life, or the preservation of a small sector of the economy'.[61] Speaking in the House of Commons in 1925, Prime Minister Stanley Baldwin cited the film industry in a speech about unemployment and stated that 'the time has come when the position of that industry in this country should be examined with a view to seeing whether it be not possible, as it is desirable, on national grounds, to see that a larger proportion of the films exhibited in this country are British'.[62]

In 1927 the government opted for a protectionist approach, following other European countries such as Germany, and introduced into law the Cinematograph Films Act 1927 (the '1927 Act'), which established quotas for the number of British films that had to be shown in cinemas. The quotas distinguished between the distributors who rented the films to exhibitors, and the exhibitors themselves, and were set in the first year at 7.5 and 5 per cent respectively. The renters' quota was higher so that they could offer exhibitors a selection of films from which to choose. The 1927 Act, or 'quota act' as it became known, allowed for the quotas to increase each year until they reached 20 per cent in 1936, whereupon they would remain the same until the 1927 Act was due to expire in 1938 (The Cinematograph Films Act 1938 replaced the 1927 Act after a review of the quota – see Chapter 3). The definition of a 'British film' was one made by a British subject or company though significantly 'the definition did not specify that control had to be in British hands, but only that the company had to be constituted in the British Empire and that the majority of the company directors should be British'.[63] There were also provisos about use of studios and the proportion of labour costs that had to be paid to British subjects. The 1927 Act also outlawed the practice of 'blind booking', by insisting that all films be registered with the Board of Trade before being offered to distributors and exhibitors. Moreover, each film to be registered had to be shown to the cinema trade first, so that both distributors and exhibitors could decide if they wanted it. With advance booking restricted to only six months hence the theory was that more space would be available in cinemas for British films.[64]

There seems no doubt that the 1927 Act immediately stimulated British film production with the proportion of British films shown increasing yearly from 4.4 per cent in 1927 to 19 per cent in 1930.[65] The increase in production was partly the result of speculative investment, though many of the newly formed film companies were not robust enough to survive for long, particularly as the advent of sound greatly increased the cost of film production. The 1927 Act was also the catalyst for the creation of Gaumont and ABPC, both of which were vertically integrated along the lines of Hollywood studios, as discussed earlier in this chapter. The significance of this was that prior to the 1927 Act British production was not sufficiently strong to supply films on a regular basis to cinema chains.[66] In part the subsequent building of the 'super cinemas' in the 1930s was a consequence of the power of the combines to secure the best British films for their chains. Since the best British films were often produced by these two combines, the British films available to independent exhibitors were often of lesser quality.

Herein lay the irony of the 1927 Act: much of the increase in film production was based upon low-budget films produced in Britain to do no more than comply with the most basic letter of the law. These films were often referred to as 'quota quickies' – a range of films made between 1928 and 1938 characterised by their low budgets and the speed with which they were made. One contemporary trade paper referred to them as made in a 'week's intensive work using unwanted scraps from other films, disengaged sets from any studio, all kinds of ingenious economies and working a star under terrific pressures for a day-and-a-half'.[67] According to Hartog, the 1927 Act's intention of stimulating production had been undermined by the fact that 'about half of the British films produced each year were made to be registered, but not shown'.[68]

The historical debates about the relative merits of 'quota quickies' are contested. Low viewed them with unequivocal disdain.[69] Glancy considered them in the context of Hollywood's own considerable output of low-budget 'B' pictures.[70] Sedgwick, in his snapshot of the market for films in 1934, was concerned that attention was not unduly drawn to the 'quota quickie' at the expense of a more measured consideration of the general state of the industry.[71] Napper considered the films as a reflection of the society and culture that produced them.[72]

Nevertheless, the main focus for the 1927 Act was the influence of Hollywood, which focused the minds of studio executives on the necessity of distributing the required percentage of British films. In the face of the quota requirement the studios were nothing if not pragmatic and they set about finding the cheapest way of fulfilling it. Two major Hollywood studios – Warner Bros. and Fox Film Corporation – had subsidiary companies in Britain which produced films; others used British production companies to make up their requisite quotas. As Glancy observed, the studios 'were willing to make British quota films, but sought to keep the costs of such films to a minimum' in order to distribute them along with their own US-produced films.[73]

Broadening the audience – a refuge from the street to a whole evening out

The 1920s are marked by a class-informed struggle for cultural 'ownership' of cinema between showmen, intelligentsia, financiers and audiences, whose different interests circulate competing critical values and aesthetic preferences.[74]

In 1914 cinema attendance stood at 7–8 million a week; by 1917 this had increased to 20.6 million a week.[75] During the war years going to the cinema was confirmed as an overwhelmingly working-class pastime, particularly amongst the large numbers of workers increasingly concentrated in the towns and cities and employed in the burgeoning war-related industries. However, the war also encouraged more middle-class patrons to visit the cinema: as MacKenzie observed, 'War enhanced the cinema's popularity, and the public needed little encouragement to attend in their millions.'[76] As war gave way to peace attendance fluctuated significantly, but the trend was for a steady increase in middle-class cinema-goers (many of whom had been keen theatre-goers).

In the period after 1910, what was known as the 'legitimate' theatre (a term used to differentiate it from music hall) had been the bastion of middle-class respectability.

While this was still true in the 1920s the main building phase of new theatres in London had already peaked by 1920.[77] In the regions, theatres were to be found in considerably fewer numbers, the case even in the larger cities like Birmingham and Manchester, and everywhere the newer post-war cinemas offered comparative or indeed greater luxury than the best live theatres. Increasingly, middle-class patrons were to be found going to the newer cinemas; the existence of a clientele of similar social standing was important in fostering the cinema-going habit. There was not universal approval for this new cultural trend. In 1919 the Editor of *The Play Pictorial* visited several cinemas and found 'the audiences at the respectable theatres average specimens of middle class life. Presumably they were intelligent beings, though how any intelligent person can become cinema habitués [sic] I fail to understand.'[78]

For working-class and poorer audiences the environment of the cinema was just as important, albeit for different reasons. For many of them the cinema offered a warm and comfortable refuge which, at prices averaging 4d, was an affordable luxury and unlike the theatre the cinema had no dress code or apparent formality. Since many poorer patrons went in their work clothes or did not practice the kinds of personal hygiene common amongst the middle classes, the smell in the cinema was often bad and it was not uncommon for cinemas to be sprayed with disinfectant before, during and after performances. At matinée showings unemployed men often attended in order to sleep and pass the time in a place of warmth and relative anonymity. People also sought privacy in the cinema, as the darkness allowed young men and women to meet away from the critical gaze of parents and guardians. What is significant about much of this audience behaviour in the earliest days of cinema was that many people bought time in the cinema rather than buying films and that time was utilised for a variety of activities.[79]

In the 1920s as the newer, larger cinemas were built and the older cinemas closed the exhibition industry sought to differentiate the audience and increasingly physically separate the middle-class patrons from those of the working class. This was done largely through ticket pricing but also through the programming of films and the developing sophistication of the film narrative that had begun to take place before 1914. As Hiley argues, the socially mixed audience was one that lacked a clear sense of communal identity and the increasingly regulated and disciplined environment imposed upon this audience both a docility and lack of participation.[80]

The regulation of audience behaviour was also engendered by changes to the films, which with the coming of sound became more naturalistic and encouraged a new form of spectatorship. Audiences were presented with what Denzin called a 'new regime of realism' in which certain ideas and representations, which were already present in dominant discourses, were naturalised on screen.[81] For the middle classes the images on screen were increasingly familiar, especially as many filmmakers in the 1920s turned to classic literature for its subjects. Moreover, the themes and ideological frameworks steadily adopted by British cinema, partly in opposition to Hollywood, provided a largely middle-class worldview against which other forms of cinema were judged. For the working-class spectator the screen increasingly offered models of behaviour and inscribed forms of identity such as those of gender, class or nationality. Further, films themselves became an important context for the articulation of morality. Morality on screen was a powerful influence on morality off screen.

Broadening the audience – alternatives to the commercial cinema

Throughout the inter-war period and in the wake of the establishment of the BBFC, there was a continued debate about morality and censorship, particularly in relation to cinema's potential as a vehicle for propaganda.[82] Many of O'Connor's rules, formulated at the height of the First World War, were only intended to last until the war ended. The revolution in Russia, political upheavals in Germany and middle-class anxiety about the 'masses', due in part to the fact that the working class now formed the majority of the electorate, meant that they were never rescinded.[83] In 1919 the BBFC, in a letter to producers and local authorities, made explicit its emphasis on the suitability of films for a largely working-class audience by comparing cinema censorship with that of the theatre.[84] The letter explained that the 'audience at the cinema is very differently constituted from that of a theatre, being composed largely of young people and family parties, who, more often than not, have no knowledge beforehand of the programme which is to be put before them.'[85]

In the fevered aftermath of the general strike in 1926 the BBFC, in connivance with the then Home Secretary Sir William Joynson-Hicks, refused a certificate for Eisenstein's *Battleship Potemkin* (*Bronenosets Potyomkin*) (1925). For those interested in seeing the film and others that dealt with 'industrial relations', one answer was to form a film society which would hold screenings of films for members only. This enabled films like *Battleship Potemkin* to be shown even though it had been banned by both the BBFC and a number of local authorities. The Film Society in London, started by Hugh Miller, Ivor Montagu and others in 1925, was one of the first such societies.[86]

In part the emergence of the Film Society reflected a nascent alternative film culture, which was beginning to find a voice in some newspapers, such as the *Observer* and *The Times* with the writing of film critics like Ivor Montagu and Iris Barry. Indeed, many of these critics were members of the Film Society and reflected the distinct middle-class complexion of this alternative film culture. Its value, according to Sexton, was that it helped establish a critical discourse about alternative film and in particular aesthetics.[87] It was followed in the 1920s and 1930s by other film societies in cities across Britain including Cambridge, Edinburgh, Manchester and Oxford. Such was the success of some, that in 1932 the Leeds Film Group came into conflict with the mainstream exhibition trade who sought to prevent the group from showing films. Their venue, the Savoy Theatre, was taken over and reopened as the Leeds Academy Cinema.[88] In the same year an attempt was made to form a Federation of Film Societies but this failed (though a Scottish federation was formed in 1934 as the Scottish Films Council). Ultimately the British Federation of Film Societies (BFFS) was constituted in 1937.

Despite its middle-class make-up the Film Society can also be seen as a precursor of a number of subsequent workers' film societies, modelled in part on similar movements in France and Germany.[89] In 1929 the Federation of Workers' Film Societies was formed by the Minority Movement, a Communist-led trade union organisation, in order to facilitate not only the showing of films but to 'encourage the production of films of value to the working-class'.[90] In the same year the Masses Stage and Film Guild (MSFG) was established by the Arts Guild of the Independent Labour Party to bring international films to working-class audiences. The MSFG was not an enduring success, especially since it made none of its own newsreels or films. Its activities, particularly its efforts to show banned Soviet films, did illuminate some of the class bias inherent in the practice of censorship in the 1920s. In 1928 the MSFG applied to show Pudovkin's *Mother* (*Mat*) (1926) at the Regal Cinema in London but it was refused a licence by the London County Council. After a protracted campaign that enlisted the support of Bertrand Russell, George Bernard Shaw and others, it became clear that the issue was, according to Hogenkamp, an 'interpretation of "public" and "private"'.[91] The low admission prices and membership put attendance within reach of the working class, which was the realm of the 'public' and distinctly worrying to those in authority.

Many of these developments were consolidated in the second half of the 1920s. Britain witnessed the possibility that cinema could be embraced by individuals, groups and organisations seeking to imbue it with an artistic, critical and political perspective. As Samson observed:

> In 1925 there were no film institutes, film archives or film festivals. Serious newspaper criticism of film did not exist; nor did specialised cinemas for minority audiences, film libraries, or educational attention to film. By 1939 all of these things had been established. Moreover, there was now a national network of film societies and workers' film societies, which meant that to a large extent the work of the Film

Society was being successfully continued by many different groups in various parts of the country.[92]

'Americanisation' in the cinema

The promotion and defence of overseas markets was the responsibility of the Foreign Department of the Motion Picture Producers and Distributors of America (MPPDA), which had extensive contacts in the US State Department and the US Department of Commerce. As early as 1926, when the Motion Picture Division of the Bureau of Foreign and Domestic Commerce was formed, the link between Hollywood and US trade was established. The Bureau calculated that each foot of film exported and exhibited abroad yielded one dollar in purchases of US goods.[93] In 1923 the Chairman of the MPPDA, Will Hays, had visited Britain and observed that the aim of Hollywood was to 'Americanise the world.'[94]

One of the reasons for the establishment of this hegemony was that Hollywood dominated its home market. Its studios were structured along industrial lines, with standardisation and other ways of achieving economies of scale. A key element of this structure was the extent to which the industry had become vertically integrated, so that the organisation established in one part of the production chain gained control of the other parts of the production process. To this end many of the Hollywood studios came to encompass the spheres of production, distribution and exhibition, with the box-office revenues providing studios with ongoing finance. Paramount, Warner Bros., Loew's/MGM, RKO and Fox all operated first-run cinemas in major cities in order to offer guaranteed outlets for exhibition. In the late 1930s the Federal Government began an anti-trust suit against the studios concerned, viewing their dominant control of the exhibition industry as a restraint of trade. In 1948 the United States Supreme Court finally outlawed the policy (known as the 'Paramount Decrees') and the studios were forced to divest themselves of their cinemas.[95] Over the following decade the major Hollywood studios realised that distribution was the key to the film industry and while dissolving their interests in exhibition they keenly retained their distribution arms. After the Second World War, Hollywood stopped selling its films to foreign distributors. Instead, the studios established local subsidiaries of home-based distributors, which allowed for the complete control of marketing and promotion, and the retention of profits.[96]

The economic disparities between Britain and the United States were great and in a very real sense militated against the British industry from the start. By 1926, $1.5bn (£308m at 1926 rate of exchange) was being invested annually in the US film industry as opposed to £35m in Britain. Most of the British investment was in the more profitable exhibition sector with only £500,000 invested in production.[97]

Street identified an increasing 'cultural and ideological alarm' about Hollywood films during the inter-war period.[98] Speaking in 1936, R. D. Fennelly of the Board of Trade's Film Department, felt that 'from the view of British culture and ideals it was unwise to allow the United States to dominate the cinemas of this country'.[99] Implicit in this view was the perception that US culture was a mass and materially based one, which amounted to an attack not only on the 'high' culture of a British social and intellectual elite but, more importantly it seemed, on the lived cultures of the population as a whole.[100] This view was articulated bluntly in the *Daily Express* on 18 March 1927 by Lt. Col. R. V. K. Applin, who was the Conservative Member of Parliament for Enfield:

> The plain truth about the film situation is that the bulk of our picturegoers are Americanised to an extent that makes them regard a British film as a foreign film, and an interesting but more frequently irritating interlude to their favourite entertainment. They go to see American stars; they have been brought up on American publicity. They talk America, think America, and dream America. We have several million people, mostly women, who, for all intent and purposes, are temporary American citizens.[101]

In this debate there was little sense of cinema as a legitimate art form, rather it was seen as a powerful message medium that either had to be controlled or colonised by elites. Moreover, its popularity amongst the population as a whole made many of these elites fearful of its potential as a democratising force. Raymond Williams noted that the first audiences for cinema were the urban working classes, while cinema had appeared just at the time when the labour and socialist movements were growing in strength.[102] According to Williams, the Left viewed cinema from the beginning as an 'inherently popular and in that sense democratic art' that leapt over 'the class-bound establishment theatre and all the cultural barriers which selective education had erected around literacy.'[103]

In the same way that the future of the film industry in Britain was tempered by that of the US industry, the future of British high/elite culture, or so it seemed, was tempered by that of US mass/popular culture. At the heart of this debate was the New World/Old World dichotomy and the sense that the United States was a bastard civilisation, whose culture was a veneer.[104] The association between US culture and industrialisation and commerce made by critics in the inter-war years reveals a paradox at the heart of this elitist view of culture. For those in the Board of Trade and their supporters, seeking to legislate for the continuation of British cinema, the answer lay precisely in the establishment of a powerful indigenous film industry, structured along Hollywood lines, in order to project British national culture. The perceived need to protect national culture, or more importantly a particular version of it, came into sharp focus around the notion that the 'mass society' was a creation of the media. It is the media that offers a world-view, which is a potential means of manipulation but also one that can serve dominant sources of social power and authority if integrated into these very sources. The problem, it seemed, was not that mass media forms like the cinema were disseminators of propaganda but that the propaganda was *theirs* and not *ours*. Thus, the Secretary of the Empire Marketing Board, Sir Stephen Tallents, opined that: 'It is horrible to think that the British Empire is receiving its education from a place called Hollywood. The dominions would rather have a picture with a wholesome, honest British background, something that gives British sentiment, something that is honest to our traditions, than the abortions we get from Hollywood.'[105]

Many commentators were only too aware of the potential of cinema as a medium for the communication of ideas and ideology. The cinema could be used, according to Williams, to 'bypass the problems of literacy; to bypass, in the silent era, the old limitations of national languages; but above all to ensure rapid distribution of a relatively standard product, over a very much wider social and geographical area'.[106] Of course, the country that realised the commercial and ideological potential of cinema was the USA, whose film industry, John Grierson noted, pursued 'the same principles as Woolworth and Ford'.[107]

The reality, however, was that in Britain the majority of films shown throughout the inter-war years were from the USA. The outbreak of the First World War saw an increase in the number shown due to the demand by exhibitors in the face of increased attendance and the decline in domestic production. This dominance was exacerbated by the animosity between producers and renters and exhibitors. Cinema owners felt they had little obligation to programme British films, especially since US distributors could offer Hollywood films at a substantial discount because their domestic market was so great.[108] Moreover, it appeared that audiences, especially the working class, preferred to see Hollywood films since they seemed to speak more clearly to them than many of the British films that purported to express a national character.

Notes

1 W. Benjamin, 'The Work of Art in the Age of Mechanical Reproduction', in *Illuminations*, ed. H. Arendt, trans H. Zorn (London: Jonathan Cape, 1970), p. 238.

2 N. Hiley, '"No Mixed Bathing": The Creation of the British Board of Film Censors in 1913', *Journal of Popular British Cinema*, 3 (2000), 5–19, p. 7.

3 See J. Richards, 'The British Board of Film Censors and Content Control in the 1930s: Images of Britain', *Historical Journal of Film, Radio and Television*, 1:2 (1981), 95–116, and S. Lewis, 'Local Authorities and the Control of Film Exhibition in Britain in the Interwar Period', *Journal of Popular British Cinema*, 3 (2000), 113–20.

4 See D. Williams, 'Never on Sunday: The Early Operation of the Cinematograph Act of 1909 in regard to Sunday Opening', *Film History*, 14 (2002), 186–94.

5 See Hiley, 'No Mixed Bathing', N. M. Hunnings, *Film Censors and the Law* (London: Allen and Unwin, 1967), and J. Robertson, *The British Board of Film Censors: Film Censorship in Britain, 1896–1950* (London: Croom Helm, 1985), for a detailed discussion of the genesis of the BBFC.

6 R. Low, *The History of the British Film 1914–1918* (London: George Allen & Unwin, [1950] 1973), p. 126.

7 The National Board of Censorship of Motion Pictures changed its name to National Board of Review of Motion Pictures in 1915 as an exhibitors' organisation that operated a 'clearing house' for films in an effort to avoid government censorship. See www.nbrmp.org (accessed May 2004).

8 Cited in Hiley, 'No Mixed Bathing', p. 10.

9 Lewis, 'Local Authorities and the Control of Film Exhibition', p. 113.

10 Robertson, *The British Board of Film Censors,* p. 7.

11 Lewis, 'Local Authorities and the Control of Film Exhibition', p. 113.

12 Richards, 'The British Board of Film Censors and Content Control in the 1930s', p. 95.

13 See A. Kuhn, 'Children, "Horrific" Films, and Censorship in 1930s Britain', *Historical Journal of Film, Radio and Television*, 22:2 (2002), 197–202, and P. Miles and M. Smith, *Cinema, Literature & Society: Elite and Mass Culture in Interwar Britain* (London: Croom Helm, 1987).

14 National Council of Public Morals, Cinema Commission, *The Cinema: Its Present Position and Future Possibilities* (London: Williams and Norgate, 1917), reprinted in full in S. Herbert, *A History of Early Film: Volume 3* (London: Routledge, 2000), p. vii.

15 See Hunnings, *Film Censors and the Law.*

16 Low, *The History of the British Film 1914–1918*, p. 136.

17 R. Durgnat, *A Mirror for England: British Movies from Austerity to Affluence* (London: Faber and Faber, 1970), p. 6.

18 P. Corrigan, 'Film Entertainment as Ideology and Pleasure: A Preliminary Approach to a History of Audiences', in J. Curran and V. Porter (eds), *British Cinema History* (London: Weidenfeld and Nicolson, 1983), p. 29.

19 J. M. MacKenzie, *Propaganda and Empire: The Manipulation of British Public Opinion, 1880–1960* (Manchester: Manchester University Press, 1986), p. 78.

20 Hunnings, *Film Censors and the Law*, pp. 408–9.

21 See S. Popple, '"But the Khaki-Covered Camera is the *Latest* Thing": The Boer War Cinema and Visual Culture in Britain', in A. Higson (ed.), *Young and Innocent? The Cinema in Britain 1896–1930* (Exeter: University of Exeter Press, 2002) and

MacKenzie, *Propaganda and Empire.*

22 See F. Gray, 'James Williamson's Composed Picture: *Attack on a China Mission –
Bluejackets to the Rescue* (1900)', in J. Fullerton (ed.), *Celebrating 1895: The Centenary
of Cinema* (Sydney: John Libbey and the National Museum of Photography, Film
and Television, Bradford, UK, 1998).

23 N. Reeves, 'The Power of Film Propaganda – Myth or Reality?', *Historical Journal
of Film, Radio and Television*, 13:2 (1993), 181–201, p. 188.

24 For further discussion of the film see N. Reeves, 'Cinema, Spectatorship and
Propaganda: "Battle of the Somme" and its Contemporary Audience – 1916',
Historical Journal of Film, Radio and Television, 17:1 (1997), 5–28, and S. D. Badsey,
'*Battle of the Somme*: British War-propaganda', *Historical Journal of Film, Radio and
Television*, 3:2 (1983), 99–115.

25 See N. Reeves, 'Official British Film Propaganda', in M. Paris (ed.), *The First World
War and Popular Cinema: 1914 to the Present* (Edinburgh: Edinburgh University
Press, 1999).

26 Reeves, 'The Power of Film Propaganda'.

27 Low, *The History of the British Film 1914–1918.*

28 N. Hiley, '"Let's Go to the Pictures": The British Cinema Audience in the 1920s
and 1930s', *Journal of Popular British Cinema*, 2 (1999), 39–53, p. 40.

29 Low, *The History of the British Film 1914–1918.*

30 *Bioscope*, 30 May 1918, cited in *ibid.*, p. 110.

31 Low, *The History of the British Film 1914–1918*, p. 16.

32 *The Cinema: Its Present Position and Future Possibilities*, National Council of Public
Morals, Cinema Commission (1917).

33 B. Baillieu and J. Goodchild, *The British Film Business* (London: John Wiley &
Sons, 2002), p. 19.

34 See A. Eyles, 'The First National Chain: P.C.T', *The Mercia Bioscope*, 90 (February
2004), 11–18 (Mercia Cinema Society).

35 D. Atwell, *Cathedrals of the Movies: A History of British Cinemas* (London: Architectural
Press, 1981).

36 For a detailed analysis of the relationship between Europe's cinema industry and
that of the United States in this period see G. Bakker, 'The Decline and Fall of the
European Film Industry: Sunk Costs, Market Size and Market Structure, 1890–
1927', *Working Papers In Economic History No. 70/03* (London School of Economics,
February 2003).

37 K. Thompson, *Exporting Entertainment: America in the World Film Market 1907–
1934* (London: British Film Institute, 1985).

38 R. Murphy, 'Under the Shadow of Hollywood', in C. Barr, *All Our Yesterdays: 90
Years of British Cinema* (London: British Film Institute, 1986). See also PEP, *The
British Film Industry*, 1952.

39 T. Ryall, *Britain and the American Cinema* (London, Thousand Oaks, CA and New
Delhi: Sage, 2001).

40 R. Gray, *Cinemas in Britain: 100 Years of Cinema Architecture* (London: Cinema
Theatre Association/British Film Institute, 1996).

41 *Pictures and Picturegoer*, 21 June 1919, 315.

42 *Ibid.*

43 Baillieu and Goodchild, *The British Film Business*, p. 27.

44 See Hiley, 'Let's Go to the Pictures'.

45 R. Murphy, 'Fantasy Worlds: British Cinema between the Wars', *Screen*, 26:1 (January–February 1985), 10–20.

46 Baillieu and Goodchild, *The British Film Business*, p. 21.

47 *Ibid.*

48 Warner Bros. purchased the rights to the Western Electric system, which helped to establish them as one of the group of studios known as the 'majors'.

49 See R. Murphy, 'Coming of Sound to the Cinema in Britain', *Historical Journal of Film, Radio and Television*, 4:2 (1984), 143–60, and R. Low, *The History of the British Film 1918–1929* (London: George Allen & Unwin, 1971).

50 Murphy, 'Coming of Sound'.

51 Hiley, 'Let's Go to the Pictures', p. 42.

52 PEP, *The British Film Industry*, 1952.

53 Hiley, 'Let's Go to the Pictures', p. 42.

54 *Ibid.*

55 D. Sharp, *The Picture Palace and other Buildings of the Movies* (London: Hugh Evelyn, 1969).

56 *Ibid.*, p. 102.

57 J. Petley, 'Cinema and State', in Barr (ed.), *All our Yesterdays*, p. 31.

58 PEP, *The British Film Industry*, 1952, p. 41.

59 Ryall, *Britain and the American Cinema*, p. 33.

60 Miles and Smith, *Cinema, Literature & Society*.

61 Ryall, *Britain and the American Cinema*, p. 36.

62 Cited in S. Hartog, 'State Protection of a Beleaguered Industry', in Curran and Porter (eds), *British Cinema History*, p. 60.

63 M. Dickinson and S. Street, *Cinema and State: The Film Industry and the Government 1927–1984* (London: British Film Institute, 1985), p. 6.

64 See PEP, *The British Film Industry*, 1952.

65 Dickinson and Street, *Cinema and State*, p. 42.

66 PEP, *The British Film Industry*, 1952.

67 *Bioscope*, 13 March 1929, cited in Low, *The History of the British Film 1918–1929*, p. 105.

68 Hartog, 'State Protection of a Beleaguered Industry', p. 68.

69 R. Low, *The History of the British Film 1929–1939: Film Making in 1930s Britain* (London: Allen & Unwin, 1985).

70 H. Mark Glancy, 'Hollywood and Britain: MGM and the British "Quota" Legislation', in J. Richards (ed.), *The Unknown 1930s: An Alternative History of the British Cinema, 1929–39* (London: I. B. Tauris, 1998).

71 J. Sedgwick, 'The Market for Feature Films in Britain, 1934: A Viable National Cinema', *Historical Journal of Film, Radio and Television*, 14:1 (1994), 15–36.

72 L. Napper, 'A Despicable Tradition? Quota–quickies in the 1930s', in R. Murphy

(ed.), *The British Cinema Book*, second edition (London: British Film Institute, 2001).

73 Glancy, 'Hollywood and Britain', p. 60.

74 C. Gledhill, *Reframing British Cinema 1918–1928: Between Restraint and Passion* (London: British Film Institute, 2003), p. 16.

75 Hiley, 'Let's go to the pictures', p. 40. See also R. Low, *The History of the British Film 1906–1914* (London: George Allen & Unwin [1949] 1973).

76 MacKenzie, *Propaganda and Empire*, p. 74.

77 A. Jackson, *The Middle Classes 1900–1950* (Nairn: Davis St John Thomas, 1991).

78 Cited in *ibid.*, p. 267.

79 See Hiley, 'At the Picture Palace'.

80 *Ibid.*

81 N. Denzin, *The Cinematic Society: The Voyeur's Gaze* (London, Thousand Oaks, CA and New Delhi: Sage, 1995), p. 21.

82 See N. Pronay and D. W. Spring (eds), *Propaganda, Politics and Film, 1918–45* (London: Macmillan, 1982).

83 See Robertson, *The British Board of Film Censors*.

84 BBFC Annual Report, 1919, cited in Robertson, *The British Board of Film Censors*.

85 *Ibid.*, p. 20.

86 See J. Samson, 'The Film Society, 1925–1939', in Barr (ed.), *All Our Yesterdays*, and J. Sexton, 'The Film Society and the creation of an Alternative Film Culture in Britain in the 1920s', in Higson (ed.), *Young and Innocent?*

87 *Ibid.*

88 See P. Cargin, (ed.), *An Introduction to Film Societies and the BFFS* (London: British Federation of Film Societies, 1998).

89 B. Hogenkamp, *Deadly Parallels: Film and the Left in Britain 1929–39* (London: Lawrence and Wishart, 1986).

90 *Ibid.*, p. 36.

91 Hogenkamp, *Deadly Parallels*, p. 41.

92 Samson, 'The Film Society, 1925–1939', p. 313.

93 Dickinson and Street, *Cinema and State*, p. 12.

94 *Ibid.*

95 See E. Borneman, 'United States versus Hollywood: The Case Study of an Antitrust Suit', in T. Balio (ed.), *The American Film Industry*, revised edition (Madison, WI: The University of Wisconsin Press, 1985) originally published in *Sight and Sound*, 19 (February 1951), pp. 418–20 and *Sight and Sound*, 20 (March 1951), pp. 448–50.

96 I. Jarvie, 'Free Trade as Cultural Threat: American Film and TV Exports in the Post-war period', in G. Nowell-Smith and S. Ricci (eds), *Hollywood and Europe: Economics, Culture and National Identity 1945–95* (London: British Film Institute, 1998).

97 Dickinson and Street, *Cinema and State*, p. 10.

98 S. Street, *British National Cinema* (London: Routledge, 1997).

99 Cited in Dickinson and Street, *Cinema and State*, p. 8.

100 P. Swann, *The Hollywood Feature Film in Postwar Britain* (London: Croom Helm, 1987).

101 Cited in K. Bamford, *Distorted Images: British National Identity and Film in the 1920s* (London: I. B. Tauris, 1999), pp. 118–19.

102 R. Williams, 'Cinema and Socialism', in Tony Pinkney (ed.), *The Politics of Modernism* (London: Verso, 1996).

103 *Ibid.*, p. 107.

104 See Swann, *The Hollywood Feature Film.*

105 Cited in P. M. Taylor, *The Projection of Britain: British Overseas Publicity and Propaganda 1919–1939* (Cambridge: Cambridge University Press, 1981), p. 10.

106 Williams, 'Cinema and Socialism', p. 109.

107 F. Hardy (ed.), *Grierson on Documentary* (London: Faber and Faber, 1979), p. 52.

108 G. Macnab, *J. Arthur Rank and the British Film Industry* (London: Routledge, 1994).

3

Cinema as mass entertainment: 1930–50

In the 1930s the cinema interior was seen as a place of escape … The architecture provided a fantasy a world apart from the unemployment and slums without … Just as the Gothic cathedral was seen as a kind of foretaste of heaven for the illiterate masses of medieval Europe, a trailer for the forthcoming attraction, so the cinema provided a glimpse into another world, a world of beauty, dancing, music and escape. (Edward Heathcote)[1]

The 1930s was a period when the mass media – press, radio, film, and gramophone records – began to develop into the forms that we are familiar with today. Moreover, it was a period when the notion of leisure became intimately tied to these mass media forms: forms that steadily came under the ownership of burgeoning big business concerns. According to Bakker the estimated number of persons employed in the entertainment industry in 1938 was 106,855.[2] Of these new electronic media forms the cinema was the most mature and extensive, employing some 37.9 per cent of the total number of people in the entertainment industry.[3] By 1930, particularly with the coming of the 'talkies' in 1929, the exhibition industry was both well established and well organised commercially with some 4,000 cinemas in operation. It catered for a population that was increasingly placing the cinema, along with radio, at the centre of cultural life. Between 1932 and 1934 alone, some 302 cinemas were built.[4] During the 1930s the exhibition industry underwent dramatic changes in both its ownership, which became progressively more centralised, and in the nature of the cinemas themselves. After 1941 two companies – ABC and Rank – would come to dominate the exhibition industry prior to 1984.

Picture palaces and the 'supers'

In twenty five years cinema building has made such progress as has probably never been equalled in a similar period in any other branch of architecture. One could write at length on the transition from the hard, cold interiors of the early halls to the modern luxury of soft carpet, armchair seats scientifically set to give the acme of comfort in viewing the screen, projection under optimum conditions, and the tasteful lighting.[5]

When the 1930s began the cinema industry was in the process of major structural changes. There was a move away from smaller local cinemas to newer sites in city and town centres and the burgeoning suburbs. Many of the older cinemas, seating around 500 to 1,000 had begun to disappear, being replaced by new cinemas seating over 1,000, to meet the increased audience demand. These smaller cinemas were closely associated with particular localities and had fostered the first audiences; however they found it increasingly difficult to compete with the newer, more sophisticated cinemas, particularly since the advent of sound had favoured the larger chains who could afford the conversions. By 1934 there had been a vigorous 'shake out' of the cinema industry with many smaller sites closing.

Weekly audiences stood at approximately 18 million in 1930, then fluctuated during the decade to increase dramatically throughout the Second World War, peaking at 31.4 million cinema visits a week in 1946 (see Table 3.1). Though the number of people visiting the cinema stagnated during the 1930s, Hiley views the period as one of flux, when exhibition went through 'a complex transition from one pattern and style of cinema-going to another'.[6]

Table 3.1 Total annual cinema admissions: selected years 1934–46

Calendar year	Weekly admissions (millions)	Annual admissions (millions)
1934	17.37	903
1936	17.63	917
1938	18.98	987
1940	19.75	1,027
1942	28.73	1,494
1944	30.28	1,575
1946	31.44	1,635

Source: H. E. Browning and A. A. Sorrell, 'Cinemas and Cinema-going in Great Britain', *Journal of the Royal Statistical Society*, 117:2 (1954), 133–70, p. 134.

Cinemas themselves changed as companies built larger venues, which were designed to appeal to a more socially mixed audience. Developing economies of scale meant that between 1930 and 1946 the audience was increasingly accommodated in larger auditoria, screening fewer programmes to bigger audiences than the smaller cinemas could. If one considers cinemas as falling into five categories according to size, the change is evident (see Table 3.2).

Table 3.2 Distribution of cinemas by size, 1934 and 1941

| | Cinemas | | | | Seats | | | |
| | 1934 | | 1941 | | 1934 | | 1941 | |
Size of cinema (no. of seats)	No.	%	No.	%	Thousands	%	Thousands	%
up to 500	901	20.9	890	20.2	371	9.6	338	8.0
500–1,000	2,184	50.8	1,900	43.0	1,660	42.8	1,423	33.8
1,001–1,500	764	17.7	951	21.5	939	24.3	1,154	27.4
1,501–2,000	307	7.1	470	10.6	537	13.9	813	19.3
over 2,000	149	3.5	204	4.62	365	9.4	487	11.5
Total	4,305	100	4,415	100	3,872	100	4,215	100

Sources: H. E. Browning and A. A. Sorrell, 'Cinemas and Cinema-going in Great Britain', *Journal of the Royal Statistical Society*, 117:2 (1954), 133–70, p. 136, and 'Statistics of the British Film Industry', *Board of Trade Journal 13*, May 1950, cited in N. Hiley, '"Let's Go to the Pictures": The British Cinema Audience in the 1920s and 1930s', *Journal of Popular British Cinema*, 2 (1999), 66–82, p. 45.

These figures show that between 1934 and 1941 the smallest cinemas retained their popularity, but the small to medium cinemas (with a capacity of between 501 and 1,000) have suffered in particular. In contrast, the medium to large cinemas with capacities of between 1,500 and 2,000 seats increased most dramatically. Those with more than 2,000 seats also began to appear in greater numbers as the decade progressed. These were the 'super cinemas' built in the late 1930s by the newly emerging large chains and primarily focused on the newly developing suburbs of Britain's major cities. The relative fortune of the smallest cinemas was possibly because many of these were in rural or semi-rural locations where competition from newer and larger cinemas was not a viable proposition, unlike the medium-sized cinemas which were almost always situated in cities and towns and were therefore vulnerable to competition.

The advent of the 'super cinemas', which began to replace the smaller auditoriums built for silent films, necessitated greater capital investment and saw the advent of three major circuits – Gaumont, Associated British Cinemas (ABC) and Odeon. They would come increasingly to control cinema exhibition right through until the advent of the multiplex in 1985. Oscar Deutsch had plans to rapidly expand his chain of Odeon cinemas. However, his empire was only in its infancy when the other two major circuits in Britain, John Maxwell's ABC and Isidore Ostrer's Gaumont had already established themselves. There were also several large chains such as Granada, which was responsible for constructing some of the largest and most dramatic cinemas, Soloman Sheckman's Essoldo circuit, and Green Brothers, based in Scotland.

In 1934 there was one cinema seat for every 10.5 persons, a situation which remained largely unchanged until after the end of the Second World War.[7] Moreover, cinema building effectively ceased after 1939, with the exception of a small-scale building programme in the late 1950s and 1960s, though conversion of existing theatres would become widespread.

At the beginning of the 1930s, Gaumont had 287 cinemas compared to ABC's 90. By the outbreak of the Second World War, however, ABC were the largest chain with 438 cinemas compared to Gaumont's 302. More remarkable than ABC's rise, and based in part on an aggressive policy of acquisition, was the development of the Odeon chain that controlled 263 cinemas by 1939. Odeon had built 136 of their distinctive cinemas since 1933 and had acquired others, many recently constructed. Between 1930 and 1940 these three companies consolidated their control over a significant portion of the cinema exhibition industry. By 1947 the ABC, Gaumont and Odeon circuits owned 1,061 cinemas (of which 966 were in operation) and while this was only a quarter of the total, they tended to be the new generation of large super cinemas.[8]

All three of the dynamic founders of these empires were primarily financiers. The Ostrer brothers were owners of a merchant bank and Maxwell was a lawyer. Deutsch, who was a Birmingham scrap-metal merchant, was noted for starting the Odeon chain with little or no capital, forming and promoting a separate company for each cinema, raising the money locally through deals between builders and the Eagle Star Insurance Company, amongst others.[9] Ostrer, in contrast, can be seen as one of the first media moguls since along with control of Gaumont he acquired the *Sunday Referee* newspaper, Baird Television, Bush Radio and Radio Luxembourg. Unlike his two major rivals Deutsch was not involved in film production but like Maxwell he was said to know little about the cinema business. The trade joke was that if you were to put both in the same room, 'you would have together the two men who knew least about actual cinema management'.[10]

The focus on the metropolitan centre was characteristic of many of the 'super cinema' developments in the early 1930s, as city and town centres across Britain experienced the majority of new developments. The significance and legacy of many of the buildings lies in their size, the nature of their design and construction and how they redefined the site of mass public entertainment and reimagined the cinema itself. As the 1920s gave way to the 1930s the cinema introduced a form of fantasy architecture and interior design which, according to the Granada chain's promoter Sidney Bernstein, should promote the escape from reality and the hypnotic experience of film in magical surroundings.[11] In Birmingham, the Beaufort Cinema, built in 1929 and designed by Hurley Robinson, was modelled on a Tudor mansion, complete with mullioned windows, oak panels and grand staircase. *Bioscope* was so enamoured of the new building that it observed that the 'pictures are at last coming into their real palaces, not places of tawdry ornament and false decorative effects, but stately, spacious mansions in which a worthwhile atmosphere can be created'.[12] 'It all sounded a bit overheated for a Birmingham suburb', wrote Atwell.[13]

Granada's cinema in Tooting, South London, designed in 1931 by Cecil Massey with interior design by Theodore Komisarjevsky, seated 3,100 people in what resembled a Gothic cathedral. The two Astorias built by Paramount in Brixton, South London in 1929 and Finsbury Park, North London in 1930, were examples of what were known as 'atmospherics'. Taking their inspiration from the US architect John Eberson who pioneered the 'atmospheric', the Brixton Astoria's interior was that of an Italian courtyard complete with Ionic colonnade and a loggia over the stage. At Finsbury Park the cinema audience sat in what has been described as a 'Hispano-Mooresque fantasy' with cupolas, turrets and loggia topped by an enormous baroque stage surround.[14]

Twelve 'atmospherics' were built but their substantial building costs meant that they were a short-lived development. In 1930 the New Victoria Cinema (now the Apollo Victoria Theatre) was opened in London's Wilton Road by Provincial Cinematograph Theatres Ltd, one of several carrying the 'New Victoria' name across the country. Its significance lies in its design, by E. Wamsley Lewis with W. E. Trent: the exterior, with its austere elevations made of Portland stone and granite, was a significant break from the prevailing aesthetic. It was, according to Atwell, the closest cinema design in Britain came or has subsequently come to European modernism.[15] The design of the interior was equally striking in its conception and execution. 'Imagine', said the *Gaumont British News*, 'a fairy cavern under the sea, or a mermaid's dream of Heaven; something one has never seen or thought of before'.[16] This 'mermaid's palace' was a striking mixture of architectural and decorative effects, including twelve-foot glass stalactite fittings on the ceiling, sculptured plaster panels and highly decorated soft furnishings and carpeting. It seated 3,000 people. Although it was not imitated, the New Victoria cinema heralded a decade which would see the apotheosis of the 'super cinema', with its close associations with modernity, both in terms of architecture and in wider culture, but also with its attempt to reflect the dreams and fantasy world that was being increasingly expressed on the screen.

Oscar Deutsch felt that the future of cinema building lay in the rapidly developing suburbs, with the future of cinema design in embracing modernism wholeheartedly and the art deco style in particular. Deutsch was unequivocal about the importance of design, observing that Odeon cinemas should 'express the fact that they are specially erected as the homes of the latest, most progressive entertainment in the world today'.[17] Deutsch was concerned with establishing a house style or a brand in a very competitive market. He was also conscious of the criticisms of the traditional cinema design aesthetic, led by architectural critics like P. Morton Shand who argued that '[t]he cinema ought to be one of the types of building most characteristic of our age ... however, in England its design still wearily rings out the changes of already obsolescent theatre models'.[18]

In commissioning new, young architects such as George Coles, Andrew Mather and Harry Weedon, Deutsch seemed to be responding to this criticism.[19] Deutsch's inspiration lay in the rigid economy of design and the rejection of ornamental detail in the cinemas designed by Modernist architects in Germany, Holland and Scandinavia. Architecturally, Odeons had a clear identity of their own:

> The genuine Odeons (as opposed to many that now bear the name) were supremely comfortable with clear sightlines, striking exteriors leading to compact auditoriums that were functionally designed to focus attention on the screen. They represented the first clean break with the traditional, decorative styles inherited from the theatre and were at the opposite pole from the preposterous but entertaining atmospheric cinemas that sat audiences under stars twinkling in a blue ceiling traversed by cloud patterns.[20]

Other chains also embraced the modernist aesthetic, though not with the same vigour and determination as Odeon. The Gaumont Palace, opened in 1931 in Birmingham and designed by local architect William T. Benslyn, seated over 2,000 people and made a virtue of its modern design, especially in its simplicity and clean lines. A contemporary review of the cinema, headlined 'modernity the keynote' went on to stress the absence of 'ornate trappings' and 'the simplicity of massed form'.[21]

Oscar Deutsch had planned to circle London with his new Odeons and in 1933, three years after he opened his first cinema in Birmingham, the first Odeon appeared in Kingston upon Thames.[22] London's suburbs sprouted a further nine Odeons in 1934 and ten in 1935, each with 1,000 to 1,500 seats.[23] The dominant market for many of these cinemas was the burgeoning suburban middle class and in particular housewives, who attended the new matinées. With some four million new semi-detached, suburban houses built in the inter-war years, Deutsch's appreciation of this new audience was acute. Jackson observed that 'few suburbs were too select to manage without a cinema' and that as houses were built and new communities created, the cinemas came 'often enough before the churches: they were part of the very fabric of the new suburbia'.[24] As a 1935 editorial in *The Cinema Architect and Builder* opined:

> What other industry in the country is building so extensively as this of ours? Excepting private dwelling houses, there is none. Project after project in town after town: each cinema incorporating the finest new and progressive ideas to influence the future. And wherever a cinema goes up it dominates the neighbourhood; it is usually by far the largest building in the area, combining dignity and cheerfulness into an ensemble that marks a new architectural style.[25]

The start of the Second World War saw the end of cinema construction as this was considered inessential work. Indeed, at the commencement of hostilities the government, fearful of air raids, ordered that all places of public entertainment be closed forthwith, only to renege on this a week later in the face of criticism from both patrons and the cinema industry. George Bernard Shaw argued, in a letter to *The Times* (5 September 1939), that the closure policy was a 'masterpiece of unimaginative stupidity'.[26] The cinema, it was argued, had a vital role to play in maintaining the morale of the nation, while producers stressed the propaganda value of films themselves.[27] The cinema's capacity as a propaganda tool was, in the words of supporters in the Ministry of Information, the "Fourth Arm" of defence'.[28] In the absence of many rival entertainments the cinema underwent a dramatic increase in attendances throughout the war (see Table 3.1). Addressing the British Association on the eve of war, Richard Ford of the Odeon Education Department stated that:

> There is no doubt that in an emergency the national importance of all cinemas would immediately increase; even in the crisis of September 1938, the value of the cinemas was clearly evident, not only for disseminating information but in providing an antidote for worry and nervous strain. Indeed the psychological value of the cinema in combating 'jitters' may well be its strongest claim to be regarded as a public servant.[29]

While the numbers of cinemas declined slightly during the war, due to bomb damage and some rationalisation on the part of the major circuits, it was estimated that at any one point only 10 per cent of cinemas were closed.[30]

Attracting audiences: admissions and trends

> There must be millions of people every day who find entertainment, perhaps
> amusement, certainly relaxation, in this great new institution, entirely unknown to
> any previous generation.[31]

The 1930s was a period of dramatic contrast in which appalling poverty and mass
unemployment coexisted with rising levels of affluence and new forms of
consumption. In 1932 unemployment stood at 3.5 million. While the numbers in
work increased year-on-year until the start of the war the stark disparities in regional
unemployment remained. For those in work and even the unemployed the cinema's
principal attraction was its status as an affordable luxury, a luxury that the masses
could, and often did, enjoy more than once a week. The programme, which often
lasted three hours, changed twice a week and usually showed two main features,
plus a newsreel and a cartoon. This meant three hours of solid entertainment in the
warm, luxurious atmosphere of the cinema. With mass unemployment and poor
housing this respite from the grim reality of life was a significant attraction of the
cinema, especially for the working class. In 1931, when average male weekly earnings
were 56s and unemployment benefit was 17s, going to the cinema cost as little as
6d.[32]

In his study of inter-war Britain Mowat cites many examples of the attraction of
the cinema for the unemployed. Orwell, in his representation of life and poverty of
northern England, spoke of the cinema as one of several 'cheap luxuries' that provided
an escape into fantasy for working-class audiences.[33] Shafer collated a series of
testimonies from cinema-goers in the 1930s, many of which attest to the important
place of cinema-going in their weekly routines.[34] One unemployed man, in a letter
to the *Film Pictorial* in 1932, spoke of the ways in which the cinema filled a gap in
his life, adding, 'I do not hanker after luxury or wealth; these I know I can never
gain; but such films take me out of myself, out of gloomy Tyneside and provide the
escape from reality without which I should grow dull and despairing.'[35]

Rowson estimated that in 1934 annual cinema attendance stood at 963 million,
which equated to twenty-two visits a year per head of population.[36] By 1939
annual admissions had risen to 990 million, some twenty-five times as many tickets
as were sold to football matches. On average half of the population over fourteen
went to the cinema once every week.[37] Though impressive, these figures are surpassed
during the historical peak of cinema-going throughout the Second World War,
particularly between 1940 and 1943 when the number of admissions increased by
50 per cent.[38]

What the averages and the totals do not immediately reveal is that many people went more than once a week and that these more frequent attendees were overwhelmingly working-class. In a study carried out in Merseyside in 1934 it was revealed that the manual working classes went most frequently to the cinema and that working-class children 'nearly all attend at least once weekly'.[39] Perhaps the most important study of inter-war cinema-going was that carried out by Mass Observation in Bolton (named Worktown) between 1937 and 1938. Of the 559 respondents in the Worktown study, 409 said they went to the cinema regularly on the same day each week, while overall attendance varied from once a month to 24 times a month.[40]

Amongst the manual working classes the cinema was particularly important for women, not least because it was a place which they could attend freely without attracting unwanted attention. Further, it provided relief from the enforced routine of domestic life.[41] Kuhn found that amongst her female interviewees some 26 per cent recalled going alone to the cinema, with 48 per cent attending two to three times weekly.[42] A correspondent to *Film Weekly* in 1930 recounted an interview with a working-class woman who told her 'frankly that they would rather go without their dinner than their visit to the pictures'.[43]

Mayer cites one survey which revealed that during June and July 1943 32 per cent of the population went to the cinema once a week or more, 12 per cent once a month and 26 per cent less frequently.[44] This means that some 70 per cent of the population visited the cinema during this two-month period. The dominant trend revealed by this research was that the overwhelming majority of cinema-goers were under forty (with 79 per cent of fourteen- to seventeen-year-olds visiting the cinema once a week).[45] People attended the cinema less frequently as they got older. A further trend which emerged in the 1930s and continued during the 1940s was that income had a direct impact on attendance. Mayer observed that 35 per cent of those in lower income groups visited the cinema once a week or more, compared to 25 per cent of those in middle income groups and only 19 per cent in upper income groups.[46]

In 1946, at the height of the cinema's popularity, Box's study also reported that cinema-going was largely habitual, with 25 per cent of people going to the same cinema regularly (once a month or more) whatever the film.[47] The cinema-going habit was established at a young age and this carried on into adolescence, which was recognised as the peak period for cinema-going, since young workers had access to their own money. It is clear, therefore, that the majority of the population went to the cinema occasionally, but that the main attendees were the young, urban working class.[48]

Table 3.3 Frequency of cinema-going by age in 1946 (%)

	16–19	20–29	30–39	40–49	50–59	60+
Once a week or more	69	57	35	28	22	11
Less than once a week	28	34	46	52	43	28
Not now, never	2	9	19	20	35	61
Sample no.	116	537	692	685	508	596

Source: K. Box, *The Cinema and the Public* (An Inquiry into Cinema Going Habits and Expenditure made in 1946), New Series 106 (London: Ministry of Information, 1946, p. 3).

By the end of the war cinema-going was enjoying a boom; since there were few alternative sources of leisure, people flocked to the cinema. With an average seat price of 1s 9d the annual expenditure of the civilian population of Great Britain on cinema in 1946 was estimated at something over £100 million.[49] This contrasts with the figure of £41.5 million for 1938.[50]

Encouraging the middle-class audience

Despite the cinema's popularity amongst the working classes the major cinema circuits had been anxious to encourage greater attendance amongst the middle classes. The purpose of this was two-fold; first as a way of recouping the costs of construction, and secondly to establish the cinema's respectability. In large part this was achieved by constructing new cinemas in middle-class suburbs. Oscar Deutsch had been instrumental in promoting the cinema as a respectable leisure activity. He did this by building cinemas which, according to Murphy, 'were modern, fashionable, functional and stylish – everything that his expected audience strove for in their bright, new homes'.[51]

In encouraging a more 'respectable' audience, particularly housewives and the growing professional classes, Deutsch and other owners broadened the social appeal of the cinema considerably. However, here we must note one of the many myths about cinema-going in Britain during the 1930s, that of the cinema audience as classless. Richards points out that while the audience embraced all classes, they rarely mixed in the cinema.[52] The increase in middle-class attendances was almost entirely due to new well-appointed cinemas in their own neighbourhoods, as well as the well-established, prestigious cinemas in London's West End and other major cities. This is evidenced in particular in Harper's study of the Regent cinema in

Portsmouth, in which the cinema's position in one of the most 'genteel' parts of the town meant that its audience was drawn primarily from a district dominated by owner-occupiers.[53] It was common for localities to have a social hierarchy of cinemas, where audiences were often delineated along lines of income and occupational status.[54] Mass Observation's Worktown study identified a range of cinemas in Bolton that appealed to different social classes, including the Odeon, which judging from the 'literary fluency' of the answers in the questionnaires, along with the higher seat prices, suggested a more middle-class clientele.[55]

Within the cinemas themselves seat prices varied considerably which also acted to separate audiences along income, and therefore social, lines as well.[56] Box found that although less frequent attendees than the lower and middle-income groups, the higher- income groups paid more for their tickets – an average of 2s 2d, as opposed to 1s 9d for middle-income groups and 1s 7d for lower income groups.[57]

Legislation and government intervention

In the period prior to the Cinematograph Films Act 1927 (the '1927 Act') and the introduction of quotas for British films, the major Hollywood studios had established distribution arms in Britain that operated a series of agreements with cinema chains, which were often characterised by the practices of 'block booking' and 'blind booking' (see Chapter 2). The success of these arrangements was built on the popularity of Hollywood films amongst British audiences, particularly the working classes. This was partly a result of the perception, held by both middle-class critics of popular culture and the working-class cinema-goer, that Hollywood cinema was essentially classless. Far from inscribing cultural differences between the United States and Britain the introduction of sound exacerbated the sense of difference between social groups *in* Britain. As Maltby and Vasey observed, it 'brought accents into play as unavoidable signifiers of social class'.[58] In Bolton, the Worktown study revealed that 63 per cent of respondents preferred US films, while amongst those described as working class the proportion was greater, at 75 per cent.[59] Insofar as working-class cinema audiences were concerned, particularly those in the north, Murphy observed that their liking for US films meant that 'they found more to identify and relate to in the films of, what was seen in the 1930s as, an alien culture'.[60]

The relationship between Britain and the United States was further complicated by the fact that the British film market was vital to Hollywood producers. Since their films usually covered their production costs at home, Hollywood was able to generate substantial profits from films in Britain without the necessity of having to invest in production or exhibition.[61] Indeed, despite fears of such intervention in production or exhibition Hollywood did not do so prior to the quota legislation because they effectively monopolised Britain's cinema screens through distribution alone.[62]

The introduction of the 1927 Act changed the context for US involvement in British cinema. Throughout the inter-war period the relationship between Hollywood and the British film industry became more problematic, although the public's appetite for Hollywood films did not diminish. Since the quota legislation stipulated that Hollywood distributors had to offer a proportion of British films alongside their own, the predominant view amongst film historians is that this prompted the Hollywood studios to adopt a more interventionist role in both exhibition and production in Britain. The importance of exhibition to the Hollywood studios was enunciated in a report of 1930, which stated that it 'is obvious that the only way of stabilising American film interests in Great Britain is by the continuance of the acquisition or construction of cinemas, and direct control over the distribution and exhibition of the American films'.[63] Fox Film Corporation acquired a substantial holding in Gaumont in 1929. United Artists, which was particularly reliant on the British market due to their small size and position as primarily a distributor, purchased a share of the Odeon chain.[64] Paramount undertook to construct a small chain of prestige cinemas in Britain's major cities in order primarily to showcase their films.[65]

Production of British films was indeed stimulated by the existence of quotas in the period between the 1927 Act and that of its replacement the Cinematograph Films Act 1938 (the '1938 Act'), which was always intended to review the operation of the quota. The study undertaken by the Political and Economic Planning Office (PEP) detailed considerable increases in investment in British film production – from £500,000 in 1927 to £7 million in 1937.[66] The number of British films made annually rose from 34 in 1926 to more than 200 in 1936.[67] Dickinson and Street cite contemporary exhibitors as insisting that there was a demand for British films on the part of audiences and this was attested by their exceeding of the quota requirements.[68] What is also clear is that this was largely confined to the two large combines – ABPC and Gaumont – who could draw upon their own films made in their own studios. For the independent exhibitors and small chains the situation was often very different. They relied on US distributors which offered 'British' films that were made by Hollywood in order to fulfil their quota and a considerable number were seen as poor quality.

One of the major criticisms of the 1927 Act was that the drive to increase the production of British films was not accompanied by any 'quality' thresholds. The Moyne Committee, set up in 1936 to review the 1927 Act, was alarmed by what it saw as the continuing threat of 'foreign control' of the British cinema industry. It sought to continue the support offered to British filmmaking with the continuance and extension of the quota to 50 per cent and for ten years.[69] It also responded to contemporary criticism of the 'quota quickie' (once again blaming foreign companies) and recommended a 'quality test' which would require that the sum spent on finished film would be in the order of £2 per foot ('quota quickies', it was said, cost approximately £1 per foot of finished film). The Committee's most radical proposal was that of a Film Commission, independent of the film industry, to oversee the 'quality test'.

The committee's report instigated a vigorous debate within the industry and government, centred on the merits or otherwise of the Film Commission, and led to considerable lobbying by Hollywood and the US Bureau of Foreign and Domestic Commerce. The outcome of these debates was the 1938 Act which set the quotas for long films at 15 per cent for renters and 12.5 per cent for exhibitors. The quota system was also refined to include double (£3 per foot) and treble (£5 per foot) quota films that were equivalent to twice or three times their length for the renter's quota.[70] A notable absence was a wholly 'independent' Film Commission. Instead, provision was made for the Cinematograph Films Council – consisting of independent members and those from the trade – to keep under review the British film industry and make recommendations to the Board of Trade. A little over a year after the 1938 Act became law, Britain was at war and the concerns inherent in the period leading up to it were superseded by the necessity of war planning. The responsibility for the British film industry was split between the Board of Trade, which oversaw the economic well-being of the industry and the Ministry of Information, which was to mobilise the cinema in support of the war effort. Cinema-going during the war would become a major force for the dissemination of propaganda and a vital morale-booster, which would see the development of an increasingly concentrated and vertically integrated industry.

Cinema and morality

[The] least studied feature of the relations of cultural production – the audience – is, where mentioned, characteristically reduced to two unequal parts: a mass of consumers and a minority of critics.[71]

The development of cinema took place in the context of many fears and anxieties about the supposed power of the mass media. Its consolidation throughout the 1930s and 1940s was achieved in the face of much opposition from various groups within both society and the establishment. These fears and anxieties included specific concerns with (a) the morally corrupting influence of cinema and its effects on the 'weak', in particular children; and its challenge to religion as the medium through which people learnt how to behave and relate to the world, (b) the commercialisation of leisure and culture and the diminution of what was seen as lived culture, and (c) the continuing and developing economic and cultural dominance of Hollywood and 'Americanisation'.

Throughout the inter-war period the impact of the cinema was widely discussed and its influence was quickly accepted as significant by many. Comparing working-class life in the 1930s with that in the early part of the twentieth century, Branson and Heinemann observed that on the whole it was less monotonous and drab.[72] However, they added that in contrast:

> Never had it been made so easy for the factory or office worker to live a complete fantasy life in substitution or compensation for the hardships of the real world. Even the unemployed found pennies somehow for the cinema. Cheap Saturday morning shows for the children were crowded in the Distressed Areas as everywhere else. Cinema, rather than religion, was 'the heart of a heartless world, the opium of the people'.[73]

The notion that cinema conferred upon the filmmakers a particular power and influence over the cinema-goer was important within the debate about cinema in the 1930s. It was seen as a powerful educating force, spreading a national culture. The Moyne Committee saw cinema as 'presenting national ideas and customs to the world'.[74] Those who viewed the cinema with fear and hostility were referred to by Richards as "the authorities", i.e. teachers, clergymen, magistrates, politicians and public bodies of various kinds'.[75] The primary considerations of these groups included the way in which the cinema might offer a challenge to the accepted notions of morality and decency.

Many contemporary observers saw cinema as analogous to religion in which cinemas were 'the cathedrals of the movies' and the notion of star 'worship' assumed cultural importance. A contemporary social survey drew a parallel between the role of the cinema manager and a cleric: 'The manager of a high-class cinema has many opportunities nowadays for useful service and there is really no reason why his social relations should not be somewhat similar to those built up around the modern parson.'[76]

The association was not a welcome one amongst those committed Christians and members of the clergy who criticised and fought the cinema as an alternative to religion that would tempt away the flock. This criticism stemmed from jealousy over the power exercised by cinema (and Hollywood in particular), which they would have liked to exercise themselves. As Macnab observed, the 'problem was not so much with the medium as with the message'.[77] In 1933 the Religious Film Society was formed as a voluntary body chaired by the Bishop of London. One of the ironies in the development of the cinema in Britain was that the honorary treasurer was none other than J. Arthur Rank. He had been attracted to the cinema initially by his conviction that the cinema could get through to people in a way that the church no longer could.[78] The Religious Film Society, it was hoped, would provide alternatives to the poor quality of religious films on offer. It was steadfast in its opposition to mainstream cinema.

In 1932 R. J. Burnett (who was on the Religious Film Society's committee) and E. D. Martell published an influential polemic entitled *The Devil's Camera: Menace of a Film-Ridden World*, in which cinema was seen as wallowing in vice, moral corruption, immorality and blasphemy, amongst other horrors. The blame for the prostituting of the film camera was laid at the feet of 'sex-mad and cynical producers', criticism that reveals a deep-rooted anti-Semitism: 'Most of the actors and actresses seem ready to go to any length in decadence and nakedness to earn the salaries doled out to them by the little group of mainly Jewish promoters who control the greater part of what is now one of the most skilfully organised industries in the world.'[79] While patently extremist and virulently racist in its assertions, *The Devil's Camera* echoed the sentiments of many moralists. The *Methodist Times*, edited by the Reverend Benjamin Gregory (also on the committee of the Religious Film Society) supported Burnett and Martell. *Methodist Times*'s critic Mr G. A. Atkinson observed that "crimeless and sexless films" had not been given a chance since the arrival of the talkies'.[80]

The subtext for this attack on the immorality of the cinema was the supposed need for greater cinema censorship and the preservation of national purity. Burnett and Martell were acutely concerned by how the 'English-speaking civilisations' might be undermined by the cinema, particularly 'the effect on natives of films showing whites in a state of degradation'.[81] What was needed, many felt, were more films in which the dominant images displayed a clear sense of national identity as identified with Empire.[82] Films needed to reinforce essentialist notions of a British character and British history, rather than its debasement by exposure to crime and sex, as exemplified by the plots of Hollywood movies. Particular versions of a public morality were intertwined with notions of an essential Britishness, though many commentators talked of Englishness rather than Britishness. If these qualities were to be encouraged then images that allegedly challenged them needed to be expunged from the screen.

In 1930 a group called the Birmingham Cinema Enquiry Committee (BCEC) (later to become the National Cinema Inquiry) was formed under the Chairmanship of the Vice-Chancellor of Birmingham University, Sir Charles Grant Robertson. It adopted a profoundly moralist stance in its examination of cinema. It sought to persuade the Home Office to hold an inquiry into film content. However, as Richards points out, the Committee displayed a lack of objectivity, since most of the members had already formulated clear ideas about the link between films and deviant behaviour.[83] Conscious of the need to document more than their own personal experiences, one of the first acts of the BCEC was to institute a 'scientific and comprehensive enquiry' into the effects of cinema on the young and adolescents.[84] This involved a group of 'investigators' attending cinemas across Birmingham, where young people were chiefly present, in order to observe their behaviour and talk to them. In addition, a questionnaire was distributed to schools, uniformed groups and youth clubs asking, for instance, how often respondents went to the 'pictures', why they liked going, what they learnt, whether the 'pictures' kept them from sleeping and how the cinema might be improved.

The inquiry report boldly outlined that many young people were attracted to films about war and crime, and what they termed 'fighting pictures' and 'frightening pictures'.[85] However, it was the question of what respondents had learnt from the cinema that focused the mind of the BCEC. Grouping them into 'General Knowledge', 'Film Philosophy' (sound and otherwise) and 'Impressions with Regard to Sex' the report invokes psychoanalytical theory and stated the following:

> Only psychologists could satisfactorily determine the full implication of this mass of comment and suggestion, and yet everyday common sense, even without much imagination, can see in these children's remarks the far-reaching usefulness or injury of the film. Without entering into that scientific realm of the perception of impressions which, stored up in the unconscious, may appear in later years, given the opportunity, all will agree with the crisp and far-sighted reply of one lad: 'I have learnt many things. If I see anything I have not seen before I am bound to learn, whether it is good or bad'.[86]

Like so many objectors to cinema on grounds of morality the essential elements of their criticisms were their own subjective observations. Of the 285 films reported on, 79 were deemed 'unsatisfactory' since they over-emphasised, for instance, 'crime and sex', 'unhealthy excitement', 'drunken women', 'sex and indecency' and 'murder'.[87]

In 1932 the BCEC held a national conference at Birmingham University on problems associated with the cinema with representatives from a range of social welfare, educational, religious and medical bodies, as well as local authorities. The demand was for state censorship and the proper regulation of cinema in opposition to the arms-length structure of the trade-financed British Board of Film Censors

(BBFC).[88] Writing in 1931, Grant Robertson had outlined the aim of the BCEC as seeking 'drastic and beneficial changes in the regulations at present governing the exercise of the "censorship"'.[89] With concerted lobbying from the BCEC and a range of other organisations the issue of greater regulation and censorship was forced on to the political agenda. However, the Prime Minister Ramsay McDonald was reluctant to order an official enquiry, especially since all the evidence from local authorities was that very few films passed for exhibition had been banned by them or received complaints from the public, thereby vindicating the adopted standards of the BBFC.[90]

In 1920 the Motion Picture Producers and Distributors of America (MPPDA), conscious of public scandals surrounding stars such as Fatty Arbuckle had decided to employ a 'tsar' to 'purify the movies and pacify the public'.[91] The incumbent was Will H. Hays who had been Postmaster General in President Harding's administration. The most important element of what became known as the Hays Office was the Production Code, which was refined from a general series of 'don'ts' and 'be carefuls'.[92] Initially, producers could lapse from the code with impunity, especially if added box-office revenues could be demonstrated. However, after a spate of 'contemporary issue' films centred on gangsters and 'sex' the National Legion of Decency was formed in 1934.[93] It was underwritten by the Catholic Church but open to all faiths, to highlight the moral danger of the cinema. Members pledged themselves to view only wholesome films, while the Episcopal Committee of Bishops published weekly lists of films which fell inside or outside the church's list of requirements. As Thorp points out, the concern was not with the aesthetic but the moral condition of the screen, in which a clean film was synonymous with a good film.[94] The impact was dramatic with the Production Code being tightened up and strictly enforced after 1934.

Although a trade body, the Hays Office and the influence exerted by the National Legion of Decency must have been the envy of those like Grant Robertson and his committee in Britain. The effect of events in the United States led to Hollywood turning away from controversial contemporary themes towards more historical dramas and Victorian novel-inspired films, and the withering of moralist groups in Britain.[95] The films that were produced by Hollywood in the wake of the Production Code found increased favour with a British middle-class audience, especially as they began to portray women as wives and mothers, and valorise private property. As Jackson observed: 'right at the end of the 1940s, the middle classes, along with the rest of the nation, saw their social norms, patterns of behaviour and general expectations from life faithfully reflected and confirmed each time they visited the cinema.'[96]

As with many subsequent moral panics about cinema, the attitude of cinema-goers was to carry on attending regardless. By the outbreak of war many contemporary studies had shown that cinema-going was the most popular form of indoor recreation, completely eclipsing the theatre, with an estimated five-eighths of the total expenditure on entertainments in 1937–38 being accounted for by the cinema.[97]

Cinema and the 'high' and 'low' culture debate

In 1929 the Commission on Educational and Cultural Films (CECF) was formed as an unofficial body by a conference of some 100 educational and scientific organisations 'who felt that the film had become, for good or evil, a powerful force in national life'.[98] In seeking to reposition the cinema as a medium worthy of consideration the CECF observed that:

> Fewer people talk of moving pictures as 'those things that flicker'. 'Cinema-minded' is in common use like 'air-minded'. The two words are the same age. A fellow of an Oxford college no longer feels an embarrassed explanation to be necessary when he is recognised leaving a cinema. A growing number of cultivated and unaffected people enjoy going to the pictures, and frequent not merely the performances of intellectual film societies, but also the local picture house, to see, for instance, Marlene Dietrich ... Yet cinematography has had to fight hard for its reputation: it has been treated as a bastard of the arts, and has been looked on askance by those whom it might serve. Under a moral interdict, it has created a form of entertainment which has given pleasure and solace to an audience which, in the main, never knew the theatre and read few books.[99]

This desire to lend the cinema legitimacy was expressed commercially by cinema owners like Oscar Deutsch and intellectually by organisations like the CECF and took place in the context of many debates about the role and function of the cinema as a leisure activity. In particular, widespread fears were expressed by the middle classes about the supposed commercialisation of leisure, and how ordinary people, or the working classes, were more passive in their reception and enjoyment of entertainment and culture. Critics like F. R. and Q. D. Leavis were antithetical to the cinema, indeed all mass culture that was based upon greater industrialisation. In the pages of *Scrutiny*, which the Leavises co-edited from 1932–53 and which professed to be 'actively concerned with standards', the lionising of language had no space for a language of the cinema.[100] The 'cinema in their eyes was an anathema to the active intelligence they sought to cultivate.'[101]

For many working-class cinema-goers the form of commercialised leisure provision typified by the cinema, or football, was popular because it was structured around their working patterns, involved a limited commitment and could be engaged with casually.[102] However, despite the fears of those who saw lived culture as somehow fatally assailed by new mass media forms, many other provisions, particularly municipal ones, were used increasingly by working-class people. Wild highlights the case of Rochdale where throughout the inter-war period book issues in local libraries grew, as did the building and subsequent use of parks and swimming baths.[103] Nevertheless, the story of Rochdale, as with Britain as a whole, is a story of the steady penetration of leisure time by capitalistic and increasingly centralised enterprise. The cinema was not the first such leisure provision but its speedy development and consolidation as a twentieth-century technological form is significant. For many it seemed that since it was clearly here to stay, what was needed was to recast it and diversify it so that it satisfied a range of functions.

Amongst the observations of the CECF were the emergence of large corporations and the rationalisation of all sectors of the industry. In large part this was to be welcomed since the CECF wanted to see 'British industry strongly organised into corporations, disposing of sufficient funds to plan on a big scale' with a warning, however, that 'there are grave dangers in too great uniformity'.[104] In some sense the CECF was torn between an implicit desire for greater economies of scale in cinema exhibition and production, and the desire to maintain what it felt was the distinct individuality of the independent sector. This was mediated by some clear assumptions about the abilities of the 'educated', middle-class audience to lend the cinema prestige and assist in educating the 'taste' of the 'nine-tenths' of the cinema-going public who are largely 'inarticulate'.[105]

Despite the best efforts of organisations like the CECF to promote the cinema's educational function, it seemed clear that what motivated most cinema-goers was a desire for entertainment and not education. As Richards points out, it was the intellectuals who favoured the cinema as an art form, expressed through a desire for documentaries, foreign films and nostalgia for the silent cinema; circulated in new film journals and shown by burgeoning film societies.[106] This group echoed the moralists in distrusting the commercialisation of the cinema and the ways in which this, inevitably, led to a lack of realism and a falsity in the images presented. In essence the object of the intellectuals' wrath was the movie mogul who 'manipulated the mass audience unscrupulously'.[107]

In the inter-war period the opportunities for cinema-goers to see foreign-language films widened, as selected cinemas programmed them along with more established films. Additionally, there were cinemas that showed foreign-language films exclusively, such as, in London, The Academy, opened in 1928 by Elsie Cohen, and The Curzon in Mayfair which opened in 1934. Stuart Davis, the head of a London-based cinema chain, was a significant figure in the development of what would become known as art cinema. In 1927 he started the 'Unusual Film Movement' and gave over one of their cinemas – the Avenue Pavilion – to the showing of 'Continental' and other films.[108] The audience for these films, Davis observed, was composed 'roughly of three different classes: the intelligentsia, the intellectual amateur who likes to follow new art movements, and the ordinary, average middle-class business man who doesn't go to the cinema as a rule because he does not like the fare provided for 'the masses".[109]

The commercial art cinema was certainly a metropolitan phenomenon and in reality largely a London-based one. For those patrons outside the capital who wanted to see foreign films the answer often lay in the network of film societies (or cine-clubs), which had their origins in The Film Society started in London in 1925 (see Chapter 2). Many film societies had started up during the Second World War, especially where new concentrations of people emerged, so that by the end of hostilities there were some 48 societies, rising to 230 in 1955 when Denis Forman contributed to Manvell's *The Film and the Public*.[110]

The notion that there might be an audience for 'non-mainstream' or 'progressive' cinema had found a voice in a new magazine called *Close Up*, first published in 1927.[111] The editorial in the first issue was unapologetic about the inferior quality of popular cinema enjoyed by the majority with its 'dismal and paltry stories and acting', which was counterposed by the demand by the 'minority' for 'films with psychology, soundness [and] intelligence'.[112] In the post-war period, the notion of the art film was extended beyond simply that of the foreign-language film to encompass other non-mainstream films. This in practice often meant those that were not picked up by commercial distribution and exhibition companies.

Instrumental in the promotion of cinema as art was the British Film Institute, itself a product of the efforts in the inter-war period to develop a public appreciation of cinema and its role in education. In 1932 the CECF had recommended the establishment of an independent film institute, with the British Film Institute commencing operations in September 1933.[113] In the post-war period, the British Film Institute found an active way of promoting the screening of non-mainstream film when it built the 'Telekinema' at the Festival of Britain in 1951. Though, initially a temporary structure the British Film Institute refurbished the 'Telekinema' and re-opened it as the National Film Theatre in 1952 before subsequently moving to a new site in London's Waterloo in 1957.

The debate around the educative function of the cinema, with its associated themes of the power of the cinema to misinform and trivialise, was caught up in a series of assumptions about audiences. These assumptions often adopted a class-based position, which saw the audience as the 'other' – the multitude or the 'common people', or more commonly throughout the inter-war period, the 'mass'. The mass were often seen as 'uneducated, ignorant, and potentially irrational, unruly and even violent'.[114] The cinema audience was heterogeneous in its make-up but was homogeneous in its focus of interest. Therefore, it was supposed, it could be clearly identified by those who might seek to influence it. The debates around the commercialisation of culture and the ways in which this might constitute a challenge to lived or symbolic culture were consistently framed by notions of the mass audience and a sense that culture was becoming more homogenous.

One of the most popular manifestations of this debate was the continued fear of 'Americanisation' – that the cinema was the dominion of Hollywood and that the worldview offered by the cinema was that which centred increasingly on the ideas and values of the United States. Reflecting on post-war British cinema, Raymond Durgnat saw mass media in an industrialised country as aiming for a 'cultural overlap between middle and working class attitudes … skirting tactfully around the conflicts between them'.[114] Here he identified what he saw as the key to the difference between the British and US consensus that serves to illustrate one perspective on why Hollywood was so popular amongst British cinema-goers:

> American ideology admits, indeed, romanticizes ambition, competition, conflict, tension, and moral and emotional intensity. Similarly, American films accommodate violent conflicts, while making them more melodramatic, morally more soot-and-whitewash, more escapist in topic, more sentimental in outcome, and more fixated in terms of physical violence, than the processes which they paraphrase and conceal. In British middle-class culture, most of these aspects are far less marked … British working class culture is rather more hospitable than middle-class to the violent and the cynical, with the result that American movies sometimes come much nearer the actual attitudes of British audiences than most British ones.[116]

The irony for the British cinema is that the films produced during the Second World War and in the late 1940s began to extend their range and embrace a more diverse national character just at the moment when the United States consolidated its position as the world's leading political, economic and cultural power. In the wake of this, came the fostering of US popular culture with its ideology of consumerism and hedonism; seemingly irresistible to impoverished British audiences.

The creation of an exhibition duopoly

In the autumn of 1941, J. Arthur Rank, then head of the General Cinema Finance Corporation (a consortium of financiers), had acquired a controlling interest in

Gaumont British. He was also a director of Odeon, having joined the board as a substantial investor in 1939, taking over the company on the death of Deutsch in December 1941. Rank had also negotiated control of Pinewood, Denham and Amalgamated Studios, adding to his involvement in the Anglo-American consortium, which purchased the Hollywood company Universal. Rank had realised that owning a production company was not enough and that he had to become more involved in distribution and exhibition in order to ensure a showing for his productions. Rank was able to emerge as the most powerful figure in British cinema seemingly unnoticed because, as Murphy observed, the British film industry's future in 1940 looked 'decidedly bleak'.[117] The substantial increase in attendance during the war was largely unforeseen.

Prior to the Second World War the two major film conglomerates in Britain had been Gaumont British and Associated British Picture Corporation (owners of ABC cinema chain). As in the United States greater integration expanded the capital base of the film companies and made them more susceptible to movements on the stock markets; this brought with it the possibility of take-overs and mergers. This, as much as anything else enabled Rank to build his empire in Britain.[118]

The end of the war established Rank as the king of the British cinema industry with the combined Gaumont and Odeon chains accounting for 607 cinemas across the country. The Labour government prevented Rank from amalgamating the two chains, insisting that both Gaumont and Odeon retain separate film booking arrangements and retain their separate identities. Nevertheless, the President of the Board of Trade, Harold Wilson, did allow Rank to create a new company to service the two circuits in 1948. It was called the Circuits Management Association and its prime consequence was both to end the control of the Gaumont circuit by the last of the Ostrer family and place all Gaumont employees under the control of the new company. The new company reflected the dominance of the Odeon circuit, which was larger and worth more. Where towns and cities had two Odeons, one was renamed Gaumont and vice-versa.

This polarisation of the exhibition industry, in particular Rank's control of the Odeon and Gaumont circuits, alarmed the Board of Trade, which in 1943 sought an undertaking from Rank that he would not acquire any further cinemas without their consent. The following year the Board of Trade also sought an agreement from those in control of ABC, which now included Warner Bros. that they would not acquire more cinemas than Rank or exceed the booking strength of either the Gaumont or Odeon chains.[119] In 1945 Warner Bros. increased their stake in ABC to 37.5 per cent of the issue capital. Now their share of the market in Britain was even greater than their market share in the United States: securing effective control of ABC was a matter of prudent business.[120] Every Warner Bros. film was exhibited at an ABC cinema. At the same time, MGM obtained a guarantee from ABC that its films would have as much showing time as Warner Bros.' films. Rank, on the other hand, distributed Universal, Paramount, Disney, United Artists, 20th Century Fox and their own films of course, via Rank Film Distributors. In 1949 Harold Wilson outlined his anxieties about the creation of the duopoly when he observed that the 'decision on a film's prospects of circuit release is taken in effect by two men – the appropriate authorities for the Gaumont-Odeon circuits and the ABC circuit respectively'.[121]

For the major chains the post-war period saw some profound changes. Initially all had been keen to expand. However, building restrictions due to shortages of materials and the demand for new homes meant that no new licences were issued for nine years on 'luxury' buildings. Nevertheless, the boom in attendance saw ABC, for instance, reach 246,288,711 admissions in the period between April 1946 and the end of January 1947.[122] In Portsmouth, the Gaumont admitted 913,000 patrons in 1946 and at the Gaumont Derby, 46,000 people saw *The Bells of St. Mary's* (1945) in one week.[123] What emerged during the post-war period was a duopoly in which two companies controlled over 1,100 cinemas; approximately 23 per cent of the total. Cinema-going became rapidly identified with these two brands.

Notes

1 E. Heathcote, 'The Development of the Modernist Cinema: Sideshow to Art House', *Architectural Design*, 70:1 (January 2000), 71–3, p. 73.

2 G. Bakker, 'At The Origins of Increased Productivity Growth in Services Productivity, Social Savings and the Consumer Surplus of the Film Industry, 1900–1938', *Working Papers In Economic History No. 81/04* (London School of Economics, January 2004), 67.

3 *Ibid.*

4 S. Rowson, 'A Statistical Survey of the Cinema Industry in Great Britain in 1934', *Journal of the Royal Statistical Society*, XCIX (1936), 67–129.

5 Editorial in *The Cinema Architect and Builder*, 2:6 (April 1935), 1.

6 N. Hiley, '"Let's Go to the Pictures": the British Cinema Audience in the 1920s and 1930s', *Journal of Popular British Cinema*, 2 (1999), 39–53, p. 45.

7 H. E. Browning and A. A. Sorrell, 'Cinemas and Cinema–going in Great Britain', *Journal of the Royal Statistical Society*, 117:2 (1954), 133–70.

8 PEP, *The Factual Film: A Survey by The Arts Enquiry:* (London: Oxford University Press, 1947), p. 195.

9 See A. Eyles, *Odeon Cinemas 1: Oscar Deutsch Entertains Our Nation* (London:

Cinema Theatre Association/British Film Institute, 2002).

10 A. Eyles, *ABC: The First Name in Entertainment* (London: Cinema Theatre Association/British Film Institute, 1993), p. 12.

11 R. Gray, *Cinemas in Britain: 100 Years of Cinema Architecture* (London: Cinema Theatre Association/British Film Institute, 1996).

12 *The Bioscope Beaufort Supplement*, 31 July 1929, iii.

13 D. Atwell, *Cathedrals of the Movies: A History of British Cinemas* (London: Architectural Press, 1981), p. 107.

14 See Gray, *Cinemas in Britain.*

15 Atwell, *Cathedrals of the Movies.*

16 Cited in A. Eyles, *Gaumont British Cinemas* (London: Cinema Theatre Association/British Film Institute, 1996), p. 36.

17 *Design and Construction*, March 1937, cited in D. Sharp, *The Picture Palace and other Buildings of the Movies* (London: Hugh Evelyn, 1969), p. 140.

18 Cited in Atwell, *Cathedrals of the Movies*, p. 93.

19 See R. Murphy, 'Fantasy Worlds: British Cinema between the Wars', *Screen*, 26:1 (January–February 1985), 10–20, for an overview of inter-war cinema developments and the place of Deutsch's Odeon chain within them. R. Clegg (ed.), *Odeon* (Birmingham: Mercia Cinema Society, 1985) has a series of photographs of all of the cinemas in the Odeon chain.

20 A. Eyles, 'Oscar and the Odeons', *Focus on Film*, 22 (Autumn 1975), 38–57, p. 38.

21 *Cinema Theatre and Allied Construction*, May 1931, p. 17.

22 Though Deutsch owned several cinemas, including his first in Perry Barr, the Odeon chain did not come into existence until 1933.

23 A. Jackson, *Semi-Detached London: Suburban Development, Life and Transport, 1900–39*, second edition (Didcot: Wild Swan Publications, 1991).

24 *Ibid.*, p. 143.

25 *The Cinema Architect and Builder*, 2:6 (April 1935), 1.

26 Cited in J. Richards and D. Sheridan, *Mass-Observation at the Movies* (London: Routledge & Kegan Paul, 1987), p. 137.

27 See R. Murphy, *Realism and Tinsel: Cinema and Society in Britain, 1939–48* (London: Routledge, 1989).

28 P. M. Taylor, *British Propaganda in the Twentieth century: Selling Democracy* (Edinburgh: Edinburgh University Press, 1999), p. 176.

29 Cited in Richards and Sheridan, *Mass-Observation at the Movies*, p. 140.

30 See A. Aldgate and J. Richards, *Britain Can Take It: The British Cinema in the Second World War*, second edition (Edinburgh: Edinburgh University Press, 1994).

31 Rowson, 'A Statistical Survey of the Cinema Industry in Great Britain in 1934', p. 68.

32 J. Richards, 'Cinema-going in Worktown: Regional Film Audiences in 1930s Britain', *Historical Journal of Film, Radio and Television*, 14:2 (1994), 147–66.

33 C. L. Mowat, *Britain Between the Wars 1918–40* (London: Methuen, 1976), and G. Orwell, *The Road to Wigan Pier* (Harmondsworth: Penguin, [1937] 1975).

34 S. Shafer, *British Popular Films 1929–1939: the Cinema of Reassurance* (London:

Routledge, 1997).

35 *Ibid.*, pp. 18-19.

36 Rowson, 'A Statistical Survey of the Cinema Industry in Great Britain in 1934', p. 70.

37 P. Miles and M. Smith, *Cinema, Literature & Society: Elite and Mass Culture in Interwar Britain* (London: Croom Helm, 1987), p. 164.

38 Browning and Sorrell, 'Cinemas and Cinema-going in Great Britain'.

39 *The Social Survey of Merseyside* (Liverpool, 1934), cited in Richards, 'Cinema-going in Worktown', p. 147.

40 Richards, 'Cinema-going in Worktown'. See also Richards and Sheridan, *Mass-Observation at the Movies*, p. 152.

41 See R. McKibbin, *Classes and Cultures in England 1918–1951* (Oxford: Oxford University Press, 1998).

42 A. Kuhn, 'Cinema-going in Britain in the 1930s: Report of a Questionnaire Survey', *Historical Journal of Film, Radio and Television*, 19:4 (1999), 531–43.

43 Shafer, *British Popular Films 1929–1939*, p. 18.

44 J. P. Mayer, *British Cinemas and Their Audience* (London: Dobson, 1948), p. 252.

45 J. Richards, *The Age of the Dream Palace: Cinema and Society in Britain 1930–1939* (London: Routledge & Kegan Paul, 1984), p. 14.

46 Mayer, *British Cinemas and Their Audience*, pp. 253–6.

47 K. Box, *The Cinema and the Public* (An Inquiry into Cinema Going Habits and Expenditure made in 1946), New Series 106 (London: Ministry of Information, 1946), p. 8.

48 See Box, *The Cinema and the Public*; McKibbin, *Classes and Cultures in England* and D. Docherty, D. Morrison and M. Tracey, *The Last Picture Show: Britain's Changing Film Audience* (London: British Film Institute, 1987).

49 Box, *The Cinema and the Public*, p. 2.

50 Bakker, 'At The Origins of Increased Productivity Growth', p. 68.

51 Murphy, 'Fantasy Worlds: British Cinema between the Wars', p. 15.

52 Richards, *The Age of the Dream Palace*.

53 S. Harper, 'A Lower Middle-Class Taste-Community in the 1930s: Admissions Figures at the Regent Cinema, Portsmouth, UK', *Historical Journal of Film, Radio and Television*, 24:4 (2004), 565–87.

54 See A. Jackson, *The Middle Classes 1900–1950* (Nairn: Davis St John Thomas, 1991).

55 Richards, 'Cinema-going in Worktown'.

56 See H. Richards, 'Memory Reclamation of Cinema Going in Bridgend, South Wales, 1930–1960', *Historical Journal of Film, Radio and Television*, 23:4 (2003), 341–55.

57 See Box, *The Cinema and the Public*, p. 12

58 R. Maltby and R. Vasey, '"Temporary American Citizens": Cultural Anxieties and Industrial Strategies in the Americanisation of European Cinema', in A. Higson and R. Maltby (eds), *'Film Europe' and 'Film America': Cinema, Commerce and Cultural Exchange 1920–1939* (Exeter: Exeter University Press, 1999), p. 50.

59 Richards, 'Cinema-going in Worktown', p. 152.

60 R. Murphy, 'Coming of Sound to the Cinema in Britain', *Historical Journal of Film, Radio and Television*, 4:2 (1984), p. 158.

61 See T. Ryall, *Britain and the American Cinema* (London, Thousand Oaks, CA and New Delhi: Sage, 2001).

62 M. Dickinson and S. Street, *Cinema and State: The Film Industry and the Government 1927–1984* (London: British Film Institute, 1985).

63 Cited in *ibid.*, p. 36.

64 See Eyles, *Gaumont British Cinemas* and Ryall, *Britain and the American Cinema*.

65 See Gray, *Cinemas in Britain*.

66 PEP, *The British Film Industry* (1952).

67 Ryall, *Britain and the American Cinema*, p. 45.

68 Dickinson and Street, *Cinema and State*.

69 Moyne Committee, *The Cinematograph Films Act 1927: The Report of the Committee Appointed by the Board of Trade*, 1936, Cmnd 5320 – see Dickinson and Street, *Cinema and State* for an overview of the committee's work and the subsequent Cinematograph Films Act 1938.

70 See PEP, *The British Film Industry* (1952).

71 P. Corrigan, 'Film Entertainment as Ideology and Pleasure: A Preliminary Approach to a History of Audiences', in J. Curran and V. Porter (eds), *British Cinema History* (London: Weidenfeld and Nicolson, 1983), p. 5.

72 N. Branson and M. Heinemann, *Britain in the Nineteen Thirties* (London: Weidenfeld and Nicolson, 1971).

73 *Ibid.*, p. 248.

74 Moyne Committee, *The Cinematograph Act 1927*, p. 4.

75 Richards, *The Age of the Dream Palace*, p. 46.

76 H. Llewellyn-Smith, *The New Survey of London Life and Labour*, 9 (1935), 43–7, p. 43.

77 See G. Macnab, *J. Arthur Rank and the British Film Industry* (London: Routledge, 1994), p. 13.

78 *Ibid.*

79 R. J. Burnett and E. D. Martell, *The Devil's Camera: Menace of a Film-Ridden World* (London: Epworth Press, 1932), pp. 10-11.

80 Cited in Macnab, *J. Arthur Rank and the British Film Industry*, p. 11.

81 Richards, *The Age of the Dream Palace*, p. 56.

82 See J. Richards, *Visions of Yesterday* (London: Routledge & Kegan Paul, 1973), and J. M. MacKenzie, *Propaganda and Empire: The Manipulation of British Public Opinion, 1880–1960* (Manchester: Manchester University Press, 1986).

83 Richards, *The Age of the Dream Palace*.

84 Birmingham Cinema Enquiry Committee (BCEC), *Report of Investigations: April, 1931–May, 1931* (Birmingham, 1931), p. 3.

85 *Ibid.*, p. 10.

86 *Ibid.*, p. 13.

87 *Ibid.*, p. 28.

88 Richards, *The Age of the Dream Palace*.

89 BCEC, *Report of Investigations*, p. 3.

90 Richards, *The Age of the Dream Palace*.

91 M. F. Thorp, *America at the Movies* (London: Faber and Faber, 1946), p. 117.

92 *Ibid.*, p. 118.

93 For a history of the organisation see F. Walsh, *Sin and Censorship: The Catholic Church and the Motion Picture Industry* (New Haven, CT: Yale University Press, 1996).

94 Thorp, *America at the Movies*.

95 Richards, *The Age of the Dream Palace*.

96 Jackson, *The Middle Classes*, p. 271.

97 Richards, 'Cinema-going in Worktown', p. 147.

98 Commission on Educational and Cultural Films (CECF), *The Film in National Life: Being the Report of an Enquiry Conducted by the Commission on Educational and Cultural Films into the Service which the Cinematograph May Render to Education and Social Progress* (London: George Allen and Unwin, 1932), p. 1.

99 *Ibid.*, p. 10.

100 'Scrutiny: A Manifesto', *Scrutiny*, 1:1 (1932), 2–3.

101 Miles and Smith, *Cinema, Literature & Society*, p. 93.

102 P. Wild, 'Recreation in Rochdale, 1900–40', in J. Clarke, C. Critcher and R. Johnson (eds), *Working Class Culture: Studies in History and Theory* (London: Hutchinson, 1979).

103 *Ibid.*

104 CECF, *The Film in National Life*, p. 44.

105 *Ibid.*, pp. 82–3.

106 Richards, *The Age of the Dream Palace*.

107 *Ibid.*, p. 65.

108 See PEP, *The Factual Film: A Survey by The Arts Enquiry*.

109 *Bioscope*, 27 February 1929, cited in R. Low, *The History of the British Film 1918–1929* (London: George Allen & Unwin, 1971), p. 34.

110 D. Forman, 'The Work of the British Film Institute', supplement in R. Manvell, *The Film and the Public* (Harmondsworth: Penguin, 1955), pp. 289–99.

111 See J. Donald, A. Friedberg and L. Marcus (eds), *Close up, 1927–1933: Cinema and Modernism* (London: Cassell, 1998), which is an anthology of articles published between 1927–33.

112 *Close Up*, August 1927, cited in Low, *The History of the British Film 1918–1929*, p. 33.

113 See I. Butler, *'To Encourage the Art of the Film': The Story of the British Film Institute* (London: Robert Hale, 1971).

114 H. Blumer, 'The Mass, the Public and Public Opinion', in A. McClung Lee (ed.), *New Outline of the Principles of Sociology* (1946), 188–93.

115 R. Durgnat, *A Mirror for England: British Movies from Austerity to Affluence* (London: Faber and Faber, 1970), p. 6.

116 *Ibid.*, p. 6.

117 Murphy, *Realism and Tinsel*, p. 62.

118 See Macnab, *J. Arthur Rank and the British Film Industry*.

119 Eyles, *ABC: The First Name in Entertainment*.

120 For a detailed discussion of the relationship between ABPC and Warner Bros. see V.
Porter, 'All Change at Elstree: Warner Bros., ABPC and British Film Policy, 1945–
1961', *Historical Journal of Film, Radio and Television*, 21:1 (2001), 5–35.

121 Memorandum to R. C. G. Somervell, Under-Secretary in charge of the Films
Branch at the Board of Trade, 25 September 1949.

122 Eyles, *ABC The First Name in Entertainment*, p. 70.

123 Eyles, *Gaumont British Cinemas*, p. 125.

4

From 'Golden Age' to the beginnings of decline: 1950–60

He had been faced with two depressing alternatives: the undignified status of cinema-manager; or unemployment. Being a realistic man, Mr Berkley had chosen the former. But the salt had gone out of his life. (David Lodge, *The Picturegoers*) [1]

At the cinema, where only a year or two ago patient queues had endlessly waited, the gaps in the stalls yawned wider each year. (Harry Hopkins, *The New Look: A Social History of the Forties and Fifties in Britain*)[2]

The immediate post-war period saw the zenith of cinema-going in Britain but in the 1950s the audience began to shrink, slowly at first and then more rapidly. There was a complementary decline in the number of cinemas in Britain. The context for this decline was the transformation in the make-up of post-war society, and the development of television; particularly the introduction of commercial television in 1955 and the end of the BBC monopoly. In the face of decline exhibitors looked at a variety of ways in which to maintain cinema's existing audience and encourage others back to the cinema. Emerging out of the war was the domination of cinema exhibition by the 'duopoly' of Rank and ABC, who would tighten their control of British cinema-going throughout the period.

'Golden Age' or golden myth?

During the war and up until 1946 over four-fifths of the population went to the cinema at least once a week, with a substantial portion visiting the cinema several times a week.[3] Although cinema audiences were to decline every year thereafter, the period up to the mid-1950s is still viewed by many as one in which the cinema was the prime mass leisure activity for a 'universal audience'. One of the reasons for this was that television had not yet become established as a major privatised leisure activity. In 1950 there were only 340,000 television licence holders. Docherty,

Morrison and Tracey characterise the ten-year period after 1946 as the supposed 'Golden Age' of the cinema, this in turn related to what they describe as 'the Golden Age of British public life'.[4] They state, 'this time may be known as BT (Before Television). During this Golden Age the working class lived and worked in integrated communities, the families who played together stayed together, and cinemas were pleasure domes where the British could live out their fantasies.'[5]

Nevertheless, the argument for a 'universal audience' is undermined by the fact that there were large sectors of the population who went to the cinema infrequently or not at all. In 1949 a *Hulton Report on Leisure* discovered that almost half the population over thirty-five years of age did not attend the cinema, or attended only occasionally.[6] In 1952 a *Hulton Readership Survey* found that this trend was undiminished, with those under the age of twenty-five accounting for nearly half of all cinema attendances.[7] In considering the contemporary evidence Browning and Sorrell concluded that the attendance rate was 'highest for the lower middle class and lowest for the relatively well-off'.[8] The 1949 Hulton Research (see Table 4.1) identified the most frequent cinema-goers as the lower-income group. The most infrequent attendees were from the middle- and upper-income groups.

Table 4.1 Frequency of cinema-going by social class in 1949 (%)

	upper	middle	lower
Twice a week	8	13	19
Once a week	20	24	24
Once or twice a month	23	18	14
Few times a year	34	31	24
Never	15	14	19
Total	100	100	100

Source: Hulton Research (*Hulton Reports on Leisure, 1949*), cited in D. Docherty, D. Morrison and M. Tracey, *The Last Picture Show: Britain's Changing Film Audience* (London: British Film Institute, 1987), p. 16.

Children and the cinema

All of the major cinema chains ran organised Saturday morning clubs after the war in order to stimulate the cinema-going habit amongst children.[9] The establishment of the clubs lay with the Granada chain in 1927. They were developed substantially by Oscar Deutsch's Odeon chain with the introduction of the first children's matinées in 1937. Initially, the clubs were called Odeon Children's Circles. This was soon changed to Mickey Mouse Clubs (an idea adopted from the United States) on the understanding that they had to include at least one Disney cartoon in each show.[10] In 1938 Richard Ford, an Odeon executive with responsibility for the clubs, instigated a questionnaire for cinema managers intended to collect information on the members of the clubs (which totalled approximately 150,000 children). Ford estimated that in 1939 approximately 4.6 million children were visiting the cinema every week.[11] Upon his takeover of the Odeon circuit J. Arthur Rank renamed the clubs Odeon Children's Clubs, though the basic principles stayed the same – children were asked to pledge allegiance to their club and abide by a series of rules that extended beyond the cinema itself, such as 'I will be truthful and honourable …' and 'obey my elders'.[12]

Conscious of the content of many films shown at the clubs, in particular films imported from Hollywood such as Westerns and adventures, Rank established the Children's Entertainment Film (CEF) division in 1944. The content of the films was subject to the control of the CEF's director, Mary Field, and a Youth Advisory Council, made up of representatives from the BBC, the education sector and the church, amongst others. They were concerned that the films 'would not only be entertaining but would also set a high moral tone and encourage good behaviour.'[13]

Despite Rank's good intentions the division was a considerable drain on resources at a time when they were seeking to make economies and in 1950 it ceased operating. In the same year came the Wheare Committee report. The committee had deliberated on the 'effects of attendance at the cinema on children under the age of sixteen, with special reference to attendance at children's cinema clubs'.[14] It concluded broadly that there were no obvious effects on children's behaviour as a result of attending the clubs and that 'educating children to view films with discrimination should be encouraged'. The committee also stressed the importance of dedicated children's films, which in 1951 led to the creation of the Children's Film Foundation – a non-profit-making filmmaking organisation funded by the British film industry.[15]

There were clear economic imperatives on the part of cinemas, particularly by the major chains which often ran the clubs at a financial loss, for encouraging children to attend. Their dominance in this sector is evidenced by the fact that 62 per cent of admissions to children's clubs in 1952 took place in the large chains.[16] During the period between 1948 and 1952 when total admissions fell by 13 per cent, admissions to children's performances rose by 14 per cent.[17] One of the major reasons why so many working-class young people went to the cinema was its centrality in popular public culture. Many extended families encouraged members to visit the cinema from an early age, as attested by Mayer who found that many children had started attending the cinema when they were four or five.[18] Cinema-going as a popular leisure form was largely a result of socialisation in which leisure habits were passed on to the next generation. Moreover, for many working-class cinema-goers the alternatives in the post-war period were limited.

Government regulation and intervention – responding to the decline of cinema

The end of the 1940s, in the aftermath of the Second World War, once again witnessed the government intervening in the film industry and in doing so it continued a pattern established with the Cinematograph Act 1909. The Cinematograph Films Act 1927 had set a precedent in stressing the importance of making sure that audiences saw a proportion of British films. According to an official from the Foreign Office, speaking in 1938, 'HM Government have never considered the position and influence of the United Kingdom film industry as primarily an industrial question, but rather as a cultural question.'[19] The focus for the concern in the post-war period, as it had been since the end of the First World War, was Hollywood and the dominance of British screens by US films. For the post-war Labour government and a number of committees and working parties set up after the war, there was a further concern about the power exercised by the Rank/ABPC duopoly. Both of these concerns would largely determine the nature of the intervention.

The first intervention however, was driven by economic factors when in August 1947 the government, anxious to stem the flow of sterling across the Atlantic, imposed a 75 per cent *ad valorem* tax on imported US films. This led to a boycott by Hollywood until the tax was ignominiously withdrawn in May 1948 as part of the 'Anglo-American Film Agreement'.[20] The outcome of the tax (or the 'Dalton duty' as it is sometimes referred to after the Chancellor of the Exchequer Hugh Dalton) was not advantageous for the British film industry. As Jarvie argues, the tax did not raise any revenue, but quite unintentionally stimulated the growth of Hollywood productions in British studios.[21] Among the lobbyists for repeal was the British film industry itself, particularly the exhibition sector through the Cinematograph Exhibitors Association. With no new Hollywood films, the cinema chains had three-month's worth of remaining releases, whereupon they would have to resort to reissues that had previously played on rival's screens.

Despite the apparent failure of the Dalton duty the government also sought to increase the protection for the film industry by introducing The Cinematograph Films Act 1948 ('the 1948 Act'), which abolished the quotas for distributors but increased the quota for exhibitor's main features from 25 to 45 per cent (though this was subsequently lowered to 30 per cent). The 1948 Act provoked serious criticism from exhibitors, and Rank and ABPC in particular. However, many in the film industry felt that these two exhibitors discriminated against independent distributors and producers. The Palache Committee had given serious consideration to the plight of independent producers and recommended both that a Film Finance Corporation be formed to fund and distribute independent producers' films, and that the Board of Trade legislate for a proportion of screen time in cinemas to be devoted exclusively to independent productions.[22] This issue was also taken up by the Plant Committee in 1949 which was charged with examining 'the arrangements at present in operation for the distribution of films to exhibitors and their exhibition to the public in the commercial cinemas, and to make recommendations.'[23]

The result of the deliberations was the National Film Finance Corporation (NFFC) set up under The Cinematograph Film Production (Special Loans) Act 1949. The NFFC was able to make commercial loans for film production with money borrowed from the Board of Trade. The power was extended to the borrowing of loans from commercial sources with the introduction of The Cinematograph Film Production (Special Loans) Act 1952.[24] Part of the rationale for the NFFC and other state support was the realisation that in order to fulfil the 45 per cent quota for first features, exhibitors needed a better supply of British films. Despite the creation of the NFFC the perceived need to stimulate production was also evidenced by the creation of the British Film Production Fund (BFPF), which was a voluntary agreement with the exhibitors to place a levy on ticket prices in order to help fund film production. Popularly called the 'Eady levy' it raised a proportion of the ticket price, giving half back to the exhibitors in the form of a rebate on the Entertainment Tax charged on each admission, and half to the BFPF for qualifying British films. As Swann observed the BFPF was 'the type of association between exhibitors and producers which ought to have emerged 25 years earlier. Film exhibition had always been profitable in Britain, and this was the first scheme which directly channelled exhibitors' receipts to film producers.'[25]

The Eady levy was put on a statutory footing by The Cinematograph Films Act 1957 whereupon it was collected by HM Customs & Excise and administered by the British Film Fund Agency. In 1952 the annual receipts from the fund were £2.9 million, and despite a negotiated increase to £3 million with exhibitors in 1954–55, that figure was never reached again while the voluntary scheme was in operation.[26] Nevertheless, in the first seven years of its operation the Eady levy raised approximately £18m, a respectable amount for producers. The introduction of the levy coincided, however, with the beginning of a year-on-year decline in cinema-going. Initially, a rise in box office receipts between 1950 and 1954 offset the decline in admissions, though after this period attendances declined to a point where higher seat prices could not compensate.[27] This meant that the revenue available to film producers was 'never as much as had been hoped, or as much as they considered to be necessary to give them a reasonable measure of stability'.[28] When the Eady levy was put on a statutory footing in 1957 the sum to be given to producers was set in the first year at £3.75m and in subsequent years at £2–5m.

According to the PEP, the Eady levy, which was not abolished until 1985 (discussed in Chapter 6), helped British cinema stay 'within reach of solvency'.[29] By the end of the 1960s the fund available to producers was between £4.2 and £4.6 million.[30] Not all of this was going to British producers, however, since its existence was a substantial incentive to Hollywood to make films in Britain. Hollywood studios increased their British-based production throughout the 1950s and 1960s, adhering to the letter of the law with regard to a 'British film' but recognising that the legislation did not distinguish between finance from abroad or Britain, or prohibit a foreign company from setting up a 'British' subsidiary. As Dickinson and Street argued, 'it seemed the Production Fund, originally intended to aid British producers, was more remunerative to the Americans'.[31] Indeed, estimates for the amount of subsidy received by British production companies in the mid-1960s put the figure at as little as 10 per cent.[32]

The beginning of the decline

As cinema attendances reached what we now know to be the high of 1946, it must have seemed to contemporary observers that cinema would remain the pre-eminent visual entertainment for a mass audience. Television was in its technological infancy in 1946, with the fledgling service offered by the BBC having been curtailed during the war. However, as we have seen, the cinema's audience was by no means as broad-based in its profile as was suggested by general admission statistics. The people who visited the cinema most often were the young working class, who lived in established urban centres. It would be this very group and these very areas that would see the greatest demographic, social and environmental upheavals in the twenty years after the war, as Britain's towns and cities were redeveloped and the population dispersed. The cinema industry would need to respond to these movements if it was to maintain its presence in people's lives. This, and the inevitable development of television beyond its experimental beginnings, would establish the context for the development of cinema from 1946 onwards. The question was *how* the cinema industry would respond.

Table 4.2 Total annual cinema admissions: selected years 1945–84

Calendar year	Admissions (millions)	Calendar year	Admissions (millions)
1946	1,635.00	1966	288.80
1948	1,514.00	1968	237.30
1950	1,395.80	1970	193.00
1952	1,312.10	1972	156.60
1954	1,275.80	1974	138.50
1956	1,100.80	1976	103.90
1958	754.70	1978	126.10
1960	500.80	1980	101.00
1962	395.00	1982	64.00
1964	342.80	1984	54.00

Source: E. Dyja (ed.), *BFI Film and Television Handbook 2003* (London: British Film Institute, 2002).

By the middle of the 1950s the annual cinema audience had fallen to 1,101 million, still a considerable number, but a decline nevertheless of 500 million in ten years (see Table 4.2). In reality the decline in the first years of the 1950s was less dramatic compared to the late 1940s, though the mid-1950s onwards signalled a sharper fall.[33] Nevertheless, it seemed that even amongst the core audience group the attraction of the cinema was waning. As Harper and Porter pointed out, cinemas 'could no longer take their audiences for granted'.[34] The social habit of cinema-going began to rupture due to a combination of external forces, one of which was the 'dictates and rhythms of family life'.[35] In general, the pattern of attendance was that young couples would attend the cinema when courting and perhaps in the initial period of marriage. After this the introduction of children would distract the parents and resources would be re-directed away from leisure into the bringing up of the young family. Attendance might pick up again when the children were young, only to tail off as the couple got older. In many respects this pattern had remained the same for four decades, though the way in which cinema-going was traditionally linked to the extended family had changed with the development of the nuclear family.

In posing the question 'The Best Place to See a Film?' Wally Olins argued that the blame for the decline in cinema-going since the Second World War had been laid at the door of a series of culprits. These were: (a) black and white television; (b) the development of colour television; (c) the comfort of the home as against the lack of comfort in the cinema; (d) the price of going to the cinema when films could be seen for free at home; (e) the 'product' (in that films are not what they used to be and people did not want to see them), and (f) the arrival of video, which meant that people could watch good films at home.[36] Olins felt that the industry had neglected what he suggested was the main reason: that cinemas were no longer pleasant places to be. He argued that the degree of decline, lack of investment and neglect could be best appreciated by drawing an analogy with another trade:

> If most of the restaurants in this country were built in the 1930s, had hardly been touched since then, except for minor, shoddy alterations and were monopolised, let us say, by Grand Met and Trust House Forte, what state would the restaurant business be in today? It would probably be as rundown, dreary and generally unprofitable as the cinema business.[37]

Persuasive though Olins' argument is, it falls into the trap of reducing a complex cultural phenomenon to that of a simple issue of investment. In reality the decline of cinemas was the result of a complex set of dynamic economic, social and cultural conditions developing from the end of the war. The factors identified by Olins certainly played an important part in the near collapse of cinema-going in Britain. However, we must add other factors, such as the changing demography of Britain's towns and cities, the development of other competing forms of leisure and the advent of widespread car ownership.

The cinema and a shifting population

Several commentators have pointed out the decline in cinema-going in the mid-1950s took place amongst the generation who were the cinema's most enthusiastic audience in the 1940s.[38] We can see further clues to the decline amongst this group by considering the changing environment for working-class communities. In the early 1950s many traditional working-class communities were moved out of inner-city areas as part of slum clearance programmes, often to new areas on the periphery of the conurbation. Many of these areas did not have cinemas, but they did enable many working-class residents to take part in new forms of leisure, such as participant sport or other outdoor activities. Moreover, they created the conditions for greater privatised, home-based leisure, in line with improvements in standards of living. The catalysts for these changes were The New Towns Act, 1946 and the Town and Country Planning Act, 1947.[39]

The New Towns Act, 1946 provided for the designation of areas in which new towns could be planned and built.[40] By the end of 1950 twelve sites had been designated in England and Wales, in order to relieve the populations of existing conurbations. In the meantime The Town and Country Planning Act, 1947 had extended the powers of public authorities to acquire and develop land for planning purposes and, crucially, had provided for major funds for the clearing of land. The slum clearance programmes initiated after the end of hostilities and the need to rebuild the 475,000 houses that had been destroyed or made uninhabitable, accounted for much migration of populations from inner-city neighbourhoods.[41] Between 1955 and 1974 some 1.165 million properties were demolished in England and Wales (approximately one in ten of all the homes in the country), necessitating the movement of some 3.1 million residents, most of them in established working-class communities.[42]

The exhibition sector failed to keep pace with this movement of population. In areas earmarked for slum clearance cinemas closed with the departure of the local population, while in areas of population expansion the new housing developments had no cinema nearby and no prospect of one. As Holmes argued, the new housing developments which were dominated by flats in high-rise or long deck-access blocks, 'made too little provision for the community infra-structure that was needed. As a result too many estates were built without adequate provision for schools, shops, health services and public transport and other facilities essential for successful communities.'[43]

The main problem for exhibitors was that unlike already erected cinemas, which could remain open even with a negligible return on capital employed, capital for new cinemas would need to provide a return which at least equalled the substantial returns now being generated in other leisure industries. Indeed, they had to exceed such returns, so as to compensate for the uncertainties in the future of cinema exhibition.[44]

The areas in which this absence of a cinema was most acute were the new towns. In 1962 only three new towns with the largest planned populations, namely Basildon (planned population 90,000–100,000), Harlow (80,000) and Hemel Hempstead (60,000), had been provided with or had the definite prospect of a new cinema.[45] For the other twelve new towns the erection of a new cinema was a remote and often unlikely prospect. Many of the Development Corporations for these towns had clearly defined plans for leisure facilities in their areas, which included pubs, churches, hotels and community centres, but few included cinemas. Osborn and Whittick noted that in the new town of East Kilbride the provision of cinema facilities was slow to materialise, even with the guarantee of financial assistance from the government.[46] It took seven years from the announcement of this support in 1960 to interest an exhibitor sufficiently to begin building a cinema.

If we consider the cinema as being subject to the 'dictates and rhythms of family life', in which young families' attendance declined with the arrival of children, then the situation in the new towns is instructive. Spraos called them 'immigrant towns', and their age structure was markedly different from the rest of the country, being affected by two factors: (a) the housing accommodation offered (which mainly consisted of family dwellings); and (b) the propensity to migrate of different age groups.[47]

As a consequence, the age group of 16–24 years was substantially under-represented. Since this was the group most likely to attend the cinema, the perceived demand was significantly reduced. In view of the fact that the older age groups were disproportionately tied to their new domestic sphere, one gets a sense of why cinema development, in an uncertain economic climate, did not take place. Of course, it could be argued that it was symptomatic of the lack of foresight on the part of the exhibition industry, since there would come a time when there were large numbers of potential cinema-goers in these areas. Significantly, it would be many of these new town environments that would witness the first multiplex developments in the late 1980s (discussed in Chapter 6).

Although much post-war planning policy sought to accelerate the decentralisation of populations of Britain's conurbations to new communities, the cities themselves would be rebuilt and reshaped. Much of this redevelopment was concerned with the commercial centre, which witnessed widespread rebuilding of shopping and business facilities in the 1950s and early 1960s. However, this was rarely accompanied by cinema development, especially outside London, and many cinemas destroyed by wartime bombing had not been replaced. The post-war restrictions on luxury building, which lasted for nine years, were a contributing factor, spanning the first major decline in cinema-going. Nevertheless, the cities still contained most of Britain's largest and most prestigious cinemas, which exhibitors were keen to concentrate. This post-war metropolitan focus for Britain's cinemas took place in the context of a steadily declining population in the city's central core during the 1950s, which accelerated during the 1960s and 1970s.[48] These city centre cinema sites tried to draw people in from other parts of the conurbation and outlying areas, relying on good access by public transport and the complementary attractions of the city centre.

With the minimal new cinema building that did take place and the modernisation of existing sites concentrated on metropolitan areas, the exhibitors' economic futures were tied to a large extent to those of the city. As city centres declined in importance and prestige during the 1960s and 1970s, partly as a result of economic decentralisation and poor planning, the fortunes of cinemas themselves declined. The crisis was not simply a case of depopulation (which might be seen as desirable given the high densities of poor housing that characterised many of Britain's cities) but the selective nature of this decentralisation, in which it was the younger, more skilled and more affluent who left the urban areas.[49]

Britain was not alone amongst industrialised nations in experiencing a contraction in cinema audiences after the war, nor was it alone in witnessing population shifts out of the urban areas. As in Britain, the cinema's audience in the United States declined. In the USA the suburban migration of the late 1940s and early 1950s amounted to over a million people a year, with suburbs growing at a rate fifteen times faster than any other segment of the country.[50] Many of these new suburbanites owned their new houses (more US citizens owned houses than rented by 1960), and most had young families as a result of the post-war baby boom. Not only did these suburbanites have less personal income to spend on cinema, but their new families also took away their time and interest in the cinema. These young people were the demographic heart of the cinema-going audience, but according to Gomery, they chose 'the psychic benefits of having children over other forms of consumption'.[51]

It is here, however, that the similarities between these two cinema-going nations end, since the reaction of exhibitors to these demographic and social changes in the USA was more pro-active than their counterparts in Britain. In the USA the decline in the post-war cinema audience was arrested to an extent by the development of new kinds of cinemas in the early 1950s. The most significant was the drive-in cinema, which was in large part a reaction to the increasing numbers of car-owning suburbanites and to the high cost of building new enclosed cinemas. Some 3,500 of these cinemas were built between 1948 and 1952, which more than compensated for the loss of 900 conventional cinemas in the same period.[52] By 1952 approximately four million people were attending drive-in cinemas, which acted as an important bridge between the traditional cinema and the new mall-based cinemas (the forerunners of the multiplex) which emerged later. Importantly, these drive-in cinemas helped maintain the cinema-going habit and sustain the interest in the publicly exhibited feature film. Richard Hollingshead, who patented and established the first drive-in in 1933, observed that 'the last two things Americans would give up were the car and the movies'.[53] By the end of the 1950s there were approximately 5,000 drive-ins, which according to Andrew 'helped the exhibition wing of the industry to absorb the loss of smaller downtown theatres which TV was deemed responsible for'.[54]

The developments in the USA took place in the context of the complementary threat of television to cinema audiences. Throughout the 1950s and 1960s television made strong inroads into the domestic sphere, especially as it offered entertainment to those families already in the suburbs with children to keep occupied.[55] Television was not the sole preoccupation for exhibitors in the USA. They felt that a large audience still existed that wanted to see films on a big screen. The task was to provide new facilities for this audience. In the USA, Gomery argues, there was a 'direct *substitution* between two complementary goods' as television replaced the radio as the mass entertainment for suburban families.[56] For cinema owners television was important, but it would not necessarily take away the cinema audience. The industry concluded that much of the audience was less than enthralled by the standard film. They responded by trying to deal with what Belton saw as 'the psychological factors underlying declining attendance figures – the need of post-war audiences for a new, more participatory kind of motion picture'.[57] The marketing of new technologies such as Cinerama, CinemaScope and 3D (discussed in Chapter 5) were an attempt to provide a future for cinema as a participatory event. This was a reaction to the idea that a cultural shift had taken place whereby the recreational market was characterised by 'active' leisure pursuits (e.g. sports, gardening and attendance at amusement parks) rather than 'passive' ones (cinema-going and spectator events).[58] What was important for exhibitors was to be able to respond flexibly to these demographic and cultural shifts. This, however, was not the case in Britain, as cinemas did not follow populations out of the cities and they were unable to adapt to the changing spatial context for leisure consumption.

The majority of British exhibitors saw television as the dominant threat and structured their developments and reactions accordingly, although Rank and ABC initially took a more pragmatic approach. In 1955 Rank became financially involved in the development of commercial television, acquiring a stake in Southern Television. During the same period, ABC acquired a stake in the new Midlands regional company ATV. At the same time as the two rival exhibitors were buying into television they were lending substantial vocal and financial support to the Film Industry Defence Organisation (FIDO), which had been formed in 1958 and sought to prevent producers selling their films to television.[59] FIDO had been instigated by Sidney Bernstein, head of the Granada chain, even though he was also the owner of the regional ITV company Granada Television. This state of affairs said much about exhibitors' ambivalent attitude to British film production and exhibition.

During the 1950s the companies were preoccupied to some extent with their new interests in television. Fearful of losing money on the new broadcasting venture, ABC sold land it had acquired to build a new cinema on Manchester's Oxford Road to raise a contingency fund. It also closed two cinemas in Birmingham and Manchester to make way for television studios. In 1958 Rank conducted a market survey which noted that:

It appears that the introduction of television to an area has a major effect on cinema attendances after the station has been established for about a year. As yet there are no signs of any halt in the decline in areas where television is no longer a novelty. It is clear the decline in cinema-going is not attributable to any one group although the extent of the changes in habit does vary considerably with age and social grade … It seems then that the cinema is more vulnerable to the counter-claims of television than other forms of entertainment.[60]

The impact of television

The development of television was the most obvious threat to cinema's pre-eminent position as the most popular leisure form in Britain after the war. A comparison between the figures for the decline in the post-war cinema audience (see Table 4.3) and the increase in the numbers of television licences issued seems to point to one conclusion: television killed the cinema.

Table 4.3 Television licences and weekly cinema admissions: selected years 1950–85

	Weekly cinema admissions (millions)	Television licences (millions)		Weekly cinema admissions (millions)	Television licences (millions)
1950	26.84	0.34	1965	6.28	13.25
1955[a]	22.73	4.50	1970	3.71	15.88
1956[b]	21.17	5.73	1975	2.24	17.70
1957[c]	17.60	6.96	1980	1.94	18.28
1960	9.63	10.46	1985	1.38	18.71

Notes: [a]Commercial TV began broadcasting in London area
[b]Commercial TV began broadcasting in Midlands and North
[c]First year in which sound and vision licences exceeded sound-only licences

Source: E. Dyja (ed.), *BFI Film and Television Handbook 2002* (London: British Film Institute, 2001); E. Dyja (ed.), *BFI Film and Television Handbook 2003*; and J. Spraos, *The Decline of the Cinema: An Economist's Report* (London: George Allen & Unwin, 1962).

The experience in the United States, where the prevalence of television was much greater at the end of the 1940s and beginning of the 1950s seemed to suggest that cinema did in fact decline in areas where television was received. Indeed, in 1953 the *Financial Times* estimated that in 1948 cinema attendance decreased by 40 per cent in areas with a satisfactory reception, by 22 per cent where reception was unsatisfactory, and areas without television showed a 3 per cent increase in cinema attendance.[61]

For Spraos the relationship between television and cinema-going can be seen in the context of three phases. Initially, in the early 1950s television coverage was ad hoc. Sets were relatively expensive, there was only one channel and the hours of transmission were limited. The purchase of television sets was largely confined to higher income groups who, as we have seen, were less frequent cinema-goers. Spraos nonetheless concludes that the decline in cinema-going must still be attributable to television since there was little or no decline outside reception areas.[62] The second phase started in 1955 and was the period that saw the advent of commercial television and a dramatic expansion in television ownership in working-class households. The purchase of a television set had become financially more manageable as more members of the household provided a second, third or fourth income. Spraos sees this as disastrous for cinema since the families that acquired these sets were a) larger than average and b) of an age composition (16 to 24 years) that accounted for the main cinema audience.[63] The third phase was post-1958. In this period each new television licence had a negligible effect on cinema-going since they were issued to groups who did not attend the cinema, such as pensioners. Spraos believed that from this time other factors made a greater contribution to the decline in cinema than television.

There was much debate in the 1950s and 1960s about the impact of commercial television on cinema-going. The 1958 PEP study noted an accelerated decline in cinema attendances after the introduction of the commercial Independent Television (ITV).[64] However, the greatest decline in attendances was in areas where television was introduced first. That there is an accelerated decrease in cinema attendance after the introduction of ITV might well be 'because people have held back from buying television sets until there was a choice of programmes available to them'.[65]

From this perspective at least, television's impact on cinema audiences did not rest on the increase in choice of programmes, but on the fact of television itself. Spraos concludes that it was television's convenience as a home entertainment rather than the content of the entertainment that was the factor. Moreover, the purchase of a television set would have entailed the setting aside of money for HP payments or rent which might have reduced the money available for cinema-going and other entertainment.[66] For the cinema industry television was undoubtedly a potent threat.

The notion that there is a simple causal link between the decline in cinema-going and the development of television is challenged by Docherty, Morrison and Tracey. Analysing the ratios of cinema closure to attendances and television licences to cinema closures, they discovered that each time a cinema closed 75 per cent of cinema attendances were lost.[67] The inconvenience of having to go out of one's area to visit the cinema may have deterred many people, indeed in the mid-1950s the exhibition industry was complaining about deterioration in public transport services.[68] As private car ownership was increasing so bus companies were cutting services and, crucially for cinemas, terminating services earlier in the evening. This supports the notion that the location of the cinema in a neighbourhood was important in the formation and maintenance of the cinema-going habit.

According to Docherty, Morrison and Tracey television was thus not the only reason for the decline in cinema attendances.[69] Browning and Sorrell estimated that for every television licence issued between 1950 and 1954, sixty-five admissions were lost.[70] On this basis, Docherty, Morrison and Tracey calculate that the 9 million licences issued by 1958 should have caused 585 million fewer admissions; in fact, by 1958 the cinema audience had declined by no less than 900 million.[71] If there were a simple causal link between television ownership and cinema attendance these statistics suggest that for each licence issued, two regular cinema-goers stopped attending altogether. This seems unlikely, since the bulk of the cinema audience was the young, urban working class, precisely the group that did not have access to television until later.[72] Moreover, the leisure patterns and habits of young single people below the age of twenty-four would have militated 'against them becoming heavy television viewers'.[73] The acquisition of televisions amongst the group most identified with cinema-going stabilised by the early 1960s. Thereafter it was the older and more affluent that purchased televisions, but these were not regular cinema-goers. The decline in cinema admissions continued throughout the 1960s at a pace beyond that which could be attributed solely to television. Docherty, Morrison and Tracey concluded that the relationship between the rise in television and the decline of cinema should not be seen as necessarily causal. Instead, the development of television was attributable to the same forces that had precipitated the decline in cinema-going:

> Just as the conditions for the cinema emerged during one phase of industrial capitalism, which created a working class concentrated in large industrial conglomerations, with increased leisure time and a financial surplus; so the conditions for television were created by the rise in real wages, comfortable homes and the emergence of the nuclear family, which was concurrent with the sense that the working class extended family was breaking up.[74]

In order to understand this shift in the conditions of capitalism, as it affected the cinema-going groups, it is important to recognise the role of 'affluence'. Rising incomes, increased home-ownership, home-oriented consumption, diversification of leisure and the increased popularity of motor cars characterised the late 1950s and 1960s. All can be seen as lessening the demand for the cinema in Britain. In 1951 30 per cent of the population of England and Wales owned their own home; by 1970 this had risen to 50 per cent.[75] In itself the growth in home-ownership was nothing new. There was a home-ownership boom in the inter-war years, when private builders built 2.88 million homes and yet in the same period cinema attendance had risen consistently.[76] A significant feature of the post-war situation, however, was the increased numbers of working-class people entering the housing market.

Throughout the early 1960s, home-ownership amongst the manual groups rose proportionately faster than amongst the non-manual and professional groups. By 1966, 40 per cent of skilled manual households, 33 per cent of semi-skilled households and 24 per cent of unskilled households were homeowners.[77] It was from these groups, and particularly their younger members, that the cinema derived the bulk of its audience. The increased incidence of home-ownership led to better and more comfortable housing in which people felt 'a greater psychological commitment to the home'.[78] In *The New Look* Hopkins linked the decline of cinema in the 1950s explicitly with the centrality of the home: '[t]he common man had no longer an acute need of one and ninepenceworth of vicarious luxury. With the aid of his new house, his car, the HP, his wife's magazines, and his do-it-yourself kit, he could build an only slightly less colourful – and much more satisfying – world for himself at home.'[79]

However, it was not only home ownership that affected the decline in cinema attendances. The PEP study of 1958 cited a *Sunday Times* correspondent who extended the argument to those who had moved in to the new local authority controlled rented sector, suggesting that:

> [I]f the new towns and L.C.C. estates were any guide it was not so much that television has stolen the screen from the cinema, but that many people today have new homes where the entertainment of their families and friends is more comfortable and pleasurable than anything they have known before. Most of these people, therefore, prefer their entertainment at home, to which television naturally contributes, and in the summer, particularly; they are too busy in their gardens for cinema-going.[80]

A consequence of this greater commitment to the home was a growth in what became known as 'consumer durables', including washing machines, vacuum cleaners, refrigerators and, of course, televisions. Purchases of these items had the additional effect of redirecting people's personal expenditure.[81] It was an age that heralded what Braverman called the 'universal marketplace', in which there was an increased focus on the individualised consumer and the commodification of the domestic sphere.[82] Notwithstanding the contemporary debates regarding the fragility of the boom of the 1950s and early 1960s, it seemed to many that Macmillan's Conservative government had delivered an economic growth that had 'dissolved the old class structure and created new social groups, in particular affluent workers and the technical intelligentsia'.[83] In the period 1951–64 there was full employment, average earnings increased by 30 per cent, and total production increased by 40 per cent.[84] In 1951 the number of households with access to a car stood at 13 per cent, rising year-on-year until 1970 when it reached 45 per cent.[85]

Perhaps the most potent force to impact upon cinema-going was a cultural revolution amongst the young, and the development of the 'teenager'. As has been demonstrated, the main audience for the cinema in the post-war period was the young working class. From the mid–1950s young people went from a position where they had no identifiable culture as a group to one where 'youth' became a clear and influential phenomenon. The 'teenager' had been invented largely by marketing agencies anxious to capitalise on the spending power of young people. Young people could now be differentiated by their patterns of consumption, which according to Laurie, were characterised by the fact that they 'spent a lot of money on clothes, records, concerts, make-up, magazines: all things that give immediate pleasure and little lasting use'.[86] Whereas young people might once have had few leisure pursuits to compete with the cinema, the growing access to more tangible material rewards meant the development of a series of real alternatives: ones which could be marked out immediately as pertaining to youth.[87]

Some youth groups professed a clear liking for the cinema, such as the Teddy Boys who, Fyvel argued, considered the cinema to be a secure and familiar social space, and somewhere for young men and women to meet.[88] The so-called *Rock Around the Clock* cinema riots of 1956, when violence broke out amongst Teddy Boys at showings of the Bill Haley film, were in many ways a defining moment.[89] From the mid-1950s onwards the young working class did not stop going to the cinema, indeed they still accounted for the greater proportion of cinema-goers but they stopped going as regularly as they once had.[90] According to an *I.P.A. National Readership Survey*, 63 per cent of 16–24 year-olds in 1956–57 went to the cinema regularly (defined as once a week or more); the corresponding figure for 1959–60 had declined to 44 per cent.[91] In many ways the cinema was caught in a cultural and social revolution, which from the mid-1950s onwards saw its most loyal audience begin to look elsewhere. This was not helped by exhibitors such as Rank, which provoked anger amongst teenage audiences by showing *Rock Around the Clock* (1956) with 'square' films such as Norman Wisdom's *One Good Turn* (1954), in an effort to broaden the appeal of rock'n'roll.[92] There was not a mad dash from the cinema, but the seeds were sown. The slow decline in admissions from the end of the Second World War to the mid-1950s gave way to a more rapid decline from 1956 onwards (see Table 4.3).

Television and the cinema: public and private worlds

> This fellow got his hand caught in a press. He didn't look what he was doing. Of course, he's only got one eye; he lost the sight of the other looking at telly day in, day out.[93]

One of the features of British cinema's 'new wave' in the early 1960s was its antipathy towards modern mass, commercialised culture, as exemplified by mass consumption and materialism, and mass entertainment such as television.[94] Hill observes that the dominant image of the working class during the 1950s was one of decline and change, in which 'modern mass production, increasing geographical mobility and urban redevelopment were breaking up traditional working class communities, while the "economic emancipation" of the working class was being bought at the expense of a cultural subjection to the hollow banalities of mass entertainment'.[95]

For the theatre and film directors and writers who came to be known as the 'angry young men', television was the epitome of this brash new commercialised culture, a culture that was implicitly US in origin and form.[96] In *The Loneliness of the Long Distance Runner* (1962) the central character Colin (Tom Courtenay) turns his back on the television that his mother's 'fancy man' brings into the house, even though all the family gather around to watch it. In *A Kind of Loving* (1962) the central character Vic (Alan Bates) is prevented from attending his father's brass band concert by his wife and mother-in-law who insist that he watch a banal quiz show on television. The notion that a brass band constituted 'authentic' working-class culture whereas television was a direct challenge was mirrored in *The Entertainer* (1960), where the decline of the music hall is precipitated by the introduction of television.

There are several aspects of these representations of television that are interesting, not least the idea that it was seen as a direct challenge to lived culture, in the same way as the cinema was viewed in the pre-war period. Of course the films mentioned above were also a reaction to the perceived class-bound nature of British cinema, which failed to represent the working class in anything other than a clichéd and peripheral fashion. There was a particular concern on the part of intellectuals during the late 1950s who, while fascinated by the emerging youth culture, felt 'unease about the quality of leisure in urban society'.[97] For many, television was part of what was disdainfully called 'mass culture' or the 'mass society', which would inexorably replace the organic society that was seen as existing in the recent past. Hewison noted that 'essentially television as a mass medium was seen as a threat to traditional literary culture which placed such emphasis on individual discriminations'.[98] Marxist intellectuals saw television as implicated in a burgeoning capitalist structure that fetishised commodities, and was antithetical to both 'high' and 'popular' culture. In the USA, by contrast, critiques of television saw it as less of a threat, even neutral in its influence. This rubbed up against a stronger British intellectual tradition, especially when it saw television as part of this larger whole known increasingly as 'the media'.

What is interesting is that, for many, the debates centred on the *context* for entertainment. Television entertainment was qualitatively different and engendered a clearly identifiable and different mode of engagement on the part of audiences. As we have seen, the audience for cinema was substantially the same as television's by the end of the 1960s. However, for commentators such as Manvell television viewers 'soon become habituated to expect something quite different from television compared with what they expect from the cinema'.[99] What they came to expect was stock entertainment, which eschewed novelty and allowed audiences as neighbours collectively to recognise what was coming and offer the *right* response. 'Novelty', according to Manvell, 'may mean exercising one's wits rather more than usual and so failing to get the point of the entertainment.'[100] Implicit in this analysis was an assumption that television offered standardisation of content and reaction. The mode of engagement on the part of television audiences was what Williams saw as an 'undiscriminating, fundamentally bored reaction … You're not exactly enjoying it, or paying any particular attention, but it's passing the time.'[101] Cinema encouraged audiences to *watch* with rapt attention while television elicited a *gaze*.[102] The technological merits or otherwise of the cinema over the inferior image offered by television were outweighed, it seemed, because of what Williams saw as the 'social complex – and especially that of the privatised home'.[103] Television offered immediacy and access to a broad social intake such as music, news, entertainment and sport, something the cinema could not. In the context of historical debates about the representations of working-class people in the cinema, Sinfield felt that 'television was the medium through which working class people were most likely to find out what was being said about them'.[104] In this context the regionally-aware commercial ITV began to offer programmes like *Coronation Street*, which was first broadcast in December 1960.

In Britain, with the establishment of state broadcasting under the BBC, early television was subject to state regulation, unlike in the USA where commercial interests in the form of the producers of the technology were powerful.[105] This meant that the audience constructed by the BBC was very much that of the family, which very quickly came to be a powerful cultural phenomenon. As Ellis observed, television is addressed to a 'generalised audience, which is conceived in a very specific way: as isolated nuclear families in their domestic settings'.[106] In a sense the standardisation of content, identified by Manvell, might be seen as a way of constructing a mass audience, and an undifferentiated audience, but one that is viewing the same image, at the same time. Ellis felt that the image offered by a particular fiction feature film could never address more than a fraction of the mass audience, and that the audience was a differentiated one.[107] This was because cinema involved a choice about *which* film audiences went to see; a choice determined early on in the development of cinema by the specifying of audiences in two principal ways – genre and stars.[108] The argument seemed to be that television saw audiences as homogenous family units, while cinema could specify its audiences along lines of age, class, gender and nationality.

At a time when the audience for the cinema was declining, much of the debate about the relationship between television and the cinema focused on the ways in which cinema involved 'traditional' notions of leisure. Of course, this 'tradition' was only twenty or thirty years old and cinema had been criticised at its inception for its challenge to what was then perceived as 'traditional' forms of leisure. Now, however, cinema had its own tradition, a tradition of leisure activity taken outside the home that seemed to foreground the notion of individual discriminations (to paraphrase Hewison).[109] Manvell talks of the wife demanding that her husband take her out one or two nights a week rather than coming in at night 'ready for his supper, his slippers and his television'.[110] By the mid-1960s the weekly audience for the cinema stood at some 6.5 million. This was still a considerable mass audience although, as Houston observed, one needed to glance at television 'to see what a real mass public looks like'.[111] Concluding that people watched films on television in a less discriminatory manner than at the cinema, Houston opined that '[i]t is in the Odeons that the myths are made, the popular history of the cinema written; and it is in the Odeons that the future of the mass medium, the closest that the twentieth century has come to a popular art of its own haphazard and improvident making, must be decided'.[112]

What is implicit in this statement (and in similar statements made by so many commentators at this time) was the sense that a *public* form of entertainment (cinema) was being superseded in large part by a *private* form of entertainment (television). To many, the concentration on the domestic sphere as the site for entertainment was problematic for two reasons. First, there was some sense that a retreat into the home was a retreat from the unmediated, authentic social experience that was the cinema. Secondly, television was seen as having been 'seduced and distracted by the alluring image of commodities'.[113] This view was much circulated by the cinema industry, Hollywood in particular, as well as by many intellectuals. It rested on the spurious assumption that the cinema resided outside the corrupting sphere of the market: the cinema industry wanted to portray its products as residing in an autonomous aesthetic sphere.

Film producers were practising a grand form of self-delusion in not seeing their products as commodities. It should be noted that film studios very quickly got into television production. Of course, they had long been promoting products (such as Coca Cola) in their films under the guise of 'realism' – a practice later to be dubbed 'product placement'. Gradually, studios began to differentiate cinema and television by emphasising that although movies might be commodities, they were 'at least uncompromised by *external* commercial discourses',[114] while television merely existed to deliver audiences to greedy advertisers. With this in mind, we might consider Mulvey's argument that the cultural shift from the cinema (public) to television (private) in the 1950s was the moment of 'triumph of the home as the point of consumption in the capitalist circulation of commodities'.[115] For many this 'moment of triumph' was no more apparent than in the USA. Indeed, it was commonly felt that this 'triumph' was that *of* the USA.

'Americanisation' and 'mass culture'

There were many debates around the 'Americanisation' of popular culture in Britain during the 1950s and 1960s. The end of the Second World War had seen a dramatic shift in the status of the USA as a world power. Moreover, although Britain was one of the triumphant military powers of the war, its parlous financial state (including its massive indebtedness to the USA) had brought about a dramatic restructuring of the power relations between these two countries. Since the USA had effectively bankrolled Britain's war effort it felt that it was entitled to considerable influence over much of Britain's foreign and domestic policy. It was clear that the USA would demand strict conditions for the continuance of financial assistance after the war. The two powers trod the delicate terrain of post-war Europe, the general perception being that Britain was the junior partner.

It was in this political climate that many expressions of anti-Americanism found their way into popular discourse, particularly through newspapers such as the *Daily Mail* and the *Daily Mirror*.[116] During the war Mass Observation had found that in Britain Russia was consistently more popular than the USA, while surveys after the war still found considerable anti-American sentiment, especially over foreign policy.[117] There was a profound contradiction in this anti-American sentiment, given that US culture was so popular amongst so much of the population. US films, popular fiction, popular music and a whole range of commodities were enjoyed and identified with, particularly amongst the working classes. It was this popularity of US culture that would frame the debates about 'Americanisation' amongst intellectuals, politicians and those in the film industries. At the heart of these debates was a growing realisation that to 'some degree, Americanisation has been almost synonymous with both the substance and the appreciation of modern publicly available forms of culture'.[118]

The case against 'Americanisation' in the post-war period tended to be posited on the notions that (a) the commercialisation of culture was inherently 'bad', especially since it intensified the diminution of supposed traditional 'lived' cultures, and (b) the developing economic and cultural dominance of the USA would lead to the 'Americanisation' of *all* culture. The concept of 'mass culture' played an important role in this case, as people struggled to comprehend the potential of new and developing forms of dissemination. Indeed, Ross observed that 'mass' is 'one of the key terms that governs the official distinction between American/UnAmerican'.[119] Of singular importance was visual culture, particularly Hollywood films augmented by television during the 1950s and 1960s. In many respects these debates were similar to debates which had raged in the 1930s. The central difference between the debates about cinema in the inter-war and post-war periods was that cinema, both as a public leisure form *and* an expression of Britishness, now came to be seen as a form of popular culture that needed to be defended.

Although the conceptualisation of masses and mass culture existed in the inter-war period, the new broadcast technology of television intensified the debates. Moreover, the developing 'consumer society' and in particular its appeal to the young seemed to justify the sense that what was happening in the post-war period was both more intensive and more threatening. Booker saw the pivotal period as the mid-1950s, when the developing material prosperity began to introduce a host of social phenomena loosely called 'Americanisation'. This he defined as a 'brash, standardised mass-culture, centred on the enormously increased influence of television and advertising, a popular music more marked than ever by the hypnotic beat of jazz and the new prominence, as a distinct social force, given to teenagers and the young'.[120]

For Booker what 'Americanisation' unleashed in Britain was a youthful sense of hostility to every form of authority. Moreover, the USA itself became an object of consumption, particularly amongst the young and the working class, and a signifier for a whole range of aspirations, both cultural and economic. However, the USA also acted as a cipher for a whole range of what Hebdige called 'ideological themes', such as delinquency, crime and the breakdown of the family.[121] Writers like Hoggart took this approach in considering what forms of indigenous 'lived' culture were being lost in this process of 'Americanisation'.[122] Hoggart talked of an 'Older' order, characteristic of the 'community' of the 1930s, yielding place to the 'new' – namely the society of the 1950s, characterised by new forms of mass culture. These 'new' forms involved a rejection of the past in favour of a 'progressivism', which was obsessed with shiny material goods and consumption. This obsession with the 'new' was partly the result of US-style advertising, though Hoggart also recognised the power of US films in circulating these discourses.

For all his insights into the importance of popular culture, Hoggart's version of the 'past' as popularly expressed in much of British cinema was not one that most working-class people, let alone the young, could recognise as representative of their lives and experiences. We might note that in 1956, the year of Bill Haley and rock 'n roll, the major star in British cinema was Kenneth More and the number one film *Reach for the Sky* (1956) was set in the Second World War. Representations of working-class characters and the young were not widespread. The cinema industry itself was dominated by directors, producers, writers and many actors who were drawn from the middle classes and/or 'Oxbridge'. While many intellectuals and cultural critics found difficulty in reconciling themselves to 'Americanisation' and popular culture, for those involved in the consumption of popular culture there was no need for reconciliation. For people like my mother and father, living in working-class neighbourhoods in Birmingham and Manchester, identification with the pleasurable, seemingly classless and optimistic world of Hollywood films was easier than with that of a hidebound and rarefied British cinema. The late 1950s heralded the Free Cinema movement. Lindsay Anderson was its leading light and he invited audiences to consider the movement's films, 'in direct relation to a British cinema still obstinately class bound; still rejecting the stimulus of contemporary life, as well as the responsibility to criticise; still reflecting a metropolitan Southern English culture which excludes the rich diversity of tradition and personality which is the whole of Britain'.[123]

White's historical study of a working-class area of London found young working-class males identifying strongly with Hollywood cinema, which created a link between the area they inhabited and the world outside. He argued that:

> [t]he adopted American accents, dress-styles and mannerisms, which many observers bemoaned as slavish emulation of a new trash culture, can be interpreted quite differently. This borrowed 'style' was a self-conscious identification with a more

democratic discourse than anything British society (including its labour movement) had to offer them.[124]

In his influential studies of post-war cinema-going, Mayer found that many of his respondents felt an affinity with 'America' and all things 'American', which was almost exclusively derived from the cinema.[125] Addison noted that while the likes and dislikes of British cinema audiences were complex, what was clear was that at 'an impressionable age, two-thirds of the British people were subject to a powerful image of the United States as an alternative society'.[126] Going on to speculate about the power of these images Addison poses the question whether these dazzling images of America lodged in the mind 'and quietly shape expectations of the future?'[127]

The debate about 'Americanisation' polarised into a debate about the merits of popular culture. Writers like Hebdige and White considered the influence from below, from the position of those who actually consumed US popular culture.[128] This offered a very different version of uses and gratifications posited from those who considered it from above, from the point of view of those who passed aesthetic judgements.[129] Here the fears about 'Americanisation' were linked to the 'threat posed to traditional intellectual elites and their judgements about taste by the 'levelling-down process'.[130] Speaking in a broadcast in July 1945 to explain the purposes of the new Arts Council for Great Britain, John Maynard Keynes demanded 'Death to Hollywood!'[131] Implicit in his mocking comment was the sense that the movement to raise the cultural and moral standards of the nation had little place for the cinema, and that it was popular cinema (Hollywood) that had undermined standards and had little formal educative function. Indeed, the suggestion that cinema should be included in the Arts Council's initial brief met with much resistance, not least because 'the suggestion threatened a number of ideas in which the intelligentsia had a vested interest'.[132] As Jarvie pointed out, there was never any suggestion that the products of high culture needed defending or that the audience for high culture (much of it imported) was itself complicit in a 'cultural invasion'.[133]

Of course, in view of the domination established by Hollywood in British cinemas and the popularity of Hollywood films amongst audiences, this debate was academic. By 1955 it was estimated that 68 per cent of films playing in the world's cinemas were from the USA, with Britain being the biggest single market.[134] However, as we have seen, the decline in attendances year-on-year from the high of 1946 accelerated during the 1950s. Nevertheless, Hollywood's hegemony was not significantly challenged throughout this period; rather it was the domestic cinema industry that suffered. The large exhibitors still looked to the United States for their main features, while Hollywood itself took advantage of a range of circumstances and invested heavily in British film production. As Spraos observed, with only 30 per cent of first features shown in Britain classified as officially British and the remainder overwhelmingly from the USA, the 'importance of American production to the exhibitor can hardly be exaggerated'.[135] The real issue for cinema owners was not the domination of the USA but the decline of cinema-going itself.

By the end of the 1950s, argues Geraghty, cinema 'presented itself as a medium that was old-fashioned, uncomfortable and associated with past pleasures. For the general audience, cinema-going was changing from being the quintessential modern form of entertainment to an old-fashioned and somewhat marginal pursuit.'[136]

Notes

1 D. Lodge, *The Picturegoers,* new edition (Harmondsworth: Penguin, 1993).

2 H. Hopkins, *The New Look: A Social History of the Forties and Fifties in Britain* (London: Readers Union, Secker and Warburg, 1964), p. 331.

3 See K. Box, *The Cinema and the Public* (An Inquiry into Cinema Going Habits and Expenditure made in 1946), New Series 106 (London: Ministry of Information, 1946; D. Docherty, D. Morrison and M. Tracey, *The Last Picture Show: Britain's Changing Film Audience* (London: British Film Institute, 1987); and J. Spraos, *The Decline of the Cinema: An Economist's Report* (London: George Allen & Unwin, 1962).

4 Docherty, Morrison and Tracey, *The Last Picture Show,* p. 14.

5 *Ibid.*

6 *Hulton Reports on Leisure, 1949,* cited in *Ibid.,* p. 17.

7 Cited in H. E. Browning and A. A. Sorrell, 'Cinemas and Cinema-going in Great Britain', *Journal of the Royal Statistical Society,* 117:2 (1954), 133–70, p. 146.

8 *Ibid.*

9 For a history of children's cinema and children's cinema clubs see T. Staples, *All Pals Together: The Story of Children's Cinema* (Edinburgh: Edinburgh University Press, 1997), and S. J. Smith, *Children, Cinema and Censorship: From Dracula to the Dead End Kids* (London: I. B. Tauris, 2005).

10 See A. Eyles, *Odeon Cinemas 1: Oscar Deutsch Entertains Our Nation* (London: Cinema Theatre Association/British Film Institute, 2002).

11 J. Richards, 'Cinema-going in Worktown: Regional Film Audiences in 1930s Britain', *Historical Journal of Film, Radio and Television,* 14:2 (1994), 147–66.

12 G. Macnab, *J. Arthur Rank and the British Film Industry* (London: Routledge, 1994), p. 150.

13 R. Agajanian, '"Just for Kids": Saturday morning cinema and Britain's Children's Film Foundation in the 1960s', *Historical Journal of Film, Radio and Television,* 18:3 (1998), 395–409, p. 396.

14 Wheare Committee (1950), *Report of the Departmental Committee on Children and the Cinema 1948,* Cmd 7945.

15 See Agajanian, 'Just for Kids'.

16 Browning and Sorrell, 'Cinemas and Cinema-going', p. 146.

17 *Ibid.*, p. 147.

18 J. P. Mayer, *British Cinemas and Their Audience* (London: Dobson, 1948).

19 Cited in I. Jarvie, 'British Trade Policy versus Hollywood, 1947–1948: "Food before flicks"?', *Historical Journal of Film, Radio and Television*, 6:1 (1986), 19–41, p. 20.

20 See P. Swann, *The Hollywood Feature Film in Postwar Britain* (London: Croom Helm, 1987).

21 *Ibid.*

22 Palache Committee, *Tendencies to Monopoly in the Cinematograph Film Industry: Report of a Committee Appointed by the Cinematograph Films Council*, 1944, published by The Board of Trade.

23 Plant Committee, *Distribution and Exhibition of Cinematograph Films: Report of the Committee of Enquiry Appointed by the President of the Board of Trade*, 1949, Cmd 7839.

24 For details and analysis of all major film legislation see M. Dickinson and S. Street, *Cinema and State: The Film Industry and the Government 1927–1984* (London: British Film Institute, 1985).

25 Swann, *The Hollywood Feature Film in Postwar Britain*, p. 135.

26 *Ibid.*

27 See B. Baillieu and J. Goodchild, *The British Film Business* (London: John Wiley & Sons, 2002).

28 PEP, *The British Film Industry 1958* (London: Political and Economic Planning Office, 1958), p. 152.

29 *Ibid.*, p. 153.

30 Baillieu and Goodchild, *The British Film Business*, p. 83.

31 Dickinson and Street, *Cinema and State*, p. 236.

32 T. Guback, 'Hollywood's International Market', in T. Balio (ed.), *The American Film Industry*, revised edition (Madison, WI: The University of Wisconsin Press, 1985), p. 479.

33 For an overview of cinema attendance trends between the 1930s and early 1990s see B. Doyle, 'The Geography of Cinemagoing in Great Britain, 1934–1994: A comment', *Historical Journal of Film, Radio and Television*, 23:1 (2003), 59–71.

34 S. Harper and V. Porter, *British Cinema of the 1950s: The Decline of Deference* (Oxford: Oxford University Press, 2003).

35 Docherty, Morrison and Tracey, *The Last Picture Show*, p. 17.

36 W. Olins, 'The Best Place to See a Film?', *Sight and Sound*, 54:4 (Autumn 1985), 241–4, p. 241.

37 *Ibid.*, p. 242.

38 See Docherty, Morrison and Tracey, *The Last Picture Show* and Olins, 'The Best Place to See a Film?'.

39 For details of these and other acts see S. V. Ward, *Planning and Urban Change* (London: Paul Chapman Publishing, 1994).

40 See F. J. Osborn and A. Whittick, *New Towns: Their Origins, Achievements and*

Progress (London: Leonard Hill, 1977).

41 Ward, *Planning and Urban Change.*

42 *Ibid.*, p. 153.

43 C. Holmes, *Housing, Equality and Choice*, Institute of Public Policy Research (IPPR), 2003, p. 9.

44 Spraos, *The Decline of the Cinema.*

45 *Ibid.*

46 Osborn and Whittick, *New Towns.*

47 Spraos, *The Decline of the Cinema*, p. 163.

48 P. Lawless and F. Brown, *Urban Growth and Change in Britain* (London: Harper and Row, 1986).

49 *Ibid.*

50 D. Gomery, *Shared Pleasures: A History of Movie Presentation in the United States* (London: British Film Institute, 1992).

51 *Ibid.*, p. 88.

52 Browning and Sorrell, 'Cinemas and Cinema-going in Great Britain', p. 151.

53 M. Valentine, *The Show Starts on the Sidewalk: An Architectural History of the Movie Theatre, Starring S. Charles Lee* (New Haven and London: Yale University Press, 1994), p. 159.

54 D. Andrew, 'Film and Society: Public Rituals and Private Space', in R. Hark (ed.), *Exhibition: The Film Reader* (London: Routledge, 2002), p. 166.

55 Gomery, *Shared Pleasures.*

56 *Ibid.*, p. 88.

57 J. Belton, *Widescreen Cinema* (Cambridge, MA: Harvard University Press, 1982), p. 76.

58 *Ibid.*

59 See D. Puttnam, *The Undeclared War: The Struggle for Control of the World's Film Industry* (London: Harper Collins, 1997).

60 Cited in A. Eyles, *Gaumont British Cinemas* (London: Cinema Theatre Association/ British Film Institute, 1996), p. 148.

61 *Financial Times*, 5 August 1953.

62 Spraos, *The Decline of the Cinema.*

63 *Ibid.*, p. 22.

64 PEP, *The British Film Industry, 1958.*

65 *Ibid.*, p. 24.

66 According to C. Hand the mid-1950s saw government restrictions on the hire purchase and rental of consumer durables like televisions, which increased the deposits required for both. See 'Television Ownership in Britain and the Coming of ITV: What do the Statistics Show?', unpublished paper, 2002, available from www2.rhul.ac.uk/~umwf133/ (accessed June 2004).

67 Docherty, Morrison and Tracey, *The Last Picture Show*, p. 23.

68 Spraos, *The Decline of the Cinema.*

69 Docherty, Morrison and Tracey, *The Last Picture Show.*

70 Browning and Sorrell, 'Cinemas and Cinema-going', p. 151.

71 Docherty, Morrison and Tracey, *The Last Picture Show*, p. 24.

72 *Ibid.*

73 *Ibid.*

74 *Ibid.*, p. 25.

75 T. Byrne and C. Padfield, *Social Services* (London: Heinemann, 1983).

76 G. Speight, 'Who Bought the Inter-War Semi? The Socioeconomic Characteristics of New – House Buyers in the 1930s', *Discussion Papers in Economic and Social History*, 38 (December 2000), Oxford University.

77 J. Westergaard and H. Resler, *Class in a Capitalist Society* (Harmondsworth: Penguin, 1976), p. 136.

78 Docherty, Morrison and Tracey, *The Last Picture Show*, p. 26.

79 Hopkins, *The New Look*, p. 332.

80 *Sunday Times* 2 January 1958, cited in PEP, *The British Film Industry 1958*, p. 138.

81 See series of 'affluent worker' studies by J. Goldthorpe, D. Lockwood, F. Bechhofer and J. Platt, including *The Affluent Worker in the Class Structure* (Cambridge: Cambridge University Press, 1969).

82 H. Braverman, *Labour and Monopoly Capital* (New York: Monthly Review Press, 1974), cited by D. Philips and A. Tomlinson in 'Homeward Bound: Leisure, Popular Culture and Consumer Capitalism', in D. Strinati and S. Wagg (eds), *Come on Down? Popular Media Culture in Post-War Britain* (London: Routledge, 1992), p. 12.

83 A. Gamble, *The Conservative Nation* (London: Routledge & Kegan Paul, 1974), p. 61.

84 J. Hill, *Sex, Class and Realism: British Cinema 1956–1963* (London: British Film Institute, 1986), p. 5.

85 C. Lindsay, *Labour Market Trends*, Office for National Statistics, March 2003.

86 P. Laurie, *The Teenage Revolution* (London: Anthony Blond, 1965), cited in Hill, *Sex, Class and Realism*, p. 10.

87 See S. Hall and P. Whannel, *The Popular Arts* (London: Hutchinson Educational, 1964) for a near contemporary analysis.

88 T. R. Fyvel, *The Insecure Offender* (London: Chatto and Windus, 1961).

89 See R. Gosling, *Personal Copy: A Memoir of the Sixties* (London: Faber and Faber, 1980).

90 Docherty, Morrison and Tracey, *The Last Picture Show*.

91 Cited in Spraos, *The Decline of the Cinema*, p. 61.

92 Eyles, *Gaumont British Cinemas*, p. 143.

93 Arthur Seaton (Albert Finney) to his father who is watching television in *Saturday Night and Sunday Morning*, Dir. Karel Reisz, UK, Woodfall Film Productions, 1960.

94 Hill, *Sex, Class and Realism*.

95 *Ibid.*, p. 150.

96 The term 'angry young men' was a journalistic one taken from the title of Leslie Allen Paul's autobiography, *Angry Young Man* (1951).

97 A. Lovell and J. Hillier, *Studies in Documentary* (London: Secker & Warburg,

1972), p. 142.

98 R. Hewison, *Culture and Consensus: England, Art and Politics since 1940* (London: Methuen, 1995), p. 129.

99 R. Manvell, *The Film and the Public* (Harmondsworth: Penguin, 1955), p. 270.

100 *Ibid.*

101 R. Williams, *Communications* (Harmondsworth: Penguin, 1968), p. 99.

102 See J. Ellis, *Visible Fictions: Cinema, Television, Video*, revised edition (London: Routledge, 1992).

103 R. Williams, *Television Technology and Cultural Form*, second edition (London: Routledge, 1990), p. 28.

104 A. Sinfield, *Literature, Politics and Culture in Postwar Britain* (London and Atlantic Highlands, NJ: The Athlone Press, 1997), p. 269.

105 Williams, *Television Technology and Cultural Form*.

106 Ellis, *Visible Fictions*, p. 115.

107 *Ibid.*

108 *Ibid.*

109 Hewison, *Culture and Consensus*.

110 Manvell, *The Film and the Public*, p. 268.

111 Houston, *The Contemporary Cinema*, p. 171.

112 *Ibid.*, p. 170.

113 C. Anderson, 'Hollywood and the Home: TV and the End of the Studio System', in J. Naremore and P. Brantlinger (eds), *Modernity and Mass Culture* (Bloomington, IN: Indiana University Press, 1991), pp. 87–8.

114 *Ibid.*, p. 89.

115 L. Mulvey, 'Melodrama in and out of the Home', in C. MacCabe (ed.), *High Theory/Low Culture: Analysing Popular Television and Film* (Manchester: Manchester University Press, 1986), p. 98.

116 See Swann, *The Hollywood Feature Film in Postwar Britain*.

117 *Ibid.*

118 D. Strinati, 'The Taste of America: Americanization and Popular Culture in Britain', in Strinati and Wagg (eds), *Come on Down?*, p. 47.

119 A. Ross, *No Respect: Intellectuals and Popular Culture* (London: Routledge, 1989), p. 42.

120 C. Booker, *The Neophiliacs* (London: Fontana/Collins, 1970), p. 33.

121 D. Hebdige, *Hiding in the Light: On Images and Things* (London: Routledge, 1988).

122 R. Hoggart, *The Uses of Literacy* (Harmondsworth: Penguin, 1958).

123 S. Laing, *Representations of Working class Life 1957–1964* (London: Macmillan, 1986), p. 114.

124 J. White, *The Worst Street in North London* (London: Routledge & Kegan Paul, 1986), p. 33.

125 J. P. Mayer, *Sociology of Film* (London: Faber and Faber, 1946), and Mayer, *British Cinemas and Their Audience*.

126 P. Addison, *Now the War is Over: A Social History of Britain 1945–51* (London: Pimlico, 1995), p. 132.

127 *Ibid.*

128 Hebdige, *Hiding in the Light,* and White, *The Worst Street in North London.*

129 Strinati, 'The Taste of America'.

130 *Ibid.*, p. 34.

131 Cited in Addison, *Now the War is Over*, p. 134.

132 Dickinson and Street, *Cinema and State*, p. 160.

133 I. Jarvie, 'Free Trade as Cultural Threat: American Film and TV Exports in the Post-war Period', in G. Nowell-Smith and S. Ricci (eds), *Hollywood and Europe: Economics, Culture and National Identity 1945-95* (London: British Film Institute, 1998), p. 43.

134 Swann, *The Hollywood Feature Film in Postwar Britain*, p. 81.

135 Spraos, *The Decline of the Cinema*, p. 41.

136 C. Geraghty, *British Cinema in the Fifties: Gender, Genre and the 'New Look'* (London: Routledge, 2000), p. 20.

5

Sub-dividing and falling, and the lessons from the USA: 1960s–1984

Most of us face this harassing dilemma that we are working in a mass medium that has lost its mass audience and won't admit it. (John Houseman)[1]

Due to lack of public support this cinema is now closed. (Sign on Granada Tooting cinema)[2]

The decline in fortunes of the cinema throughout the 1960s and 1970s took place in the context of dramatic changes in British society. Changing leisure patterns, demographic shifts, the growth of consumer culture, television, and new broadcast technologies like video and satellite all compounded the decline in cinema-going and a corresponding contraction of the cinema infrastructure. The period is one in which cinema exhibitors sought to distinguish the silver screen from the television screen as a plethora of technological advancements were marketed, such as stereophonic sound and special widescreen formats. It is also at the end of this period that sees not only the emergence of the video cassette recorder (VCR) but also sees the conditions created for the development of a new kind of multi-screen cinema, pioneered in the USA.

The exhibition industry: adapting to decline

In 1960 annual cinema attendances stood at 515 million, a collapse of over 50 per cent in less than five years. Exhibitors adopted a variety of approaches to arrest the decline; each based on a careful rationalisation of the causes for the drop in attendances. This was coupled with a hard-nosed approach to the continued profitability of the companies, in which widespread closure was a key element. One significant trend in the wake of declining cinema audiences was the diversification of cinema use. Rank enthusiastically began turning cinemas into dance halls under the Majestic Ballroom banner. In 1960 ABC opened Britain's first bowling alley in the former Super,

Stamford Hill in London and it converted the Princess, Dagenham some four months later. Rank also became interested in converting cinemas into ten-pin bowling alleys. Cinemas were totally gutted at a cost of approximately £300,000 each and ironically, film stars were often used to open the new bowling alleys, most under contract to ABPC.[3] Similarly, Rank converted six cinemas. Both companies, however, had been the victims of what turned out to be a passing fad. They recognised that they had made financial miscalculations. The conversion to bingo halls proved to be much more profitable and enduring: Rank's Gaumont Peckham was the first cinema to be converted to bingo in January 1961, while ABC converted the Dominion Walthamstow, London in March 1961.[4]

The prevailing view amongst many in the exhibition industry was that cinema had fallen victim primarily to the onward march of technological progress, in the form of television. Therefore, cinema had to reassert its technological superiority in the presentation of moving images. In the 1950s both of the major chains, along with many smaller companies such as Granada and Essoldo, had embraced new widescreen formats such as Cinerama and, more importantly, CinemaScope.[5] The first film made in CinemaScope was *The Robe* (1953), which had premiered in London in the same year. CinemaScope required a screen wider than the traditional 'academy ratio', therefore, conversions of existing cinema screens to larger ones were required. According to Spyros Skouras, then President of 20th Century Fox, CinemaScope would restore the public's interest in the 'greatest entertainment in the world'.[6]

The appeal of CinemaScope and other widescreen formats such as Todd-AO and VistaVision was stimulated during the 1960s by a steady procession of big budget, widescreen Hollywood blockbusters such as *Around the World in Eighty Days* (1956), *South Pacific* (1958), *El Cid* (1961) and *The Sound of Music* (1965).[7] Conversion of cinemas to CinemaScope was a costly undertaking, requiring, at the insistence of 20th Century Fox, the installation of stereophonic sound. As Wollen points out, the skilled marketing of 20th Century Fox, which went all out for CinemaScope, left exhibitors with little choice but to make the outlay. Producer Darryl F. Zanuck said the company had the 'conviction that it brings to theatre-goers a new type of entertainment unavailable in any other medium, and so startling in effect that it truly brings a new dimension to the motion picture theatre. We believe it will supplant all other types of film.'[8]

In 1954 the number of cinemas equipped for CinemaScope in the USA was 3,500; twelve months later it had risen to 13,500.[9] This constituted approximately half of all cinemas. CinemaScope was seen as establishing an entirely new market for film, so much so that three months after its launch 20th Century Fox was actively considering selling its entire back catalogue of film titles to television. For cinema exhibitors the new process 'enabled them to present a seductive big-screen spectacular event for which they could charge more at the box office'.[10] In Britain the conversion of cinemas was initially confined to large premier city centre venues due to the cost. Rank, for instance, had equipped approximately seventy of its cinemas by the beginning of 1954 and Granada agreed to equip a third of its circuit with CinemaScope along with the most advanced stereophonic sound in May 1954.[11]

The underlying idea in the application of these new forms of technology was that audiences had to be reminded that the projected, photographic image was superior to that of the broadcast television image. It was necessary therefore, to emphasise the large size of the cinema screen in relation to the small size of the television screen. Audiences for films made in CinemaScope were presented with a panoramic image up to eighty feet wide and with stereophonic sound, at a time when the average television broadcast was in black and white, on a screen twelve inches wide. Initially, the reaction of audiences to CinemaScope, marketed as 'putting you right in the picture', was strong with many cinemas reporting substantial increases in attendance. At Granada's flagship Tooting cinema in London the numbers attending in 1955 had risen for two consecutive years in the context of a national decline.[12] As Ellis points out, there had been a steady 'tendency towards elaboration of the image and soundtracks', which reached its apotheosis in the widescreen spectaculars of the 1960s.[13] It must have seemed to the industry that people were bound to return to the cinema.

Three significant factors weighed against arresting the decline in cinema-going in Britain during mid-1960s. The first was the spiralling cost to the studios of making CinemaScope and other widescreen epics, particularly in the wake of films such as *Cleopatra* (1963) and *Doctor Dolittle* (1967) that did not recoup their considerable production budgets. Second, was that the novelty of these films soon wore off and as widescreen was steadily taken for granted the films themselves came under greater critical scrutiny. As Andrew argues, producers were less concerned about the narrative possibilities of CinemaScope than they were about 'reinvigorating the ritual of going to the movies'.[14] Third, was that the industry did not build new cinemas in the areas to which many city dwellers had moved, such as the new towns and suburbs. It would be the US and Canadian multiplex owners who, realising the potential, would ultimately build cinemas in this new Britain.

In 1984 there were 660 cinemas in Britain, down from approximately 4,750 in 1947. The peak period for closures was 1957–60, when the total fell from 4,194 to 3,034.[15] Between 1952 and 1964 the total seating capacity of all cinemas halved from 4.2 million to 2.1 million and by 1982 seating capacity had shrunk further to around 600,000.[16] As the cinema sector declined overall, the dominance of Rank and ABC increased so that by 1965 Rank and ABC controlled over two-fifths of cinema seats.[17]

The dominance of the exhibition sector by these two companies was built upon their almost total control of cinemas with seating capacities of 2,000 and over, which were the key to the whole release pattern for film distributors. Such was the role played by these two companies that in 1966 the Monopolies Commission investigated their ownership of cinemas.[18] The Commission concluded that there was no real competition between the two major circuits in obtaining a supply of films, since a series of bars were operated by Rank and ABC in respect of other exhibitors. If an independent cinema had an ABC or Rank cinema in its location then it found competing difficult or impossible and many closed down as a result. In simple terms a duopoly, created in the period after the Second World War, was operating in respect of distribution and exhibition, since each company had exclusive access to the films of particular distributors. As Tunstall observed, the Commission found that 'while getting your film on to the Rank or ABC circuit did not guarantee success, not getting it on either circuit did guarantee failure'.[19]

Notwithstanding the tepid recommendations of the Commission's report, Rank and ABC consolidated their dominance of the exhibition sector. This led to a series of developments that ran in tandem with the technological improvements discussed above. These included the building of some new prestige cinemas, such as the ABCs in Sheffield (1961), Bristol (1966) and Newport, Gwent (1968) and the introduction of dual-use sites (bingo and cinema). As in the 1950s, the context for these developments was an inexorable decline in cinema admissions. The building of new cinemas took place in cities where either ABC or Rank had no presence and the designs reflected a change in the way in which the 'dream palace' was perceived. There was little design that could be considered radical and in general the construction of cinemas in the 1960s was dominated by the necessity of incorporating them into other developments, usually offices. In London, where land prices were accelerating fastest, the Curzon Mayfair built in 1966 was located underneath an eight-storey office and residential development. The Odeon Marble Arch, opened in 1967, was the largest cinema built in the capital since the 1930s but this too was hidden beneath an office block. A notable exception was the Odeon in London's Elephant and Castle. With the planned closure of the 3,329 seat Trocadero cinema in 1963, Rank had commissioned plans for a two-level 1,050 seat cinema, coffee bar, underground car park and eight-storey office building. It opened in 1966 and unlike other 'multi-use' sites the design by Hungarian architect Ernö Goldfinger, was brilliantly simple and expressive, with the cinema's identity clearly delineated from that of the accompanying structure.[20]

In the new cinemas there was little if any ornamentation and a greater accent on technology. Sight lines were usually excellent and the screen sizes were impressive, particularly at the Odeon Marble Arch. Paradoxically, where cinemas were upgraded and improved, the key to making them more inviting was to reduce the seating capacities. ABC introduced 'luxury lounges', whereby the area of the cinema previously occupied by the stalls was modernised and spaced out, and the circle was often downgraded in order to attract the rowdier elements away from what was now the luxury area.[21] Nevertheless, the numbers of cinema-goers was still judged to be too low to justify the total seating capacities available, and Rank and ABC closed many cinemas (especially Rank which often had both an Odeon and Gaumont in the same town or city). Rank had concluded that what were required were smaller cinemas and in 1965 came up with the idea of sub-dividing an existing cinema into two smaller auditoria at its Nottingham site (followed by others in Leeds, Liverpool and Sheffield in 1968). ABC followed in 1969 by dividing its Edinburgh Regal site into three auditoria. Rank accelerated its closure programme as twinned and tripled Odeons and Gaumonts forced the demise of each other. This culminated in the loss of the Gaumont name altogether in 1987 in favour of the Odeon brand.[22]

Billed by ABC as 'The ultimate Cinemas of the Seventies' sites such as the ABC 1 & 2 in London's Shaftsbury Avenue and the ABC Edinburgh were luxurious. After ABC was sold to EMI in 1969, the company introduced an accelerated policy of closure and conversion, as competition with Rank heated up. The costs of conversion were often substantial and exacerbated by the necessity of closing the cinema for up to nine months. Initially, the majority of the conversions created twin auditoria by dividing the existing building horizontally and extending the circle forward to create one auditorium on top of another. Purists argued that this had the catastrophic effect of removing all traces of the cinema's existing decor. In some larger sites there was enough room to sub-divide the circle and create a bingo hall in the area previously occupied by the stalls, or create four screens. However, concerned at the loss of business due to temporary closure, Rank introduced the 'drop-wall' conversion technique in 1972. This created three screens by blocking off the space beneath the circle and dividing it down the middle to create two smaller cinemas, leaving the rest of the building to become the largest of the three.[23]

There were significant drawbacks to many conversions. Poor sight lines in the lower auditoria were caused by the necessity of off-centring the screen to make way for an emergency exit and aligning them with a shared projection box located at the corner. The low ceilings and narrow halls also meant much reduced screen sizes. Audience reaction was often poor, especially for those who did not occupy one of the few seats that could be described as halfway ideal. Upstairs, in what had previously been the circle, things were a little better, although there was often a large void in front of the screen where the front of the former stalls had been, which could play havoc with the acoustics, especially for those sat at the front.

The shared projection box was often a pragmatic, cost-saving necessity but at Rank's Nottingham Odeon it also introduced an interesting feature that would be a precursor of the multiplex: a fully automated projection control system. Dubbed the 'cinema of the space age' the Odeon incorporated a new process called 'Cinemation' in which an electronic system controlled the lighting, focusing and sound, as well as ventilation, heating and the opening and closing of the curtains in the auditorium.[24] 'Cinemation', which was also marketed as 'Projectamatic' by Granada cinemas, was based upon technology developed by the Essoldo circuit which dubbed its version 'Essoldomatic'.[25]

Though ABC did adopt some 'drop-wall' conversions at less prestigious sites, it was far more inclined to undertake more expensive conversions. This meant that it could re-launch the sites as entirely new film centres, thus avoiding the 'postage-stamp' size of some of Rank's auditoria.[26] Additionally, the move to the twinning and tripling of cinemas also reflected a shift in booking practices for cinemas, particularly for new releases. Increasingly, 'Roadshow' arrangements were introduced whereby prestige films ran for extended periods as part of separate programmes and a seat could be booked in advance.[27]

Throughout the 1970s there was a steady decline in cinema attendance and both ABC and Rank rationalised their operations, instigating sub-dividing of cinemas and widespread closures. Nevertheless, both continued to stress the element of more choice for cinema-goers. The number of cinema buildings fell from 1,492 to 660, although the number of screens remained fairly constant due to the accelerated process of 'twinning' and 'tripling' (see Table 5.1).[28]

Table 5.1 Number of cinema sites and screens in Britain, 1969–84

Year	Sites	Screens	Year	Sites	Screens
1969	1,559	1,581	1977	1,005	1,510
1970	1,492	1,529	1978	985	1,519
1971	1,420	1,482	1979	978	1,564
1972	1,314	1,450	1980	942	1,576
1973	1,269	1,530	1981	877	1,533
1974	1,176	1,525	1982	803	1,439
1975	1,100	1,530	1983	707	1,304
1976	1,057	1,525	1984	660	1,271

Source: Board of Trade/Department of Trade and Industry cited in 'Cinema and Film Statistics', *Screen Digest*, October 1990.

Not all of the innovation in cinema design was attributable to Rank and ABC. In 1969 Compton Cinemas (a small but vertically integrated producer and distributor of mainly horror, erotic and science fiction films) opened a new cinema in London's Panton Street. It was the first of an innovative chain of cinemas under the company's new brand called Cinecenta. The Cinecentas were unique in that they were designed as multi-screen cinemas (the Panton Street site had four screens). The auditoria often had small numbers of seats (up to 250 though Panton Street's had 150 each) but the company reasoned that it could fill its auditoria while Rank's and ABC's larger capacity cinemas were often poorly attended.

Cinecenta paid a great deal of attention to design (the cinemas were dubbed 'Boutique Cinemas') and introduced glamorous usherettes called 'Cinegirls' in an effort to reintroduce an element of showmanship as well as brand identification.[29] According to Hughes-Stanton, writing in *Cinema* in 1969, Cinecentas were 'aimed at the young and unmarried, those who want a choice of film, and the idiom is strictly fashionable'.[30] In line with their policy of attracting younger audiences, Cinecentas offered a more eclectic and non-mainstream film programme, including foreign-language titles and independent productions. Though now seen as having a considerable impact upon subsequent cinema developments, Cinecenta survived as an independent for only ten years before being taken over and many of its cinemas sold to rivals.

Come back to the cinema – please!

> The interest, indeed fascination, with films and filmmaking in this country undoubtedly exists. Our job as an industry, in British Film Year, is to harness that fascination to its proper focal point: the cinema.[31]

In 1985 British Film Year (BFY) was launched with the slogan 'Cinema – The best place to see a film'. A general campaign to revive cinema-going in Britain was joined with an attempt to highlight filmmakers and facilities as one of Britain's great national assets.[32] The *BFY Broadsheet*, published in July 1985, was explicit about the place of cinema, stating that:

> BFY is celebrating film in its first and natural home – the cinema. Here, and only here, with the dimming of the house lights, comes that electric concentration – the tears, laughter, and shared excitement, which only the big screen can command, and an audience create. The audience is vital to that sense of occasion, and the three main cinema chains are spending £1 million a month during 1985 to entice film lovers away from their homes and back to the magic of the silver screen … Film artistry translated into moving pictures on a large screen weaves a unique spell. BFY

is dedicated to continuing that spell – by keeping the cinema alive at the heart of the community.[33]

As Docherty, Morrison and Tracey pointed out, the BFY campaign assumed the level of a 'moral crusade: a cry to the masses to renew their faith in film by returning to the place of true worship – the cinema'.[34] In many ways the rhetoric used by the organisers of BFY takes us back to the halcyon days of the 1930s and 1940s when everyone went to the cinema. Indeed, Richard Attenborough stated that the purpose of BFY was to 'revive cinema-going as a national habit' based upon the notion that 'films are made to be shown in cinemas, on the big screen as a communal activity'.[35] The rhetoric confers on cinema a mythical status that seems to miss an obvious contemporary reality – that cinema was the 'home' of film for particular historical reasons and that now the conditions for the consumption of films had changed as a result of capitalism's focus on home-based technologies, and in particular the video cassette recorder (VCR).

VCRs had not necessarily replaced cinema-going; rather video offered a new way to enjoy film that was closer to television in its mode of consumption. A stated preference for watching films on video or television in the home may be an assertion of the importance of the home as a site of leisure or in the fabric of people's lives, rather than a rejection of the merits of the cinema. Docherty, Morrison and Tracey's empirical study (undertaken initially in 1984–86) found that amongst those respondents who possessed VCRs some 33 per cent felt that the best way to watch a feature film was in the cinema, as opposed to 29 per cent of those who did not have a VCR.[36] Of course, watching a film on video allows the viewer to stop it while they make a drink, watch it when they want or rewind it if part of the narrative was confusing or unclear. The freedom conferred on the viewer is at odds with that of the cinema, since it undermines the 'rules' of watching a film that have been established by the experience that is cinema.[37]

Prior to the mid-1980s there had been consistent attempts to reassert the position of cinema as not only a distinct leisure form but an important national cultural form as well. The discourses of BFY were a particularly interesting example of this in that they attempted to fuse these with the commercial imperatives of Thatcherism. Two points were being articulated. First, that the cinema should be naturalised as the 'home' of the film. Secondly, that the cinema had what Higson described as a 'profoundly nationalising (and naturalising) ideological function' in which a chain, which ran from the film industry via notions of audience and community to nation, was implicitly contained.[38] Despite the plans to champion British films via a series of national and international events, including roadshows and British Film Weeks, the cinema industry, according to Howkins, thought of cinema 'merely as an outlet for their latest product. They do not want to engage with the public who may, if the circumstances are right, go to the cinema and form an audience.'[39] With regard to the exhibition sector the prevailing view was that, in Howkins' words, it was both 'fragmented and hapless'.[40] The Association of Independent Producers argued that the aims of BFY would be undermined 'unless the major exhibition circuits … make tangible commitments to improve the quality of their cinemas and the sound and projection equipment in them'.[41] Higson observed that the turn to the USA during BFY to increase cinema admissions ran in tandem with the imperative of getting British films shown there in order to raise the profile of domestic production.[42] British films, it seemed, were intended for the US market and for many cynical observers BFY was a 'vision of cinema dominated by economic interests, and cloaked in the glamour and excitement of showbiz'.[43]

The context for BFY was a small rise in cinema admissions, though the irony in the nationalistic and jingoistic approach was that the increase was achieved largely on the back of a number of major Hollywood releases such as *Ghostbusters* (1984) and *Back to the Future* (1985). *Sight and Sound* went as far as to suggest that British cinema managers 'ought to be giving all their thanks to Steven Spielberg and a few of his colleagues' for the increase in admissions.[44]

Much of the smaller audience in the 1970s and early 1980s had not rejected cinema as a special place in which to see a film; rather most of the films that had come along in the intervening years were not recognised as cinematic enough to tempt them out. Moreover, for many young families having their first mortgaged house, small children and a television set had meant that the domestic sphere was important to them, for practical and emotional reasons. Going out 'to the pictures' became a special occasion, taken annually or bi-annually, and was no longer the social habit it had been when married couples were young and courting. Consistent with this new attitude, prospective cinema-goers became more discerning in their choice of film.

Notwithstanding all that has been said about television, the primacy of the domestic sphere and shifting leisure patterns, the root of the trend away from cinema-going was simply that for many people most cinemas were not pleasant places to be. In part this was a result of the less than satisfactory conversions that took place in a significant number of cinemas in the 1960s and 1970s. For Olins, a cinema designer himself, part of the responsibility for the decline of cinema-going from the 1960s onwards lay firmly with the two companies who dominated the exhibition industry – Rank and ABC's successor Thorn-EMI.[45] Both were large conglomerates with interests in a variety of other fields which had somehow neglected their cinema businesses, and worse, failed to listen to outside advice. According to

Olins, 'the revolution in the customs, habits and tastes of the British people, which took place between the 60s and 80s completely, passed them by. They remained pickled in aspic with Clark Gable and Marilyn Monroe, somewhere in 1961. British cinema somehow got stuck in some monstrous time-warp.'[46]

Olins was writing on the eve of the new multiplex development in Milton Keynes. His central tenet, that the cinema industry was dominated by two major companies who had failed to market cinema and lacked imagination, was about to be challenged by North American corporate power. The implicit claim was that cinemas themselves were often unfit for their stated purpose being both poorly designed and maintained. Olins was not alone in describing what he regarded as the potential collapse of the industry. For one Hollywood executive the trend towards conversion and closure throughout the 1970s could prove to be the death-knell for the exhibition industry. Speaking at the time of a temporary upward swing in attendances on a wave of box-office hits in 1978, Ascanio Branca, the head of 20th Century Fox in London, told *Variety*:

> No country in Europe is so badly served as Britain as to the condition of its theatres. Many of the multi-auditoria put up here are lousy. There are continual complaints about sound and comfort. It is pitiful … [British Exhibitors] have no faith in the business. If they don't react now and build new theatres when things are going great they will eventually be proven right and the business will collapse.[47]

Branca looked at Britain from the perspective of someone who had experienced developments in the United States where major changes had taken place in the exhibition industry. In 1984 an article in *Screen Digest* identified these developments, which had led to a twenty-one year admission peak in 1982 suggesting that they were 'radical' in the context of Britain's exhibition industry. They were:

1   resiting City centre cinemas into suburban areas;
2   ensuring close proximity to fast food, shops and parking;
3   installing six ten-screen complexes to give wider choice;
4   improving the convenience and fabric of the total viewing experience.[48]

The article went on to observe that in this context it was 'interesting to note' that Rank had decided that half of its Odeon cinemas in the London suburbs were to be closed and their sites redeveloped for their real estate value. In the absence of proposed radical changes based on the US model, the British cinema industry initiated three schemes: the change from Sunday to Friday film openings; the CAVIAR (Cinema and Video Industry Audience Research) project and a new advertising campaign. The latter involved placing joint whole-page advertisements in up to five major daily newspapers, in an effort to reach 70 per cent of potential audiences. Thorn-

EMI went further and instigated a policy of releasing '36 of the best films of the year', divided into categories according to market potential. Films were categorised as six 'Super As', six 'As', 12 'Bs' and 12 'Cs'. Instead of programming them all in major holidays they would be spread out across the year so that 'destructive clashes of subject matter' were to be avoided'.[49] It was hoped that returns could be maximised by capitalising not just on distributors' marketing strategies but on editorial impact in other subsidiary media such as newspapers. This strategy recognised that with cinemas at 80 per cent below capacity a significant increase in admissions could be accommodated at existing sites. There were no plans for capital developments beyond further modest refurbishment and closures were not ruled out.

In 1983 the Monopolies Commission once again examined the concerns of critics like Olins about the state of the domestic exhibition sector, and in particular the power exercised by the Thorn-EMI/Rank duopoly. Like its predecessor in 1966, the *Report on the Supply of Films for Exhibition in Cinemas* was almost bound by its terms of reference to take a conservative view.[50] Since the industry was in such decline, due to a combination of lack of inward investment and a lack of managerial initiative, there seemed little real room for manoeuvre. The Commission found a growing concentration of distribution interests, with three major conglomerates (Columbia-EMI-Warner, United Pictures International and UK Film Distributors) and three 'minor majors' accounting for 90 per cent of all film rentals. Moreover, this was bound into a system of 'alignments' with the two major exhibitors, Thorn-EMI and Rank.

There seemed little doubt that this system operated against the public interest, however, the report was ambiguous in its recommendations, concluding that little should or could be done to reform a declining industry. It rejected as impractical the call for the creation of an effective competitor to Thorn-EMI and Rank by forcing them to divest themselves of cinemas, preferring to call for the ending of the system of 'bars' and restricting the length of exclusive first-runs outside London's West End. As Ian Christie pointed out, the report seemed to recognise that the industry was 'hiding its head in the sand' as it raised seat prices to compensate for falling attendances, undertook cheap conversions, closed cinemas and eliminated competition through a system of 'alignments'.[51] Christie went on to observe that such a response was 'easier in the short term than undertaking the major reconstruction of cinema that has taken place in the United States and with the backing of governments of all hues, throughout much of Europe'.[52]

By 1984, cinema attendance had plummeted to fifty-four million admissions. Thorn-EMI's ABC circuit had shrunk to 107 sites and 287 screens, and the Rank circuit to 75 sites with 194 screens. In 1984 it was estimated that approximately a quarter of the population now lived twenty miles or more from a cinema.[53] It was at this time, in the context of a prolonged contraction in the exhibition industry and at the moment when attendances reached their nadir, that American Multi-Cinema (AMC) in partnership with Bass Leisure Holdings, laid plans to build a new ten-screen cinema, called The Point, in Milton Keynes (see Chapter 6 for an examination of the development of the multiplex in Britain). The Point was officially opened in November 1985 and in every way marked a departure from previous cinema orthodoxy. Although the 'twinning' and 'tripling' of existing cinemas was seen as giving multi-cinemas a bad press, the multiplex was seen as banishing this due to the design of the auditoria. The Point was designed and built with the benefit of the experience of twenty years of evolution in cinema-going in the USA and Canada, an evolution which had culminated in the development of the multiplex cinema in suburban and out-of-town centres.

Multiplex corporations did one important thing that the British film industry and BFY, in particular, did not do: recognise that film's mode of consumption had shifted decisively under contemporary capitalism into a commodity that had its emphasis in home-based technological forms and entertainment. Film viewing as a popular cultural activity was very much alive: it was cinema-going that was not. Therefore, the multiplex companies set about marketing the cinema as not only the best place to see a film but as a place to which people would want to go. This may seem obvious, but in fact this was precisely what was not happening in Britain in the 1970s. Even those people for whom the home was not necessarily the main centre of entertainment no longer saw the cinema as a popular leisure activity.

What emerges from an examination of the decline in the numbers of cinemas is that the problems for the exhibition industry and the possible remedies were too often focused on the *mechanics* of exhibition and distribution, rather than on the social and cultural *experience* of film. The industry adopted a position of technological determinism, believing that there was a direct relationship between new cinema technologies and enhanced audience appeal. However, as Corrigan points out, technological determinism and its 'associated images of the audience are totally inadequate', adding that what 'they reveal is that there are multiple determinisms at work in any history of a cultural form'.[54] In the post-war period, at the height of cinema's popularity, it was believed that there still existed a 'universal audience' in which all sectors of the population attended the cinema: the 'Golden Age' of cinema-going. The exhibition industry, dominated as it was by two conglomerates, missed what Docherty, Morrison and Tracey identified as 'one of the most important aspects of the decline in cinema attendance, namely the cultural shifts and changing material world of the audience upon which it depended'.[55]

Leaving it to the market – government film policy

The mid-1980s was a period in which the articulation of 'nation', typified by BFY, came to be superseded, in respect of the cinema, by the other prime discourse of Thatcherite ideology: the market. AMC opened Britain's first multiplex in 1985 because the company viewed Britain as a sound commercial opportunity and one in which the hegemony of Hollywood had been established, even if cinemas had been consistently closing. Writing in 1985, Roddick concluded that 'the real crisis in British cinema is not in production but in distribution and exhibition' and that 'the realities of cinema-going in this country are numbing'.[56]

In 1982 the new Conservative government announced a review of film which emerged as a White Paper in 1984.[57] Its recommendations entered into law with the passing of the Films Act 1985, which abolished both the Eady levy and the National Film Finance Corporation (NFFC).[58] The hostility of the Thatcher government to any notion of subsidy meant that the Eady levy had been particularly vulnerable. The scrapping of the NFFC had come after an unsuccessful attempt to align it more with the market, when in 1981 it had been restructured, receiving £1m from central government to be matched by £5m from the private sector. Upon termination, the NFFC's assets were transferred to a private company called British Screen Finance Limited (BSF). BSF had four major shareholders – Channel 4, Granada Television, United Artists Screen Entertainment and Rank. Its mandate was to develop potential film treatments and scripts, and present them as commercial packages.

The Films Act 1985 was an expression of a new ideology in which the British film industry would have to yield to market forces. To many in the industry, particularly the exhibition sector, this appeared realistic. The Eady levy was a case in point, since the decline in admissions during its entire existence had meant that the sums raised for production reduced accordingly. The White Paper had argued that the Eady levy constituted 'an unreasonable burden upon the cinema exhibition industry', for which exhibitors felt vindicated.[59] Many in the film industry, however, were of the opinion that a levy on cinema visits should be replaced with one on TV screenings of films and on video tapes, though this was rejected by the government as simply another subsidy.[60] In a vitriolic article on the passing of the Eady levy and the 'careless attitude to film that pervades the corridors of power', *Stills* reported the comments of one Conservative MP who confessed 'I watch lots of films but never go to the cinema'.[61]

Watching films at home – television and other domestic viewing technologies

As if to compound the fears about television in the minds of cinema exhibitors the late 1970s saw the development of domestic video cassette recorders (known as video tape recorders or VTRs in the USA). JVC launched their first Vertical Helical Scan (VHS) video cassette recorder (VCR) in Japan and the USA in 1977 and subsequently in Britain in 1978. In the same year Sony launched a rival format called Betamax that was eclipsed by VHS in terms of sales and was effectively finished as a rival when in 1986 British video distributors began offering titles on VHS only. Sony's system was widely acknowledged as technically superior but initially offered cassettes of only one-hour recording duration, unlike VHS which were three-hours. In their launch advertisement JVC (UK) Ltd listed a number of revolutionary features including the ability to record programmes using a timer (subsequently known as 'time-shifting'):

> You can set it to tune into any channel and time it to switch on automatically (and just for a moment, consider the implications of that; you could be out having dinner or flying half-way across Europe and your JVC will be sitting quietly at home recording your telly for you).[62]

The development of affordable VCRs in the early 1980s coincided with a significant drop in cinema admissions, from 101 million in 1980 to 54 million in 1984. Between 1981 and 1985 some 28 per cent of British homes acquired a VCR and by 1990 it had reached 62 per cent.[63] The British took to the VCR in greater numbers than any other country in Europe.

   Conscious of video rental's early associations with pornography and poor quality 'back street' video tape dealers, the major film producers initially shunned the technology. Moreover, the cinema industry blamed the pirate film market for siphoning off much of its potential profit in the first few years of its development. Of course, with the major studios not making films available the demand for pirate copies of major releases was fuelled. Nevertheless, in 1983 video film rental and sales was worth approximately £283m, which was more than twice the amount spent on cinema-going – £107m in 1982.[64] In Britain, as in the USA, the growth in video rental was built upon the proliferation of outlets that sprang up in many locations. With little capital outlay required, especially for existing shop owners, renting videos conformed perfectly to the entrepreneurial spirit of the early 1980s.

   The eventual decision by the major Hollywood studios to make films available for video was a result of their desire both to control the distribution business and restrict copying of their films and television programmes. As part of their efforts to restrict copying, MCA/Universal entered into a protracted legal battle with Sony Corporation that went all the way to the US Supreme Court in 1984. With the judges far from unanimous, and with an accompanying recommendation that Congress debate the issue, the decision eventually went in Sony's favour; the Supreme Court held that the 'sale of the VTR's to the general public does not constitute contributory infringement of respondents' copyrights'.[65] With such potential profits to be made the major studios finally accepted video as a legitimate medium, releasing many mainstream titles on to the market, albeit on terms that were extremely favourable to them. The studios' move into the video sector was important since they managed to establish as standard a distribution deal which gave them 75 per cent of the wholesale revenues from video – more than twice the revenue share they received from cinema and television distribution.[66]

In the 1980s the small business nature of video rental also changed so that by the end of the decade this was increasingly the domain of large chains and business concerns. Blockbuster video, formed in Texas in 1985 with one store, was a case in point. The company grew phenomenally quickly, coming to occupy the corners of many streets in the USA. In 1990 Blockbuster acquired the Ritz chain in Britain as part of a major overseas expansion. Operating some 1,000 stores worldwide, it was taken over by Vivendi, then owners of Universal Studios, in 1995.[67] In Britain video rentals and sales climbed to £445m in 1986.[68] Attendances at the cinema were seventy million a year in 1986, however the British were renting 350 million video films; with three people watching each on average, this totalled 1,050 million screenings.[69] On the surface the argument seemed clear: video technology would be the final nail in the coffin of the cinema.

Like the previous technologically determinist arguments based on the development of television, the debate around the pre-eminence of VCRs was undermined by some significant factors. These included: (a) the development of the video market took place in the context of a continuous rise in cinema admissions after 1984 and the development of new cinemas; (b) the marketing strategies of video films by the large Hollywood producers and distributors were closely tied to their recent exhibition in cinemas, thereby stimulating interest in the latter; (c) people still had good reasons for wishing to undertake out-of-the-home leisure activities even after the advent of VCRs, and (d) video is closer to television than it is to the cinema, thereby protecting the cinema and the experience it affords. Let us examine these four points in more detail.

After their initial scepticism the major Hollywood producers established the video rental and sales sector as part of a sophisticated market relationship with the cinema, in which the pre-eminence of the single feature film was actually strengthened. One of the effects of their entry into the video sector was that the major studios, along with the independents, began to market films more vigorously and in ever more sophisticated ways. In 1983 Thorn EMI Screen Entertainment commissioned a survey on 'the scope for promotional activity'.[70] The survey dismissed the potential threat to cinema from the newly emergent video sector. Posing the question 'How can a distributor contemplate a £500,000 national marketing campaign when cinema admissions are averaging less than 1.5m a week against video rental transactions estimated to be 5m?' the survey identified the following answers:

1   Cinema and theatrical distribution is the shop window for every new film.
2   Demand for films through video has only increased through widespread availability and previous word of mouth success.
3   Major studios and distributors will increase all their values of ancillary rights by maximising their theatrical launch.[71]

In his discussion of the relationship between cinema and broadcast television, Ellis points out that 'the space for representations opened up by cinema, and vastly expanded by the advent of TV, contains both cinema and TV in a series of mutually defining, and mutually dependent relationships. TV needs cinema, cinema needs TV.'[72] Although Ellis is considering the cultural spaces that the two forms have established, films and video are mutually dependent on every level. Despite the fact that we are more likely to watch a feature film on television (either on terrestrial and/ or satellite channels) or on video/DVD, the film is always referenced to a notion of cinema.[73] The single narrative fiction that is the feature film is a creation of the cinema and continues to be associated with the performance that is the cinema. Audiences are aware that the experience of watching a feature film afforded by the television is distinctly different from that of a cinema, not just in a technological sense but spatially and culturally.

The industry (primarily Hollywood) has come to rely heavily on the video sector to boost profits. For example, in 1980 the major Hollywood studios collected approximately $20m from the worldwide sale of video cassettes; by 1986 this had risen to over $3bn.[74] Throughout the 1980s in its relatively short time as a major market sector, video underwent a significant series of changes, not least as the numbers of rental transactions in Britain rose year-on-year to reach a peak of 289 million in 1989. The trend reversed during the 1990s so that by 1999 it stood at 186 million transactions.[75] In the same period the video retail sector boomed, with 96 million transactions in 1999, worth some £1.1bn as compared to 6 million transactions, worth £55m in 1986.[76] Despite the fact that the retail sector of the market was largely dominated by non-feature film material such as music videos, television programmes and special interest material, many of the largest selling titles were feature films, a number of which were hugely successful on their cinema releases.

During the 1980s Britain began to experience the development of both domestic satellite and cable television. In 1983 the government awarded eleven regional cable franchises, which were taken up by eight companies by 1985. Almost all of these were owned or operated by US companies. Take-up was initially poor, mainly because video offered the possibility of viewing films conveniently and cheaply. Further, the terrestrial television companies, including the recently launched Channel 4, offered a broad range of programming, particularly sport. What was significant about the early development of cable systems was that the programming offered originated on satellite stations, notably Rupert Murdoch's Sky, which he acquired in 1984.

When direct broadcasting by satellite was proposed by the government in 1982 a licence was granted to the BBC, though ultimately the costs of the technology itself were considered too great. When a British-based service was proposed again it was a consortium of private companies which in 1986 formed British Satellite Broadcasting (BSB), with a view to having a service up and running by 1990. In the event they were trumped spectacularly by Murdoch's Sky TV system, which operated on the Astra satellite and, crucially, was based outside of Britain, beyond the scope of the regulatory body the Independent Broadcasting Authority. Unencumbered by the financial burden of having to offer original programming, Sky TV drew upon programming from the USA and acquired the rights to major Hollywood films in order to offer dedicated film channels. BSB collapsed in 1990 and was taken over by Sky. A new company, British Sky Broadcasting (BSkyB), was formed offering a range of channels including two showing films. These channels were able to screen major releases after they had been available on video but before they were available for broadcast on terrestrial television.

In many of the debates about the relationship between home-based media technologies and the cinema, a key assumption seems to be made: that radio, television and video are competing forms of mass media and challenges to cinema's monopoly.[77] However, as Maltby points out, the 'movies have never in their history had a monopoly in the business of turning pleasure or leisure into a purchasable product, and it would be more accurate to describe television and video as alternatives to cinema rather than as competitors or rivals'.[78]

Television arrived just at the point when the major studios were being forced to divest themselves of their cinema chains under the Paramount Decrees (see Chapter 2). This meant that their power base moved from production and exhibition to production and distribution. The consequence was that the interests of exhibitors became less of a concern to the studios. This in turn pitted cinemas against television as an outlet for Hollywood films. Television was embraced as a new market for much of the studios' minor product ('B' movies, newsreels etc.) with the cinema being reserved for larger scale features. According to Maltby this permitted a 'publicly repressed hostility between production and exhibition to reappear as a much more explicit discourse of hostility between the film and television industries, sustained in part by the cinema's commercial need to justify its cost premium by differentiating the two media'.[79]

Writing in 1983, Blanchard called for the rejection of a simple dichotomy, which identified cinema as public and therefore 'good', and television as private and therefore 'bad'.[80] He argued that we should be developing what is worthwhile in both, while recognising that cinemas were most in need of attention. As one element of a plan of action he observed that:

> It is neither possible nor desirable to think in terms of a return to what could be called 'the spirit of 1946'. Support for cinema-going has to amount to much more than devising a life support system for 'actually existing cinemas'. If the publicly shared viewing of large moving images is to continue, it will have to work out for itself a carefully chosen space amongst the developing array of new communications media.[81]

Blanchard also prophesised that 'what seems unlikely to survive in these circumstances is any claim that cinemas still have to be considered as a significant cultural force enjoying broad popular support'.[82] In many ways this sentiment helps us to pinpoint a particular moment in the story of cinema-going in Britain, a moment when it seemed that the cinema had lost its privileged place in the social fabric of the nation. From Blanchard's vantage point there seemed little more that could be said or done in favour of the cinema. On the eve of the multiplex Blanchard's polemic identified two broadly overlapping arguments for cinema exhibition: the cinema's place as part of the 'wider mosaic of public cultural life' and the need for cinema to remain open as 'part of a strategy for preserving and extending spaces and options outside the domestic and largely familial context and assumptions of TV'.[83]

This attitude was what the multiplex would subsequently have to contend with as it strove to generate interest and, more importantly, profits. However, the multiplex companies eyeing up Britain were doing so from a position where they had seen their own domestic market change drastically in the face of new cinema developments. Their experience convinced them that the poor state of the exhibition industry in Britain, and Western Europe more generally, reflected a decline in the attraction of cinemas *not* of feature films. The multiplex companies could base overseas expansion on lessons learnt in their own markets, ones that had demonstrated the value of a radical response to the social and cultural shifts of the cinema's audience. The response itself was a new form of cinema in a new landscape, aimed at a new audience. This cinema was the multiplex and its antecedents were in the post-war suburbs of the USA.

Beginnings of the multiplex in the USA: into the shopping mall

The development of multiplex cinemas in the USA ran in tandem with two phenomena – major changes in retailing during the 1960s and 1970s, and the post-war development of suburbs. Historically, the majority of cinemas had been located in downtown shopping and residential areas that were well served by public transport. In contrast, the growth of suburbs in the 1940s and 1950s was built around the car and single-family housing, giving rise to the development of the shopping centre. The 1950s had witnessed a phenomenal growth in not only suburban developments but in the wealth of those living there, as suburban families earned incomes 70 per cent higher than those of the rest of the USA.[84] Unlike their British counterparts, cinema companies in the USA followed this movement of large sections of the population into the burgeoning suburbia. As Maryland-based circuit owner Irwin R. Cohen observed, '[t]he industry moved to where the public was'.[85]

The focus for new cinema building was the shopping centre, or mall, which numbered only a few hundred in 1950 but totalled approximately 3,000 by 1958. This growth continued apace during the 1960s and 1970s until the number of out-of-town shopping centres reached 22,000 by 1980, many of which were located at the intersections of major highways, built under the 1956 Federal Highways Act.[86] The concept of the enclosed, climate-controlled shopping centre was introduced in Minneapolis's Southdale Shopping Centre in 1956. The development of the shopping centre heralded the introduction of new cinemas and chains that took their aesthetic inspiration from the malls themselves. As Gomery observed:

> The look of the shopping center was pure international style. Function dictated. Stylistic considerations were set aside. For the movie theatre this meant stripping all the art deco decoration that had made theatres of the 1930s and 1940s so attractive. Little survived. There was a necessary marquee to announce the films. The lobby consisted of a place to wait, a department store concession stand, and restrooms. The auditorium was a minimalist box with a screen at one end and seats in front.[87]

General Cinema was the pioneer of this new form of cinema, having established itself in the burgeoning drive-in sector prior to the Second World War. By the

1960s the mould was set, with other cinema chains being invited into prospective complexes at the planning stages. Initially, the new cinemas were single screens, albeit smaller (approximately 800 seats) than their downtown rivals, though plans were soon laid to extend the new-build concept to embrace multiple screens.

In 1963 Durwood Theaters opened the Parkway Twin in the Ward Parkway Center, a mall in Kansas City. It consisted of two auditoria side-by-side, which shared a lobby, ticket office, concession stand and projection booth. As the first designated two-screen cinema in a shopping complex it aroused much industry attention. It was judged successful enough for Durwood Theaters to embark on a programme of cinema building, which included the world's first four-screen or 'quadriplex' cinema in Kansas City, in 1966. Called the Metro Plaza, the cinema was followed by a 'six-plex' in Omaha, Nebraska in 1969. As if to symbolise the reach of their new form of cinema operation, Durwood Theaters became American Multi-Cinema (AMC) in 1969. In 1972 Stanley Durwood outlined his rationale for the new multiplex concept. He stated that the provision of four screens and later six 'enable us to provide a variety of entertainment in one location. We can present films for children, general audience, and adults, all at the same time.'[88]

Stanley Durwood had not been the first to recognise the virtues of having more than one auditorium. In Canada in 1948 the eventual co-founder of the giant Cineplex Odeon Corporation, Nathan Taylor, had taken over an unfinished cinema in Elgin, Ottawa as part of his Twentieth Century Cinemas chain. The cinema had a 1,200 seat auditorium and on a piece of adjoining land Taylor built an additional 800 seat auditorium, with the intention of showing art films. By the 1950s Taylor was introducing several innovations at the Elgin, not least of which was the showing of the same film on both screens at times of high demand. Moreover, he also recognised that a film that was initially popular in the larger auditorium could be moved to the smaller one as audiences fell. This ability to retain films for longer was important and heralded what became known as the 'move-over' film or the 'sub-run'.[89]

As to who was the 'father of the multiplex' – Stanley Durwood or Nathan Taylor – is a matter of conjecture. Although the term 'multiplex' was coined by National Amusements (which started as a chain of drive-in cinemas and who run the Showcase multiplex chain), what Durwood and Taylor undoubtedly did was usher in a revolution in cinema building in the USA and Canada.[90] Companies like AMC and Cineplex Odeon symbolised a new, aggressive form of cinema operation. They took advantage not only of relatively low-cost sites and buildings, but also of new forms of employment and managerial practices. As Gomery pointed out, a site with six screens required only one concession counter staffed by part-time students, one projectionist and one manager who also sold the tickets.[91] In common with the proliferating fast-food outlets across the USA cinema could, owners thought, be reduced to a high-profit low-cost enterprise employing largely unskilled labour.

At a time when the hegemony of Hollywood was subject to challenge from television, and in particular pay-TV, these new sites became the focus for the attentions of the major studios. Provided that a relatively small but regular number of major releases could be booked the cinemas were profitable. The main audiences for these films were teenagers and young adults, with 75 per cent of total cinema admissions in the USA in 1973 being accounted for by 12–29 year-olds.[92] The Hollywood studios saw teenagers as an easy market to reach, especially since many went to the cinema two or three times a week regardless of what was showing. Hollywood executive Samuel Arkoff identified this market as 'gum-chewing, hamburger-munching adolescents dying to get out of the house on a Friday or Saturday night'.[93]

The 1960s and early 1970s was a significant period in the development of the multiplex cinema, not simply in terms of the imperatives of design, but in the ways in which cinemas were recast with new forms of marketing, consumerism, leisure and business management. Companies that had previously been regionally based also began to look further afield, utilising market research in developing suburbs and forging alliances with large developers.[94] The result was the creation of several national chains by the early 1980s, which in terms of size and power came to replace the cinema chains once owned and run by the 'Big Five' major Hollywood studios (Universal, RKO, 20th Century Fox, Warner Bros. and Loew's/MGM).

The new US chains were based in suburbia rather than the downtown city, though according to many observers, with this new terrain came a diminished cinema experience. At a time when cinema owners in Britain were dividing up their sites via 'twinning' and 'tripling', with largely unsatisfactory results, the early US multiplexes were often compromised by poor design and building execution. Variously described as 'shoe boxes' and 'cookie cutter' theatres, the auditoria were often badly soundproofed, had poorly aligned projectors and were too small. Moreover, the imperative of function dictated that the shopping mall-based cinemas had little architectural merit compared to their forebears in the cities. There was little or no adornment and the cinema became largely indistinguishable from the shops within the mall itself. Valentine observed that in one shopping centre in Santa Fe, New Mexico a 'small marquee hidden in a protective corridor … reads simply 'The Movies'.'[95]

The entrance to the cinemas became increasingly dominated by the concession stand, which steadily assumed a greater financial importance in the profitability of the cinema itself. In 1951 sales of 'candy' accounted for 20 per cent of the revenue of a cinema and the concession stand was often referred to as the 'second box office' by exhibitors.[96] By 1991 some cinemas in the USA were reporting that concession sales accounted for 90 per cent of profits.[97] Should audiences manage to negotiate the ever-expanding concession stand, they were often presented with the new innovation of the video game that invariably filled the entrance.

Unlike Britain though, the cinema sector in the USA remained dynamic throughout the 1970s and 1980s with a year-on-year increase in the number of screens and much new cinema building. By the end of the 1980s the number of annual admissions was stable at one billion; however ticket prices had risen steadily so that the potential box-office receipts grew similarly. By 1989 the six largest cinema chains – United Artists Theatres, Loew's Theatres, Cineplex Odeon, AMC, Carmike Cinemas and General Cinema – which had all prospered in the shopping malls and entered into a building boom in the 1980s, controlled some 40 per cent of cinema screens in the United States, up from 24 per cent in 1986.[98] By the end of the 1980s there existed more screens than at any time in history, although they were primarily in multiplexes and not traditional single-screen cinemas.[99] Indeed, the development of the multiplex saw the Motion Picture Association of America (MPAA) begin to recognise screens and not cinemas. As Paul observed rather acidly, it was 'as if the actual number of theatres in the country had become an irrelevant statistic. The screen is the defining factor.'[100]

Though based on the experiences of new mall-based cinemas in the 1960s and 1970s, multiplexes in the 1980s were increasingly sophisticated, utilising new forms of materials and benefiting from better design. Moreover, these new cinemas were growing in size, and there was a trend for larger complexes featuring eight, ten or more auditoria, coupled with a realisation that the cinemas had outgrown the shopping mall. Many owners were conscious of the constraints of being located within another complex, especially one that might close before the cinema's last showings or present problems for large cinema queues clogging up aisles. What emerged was the free-standing cinema complex, though still sited adjacent to shopping malls.

The new designs involved some attempt to re-establish an identity for the cinema, in which the functional design of the malls was replaced by a more playful and postmodernist aesthetic which plagiarised many of the features of the older 'picture palaces'. The lobbies were greatly enlarged, in part to accommodate the enhanced concession counters, and to provide the complex with a focal point for forthcoming attractions. Behind the scenes, advantage was taken of new technologies such as Dolby Surround Sound, computer-controlled projectors with automated reel-change, computerised advance ticket booking and stock control. Above all, the owners trumpeted 'choice' as the dominant appeal of the new, larger multiplexes.

Commenting on the multiplex experience, US exhibitor Arthur Hertz said:

> You stand in line and you see someone just scanning the board and you realize
> what's going on … It's like going to a smorgasbord and they'll see what appeals to
> them at the moment. There is a psychology to having a lot of small auditoriums
> playing a lot of pictures. If you are sold out of one, there are still choices for people
> to come in and see something else. They're not usually going to walk away and say
> 'the hell with it, I'm going home.' They'll see something else.[101]

As the multiplex consolidated its position in suburban malls throughout the
USA, in the early 1980s the pervading view in Britain was that cinemas were the
last places that people wished to see films. Writing in 1985, on the eve of Britain's
first multiplex, Brosnan observed that the cinemas themselves might be the reason
why the British public 'avoids going to the cinema like the plague … which is in
direct contrast to other countries like America, where cinema attendances are on the
increase'.[102] As audiences plummeted to their lowest level ever, 1985 was a turning
point in the fortunes of cinema exhibition and things would never be the same
again.

Notes

1 John Houseman, cited in P. Houston, *The Contemporary Cinema* (Harmondsworth:
   Penguin, 1963), p. 169.

2 Sign on the Granada Tooting cinema, November 1973, illustration in A. Eyles, *The
   Granada Theatres* (London: Cinema Theatre Association/British Film Institute,
   1998), p. 217.

3 A. Eyles, *ABC: The First Name in Entertainment* (London: Cinema Theatre Association/
   British Film Institute, 1993).

4 See A. Eyles, *Gaumont British Cinemas* (London: Cinema Theatre Association/
   British Film Institute, 1996) and *ABC: The First Name in Entertainment*.

5 Cinerama required three projectors for three linked images, which were melded
   onto a concave screen some 7.5 metres deep at its centre. Although a spectacular
   effect, Cinerama's screen requirements meant that the optimum view was confined
   to centrally placed seats. Moreover, installation was very costly and the three linked
   images were difficult to synchronise properly. CinemaScope utilised an anamorphic
   or Hypergonaar lens, which had been developed by Henri Chrétian in 1929. The
   lens was fitted to a camera and compressed the image onto normal 35mm film
   stock. When unsqueezed by the same lens on the projector the image was 2.66
   times as wide as it was high. This compares with the hitherto normal image size of
   1.33 times as wide as it was high. See J. Belton, *Widescreen Cinema* (Cambridge,
   MA: Harvard University Press, 1982) and the 'Widescreen Museum' online at
   www.widescreenmuseum.com.

6 Cited in T. Wollen, 'The Bigger the Better: From CinemaScope to IMAX', in P.

Hayward and T. Wollen (eds), *Future Visions: New Technologies of the Screen* (London: British Film Institute, 1993), p. 12.

7 Todd-AO was a non-anamorphic lens system that used 70mm film stock, thus requiring larger cameras and projectors. Technically, it was superior to any other contemporary system but was expensive. Only 15 Todd-AO films were made in 16 years. VistaVision was also a non-anamorphic system, which used 35mm film stock that was exposed horizontally rather than vertically.

8 *Today's Cinema*, 80:6713 (10 March 1953), cited in Wollen, *Future Visions*, p. 13.

9 M. Allen, 'From Bwana Devil to Batman Forever: Technology in Contemporary Hollywood Cinema', in S. Neale and M. Smith (eds), *Contemporary Hollywood Cinema* (London: Routledge, 1998).

10 *Ibid.*, p. 112.

11 Eyles, *The Granada Theatres*, p. 155.

12 *Ibid.*, p. 158.

13 J. Ellis, *Visible Fictions: Cinema, Television, Video*, revised edition (London: Routledge, 1992), p. 53.

14 D. Andrew, 'Film and Society: Public Rituals and Private Space', in R. Hark, (ed.), *Exhibition: The Film Reader* (London: Routledge, 2002), p. 167.

15 Monopolies Commission, *Films: A Report on the Supply of Films for Exhibition in Cinemas* (HC 206, 1966).

16 S. Blanchard, 'Cinema-going, Going, Gone?', *Screen*, 24:4–5 (July–October 1983), 109–13.

17 Monopolies Commission, *Films: A Report on the Supply of Films for Exhibition in Cinemas* (HC 206, 1966).

18 *Ibid.*

19 J. Tunstall, *The Media in Britain* (London: Constable, 1983), p. 62.

20 The building was demolished tragically by developers in 1988. See R. Gray, *Cinemas in Britain: 100 Years of Cinema Architecture* (London: Cinema Theatre Association/ British Film Institute, 1996).

21 See Eyles, *Gaumont British Cinemas* and Eyles, *ABC: The First Name in Entertainment*.

22 See Eyles, *Gaumont British Cinemas*.

23 See D. Atwell, *Cathedrals of the Movies: A History of British Cinemas* (London: Architectural Press, 1981), Eyles, *ABC: The First Name in Entertainment*, Eyles, *Gaumont British Cinemas* and Gray, *Cinemas in Britain*.

24 See D. Sharp, *The Picture Palace and other Buildings of the Movies* (London: Hugh Evelyn, 1969).

25 See M. Gould, 'Loughborough Cinemas', www.merciacinema.org.uk/ gallery0305.htm (accessed January 2006).

26 Eyles, *ABC: The First Name in Entertainment*.

27 See Gray, *Cinemas in Britain*.

28 *Screen Digest*, June 1986.

29 See P. Turner, *Cinecenta Cinemas: An Outline History* (St Paul's Cray: Brantwood Books, 2000).

30 C. Hughes-Stanton, 'Four-in-one Cinema', *Cinema*, 5:3 (1969), 26–30, p. 27.

31 Richard Attenborough, in G. Adair and N. Roddick, *A Night at the Pictures: Ten Decades of British Film* (London: Columbus Books, 1985), p. 10.

32 A. Higson, 'The Discourses of British Film Year', *Screen*, 27:1 (January–February 1986), 86–109.

33 Cited in *ibid.*, pp. 89-90.

34 D. Docherty, D. Morrison and M. Tracey, *The Last Picture Show: Britain's Changing Film Audience* (London: British Film Institute, 1987), p. 66.

35 Richard Attenborough, 'British Film Year: An Explanation', *The Hollywood Reporter*, 289:2 (October 1985).

36 Docherty, Morrison and Tracey, *The Last Picture Show*, p. 67.

37 For an analysis of the place of the VCR in the domestic sphere see A. Gray, *Video Playtime: The Gendering of a Leisure Technology* (London: Routledge, 1992).

38 Higson, 'The Discourses of British Film Year', p. 90.

39 J. Howkins, 'British Film Year', *Sight and Sound*, 54:1 (Winter 1984/85), p. 8.

40 *Ibid.*

41 *AIP & Co*, 59 (October 1984), p. 15.

42 Higson, 'The Discourses of British Film Year'.

43 *Ibid.*, p. 89.

44 '35 per cent?', *Sight and Sound*, 55:2 (Spring 1986), p. 96.

45 W. Olins, 'The Best Place to See a Film?', *Sight and Sound*, 54:4 (Autumn 1985), 241–4. In 1979 EMI merged with Thorn Electrical Industries to become Thorn-EMI.

46 *Ibid.*, p. 242.

47 Cited in Eyles, *ABC: The First Name in Entertainment*, pp. 105–6.

48 *Screen Digest* (February 1984), p. 40.

49 *Ibid.*

50 Monopolies Commission, *Films: A Report on the Supply of Films for Exhibition in Cinemas*, Cmnd 8858, 1983.

51 *Sight and Sound*, 52:3 (Summer 1983), p. 152.

52 *Ibid.*, p. 152.

53 Advertising agency Rex Stewart Jeffries cited in *Screen Digest*, February 1984.

54 P. Corrigan, 'Film Entertainment as Ideology and Pleasure: A Preliminary Approach to a History of Audiences', in J. Curran and V. Porter (eds), *British Cinema History* (London: Weidenfeld and Nicolson, 1983), p. 25.

55 Docherty, Morrison and Tracey, *The Last Picture Show*, p. 82.

56 N. Roddick, 'If the United States Spoke Spanish, we would have a Film Industry …', in M. Auty and N. Roddick (eds), *British Cinema Now* (London: British Film Institute, 1985), p. 8.

57 *Film Policy*, Cmnd 9319 (London: HMSO, 1984).

58 For an analysis of film policy during the 1980s see J. Hill, 'Government Policy and the British Film Industry 1979–90', *European Journal of Communication*, 8:2 (1993), 203–4.

59 *Film Policy*, Cmnd 9319, p. 12.

60 See B. Baillieu and J. Goodchild, *The British Film Business* (London: John Wiley &

Sons, 2002).

61 *Stills*, 17 (March 1985), p. 5.

62 See www.terramedia.co.uk/video/JVC_launches_VHS_in_UK.htm (accessed August 2004).

63 BBC Broadcasting Research Department, *Annual Review of BBC Broadcasting Research Findings* 18 (1992), p. 40.

64 A. Crisell, *An Introductory History of British Broadcasting* (London: Routledge, 1997) and BFI, *Film and Television Handbook 1993* (London: British Film Institute, 1992).

65 U.S. Supreme Court, *Sony Corp. v. Universal City Studios, inc.*, 464 U.S. 417 (1984).

66 For an account of the ways in which the Hollywood studios derive revenue from a variety of distribution channels see J. Wasko, *How Hollywood Works* (London: Sage 2003) and T. Miller *et al.*, *Global Hollywood 2* (London: British Film Institute, 2005).

67 Blockbuster now operate some 8,500 stores worldwide – see www.blockbuster.com/corporate/displayAboutBlockbuster.action (accessed July 2005).

68 BFI, *Film and Television Handbook 1993*.

69 Docherty, Morrison and Tracey, *The Last Picture Show*, pp. 64–5.

70 *Screen Digest*, February 1984, p. 28.

71 *Ibid.*, p. 28.

72 Ellis, *Visible Fictions*, p. 176.

73 *Ibid.*

74 D. Gomery, 'Hollywood's Hold on the New Television Technologies', *Screen*, 29:2 (Spring 1988), 82–8, p. 84.

75 *Ibid.*

76 *Ibid.*

77 See G. Nowell-Smith (ed.), *The Oxford History of World Cinema* (Oxford: Oxford University Press, 1996) and his introduction to 'Section 3: The Modern Cinema 1960–95', pp. 463–65.

78 R. Maltby, '"Nobody Knows Everything": Post-classical Historiographies and Consolidated Entertainment', in S. Neale and M. Smith (eds), *Contemporary Hollywood Cinema* (London: Routledge, 1998), p. 28.

79 *Ibid.*

80 Blanchard, 'Cinema-going, Going, Gone?', p. 111.

81 *Ibid.*

82 *Ibid.*, p. 109.

83 *Ibid.*, pp. 110–11.

84 B. Austin, *Immediate Seating: A Look at Movie Audiences* (Belmont, CA: Wadsworth Publishing, 1989).

85 B. Stones, *America Goes to the Movies: 100 Years of Motion Picture Exhibition* (Hollywood: National Association of Theater Owners, 1993), p. 215.

86 Gomery, *Shared Pleasures: A History of Movie Presentation in the United States* (London: British Film Institute, 1992).

87 *Ibid.*, p. 95.

88 *Boxoffice*, 18 September 1972, E-9.

89 P. Turner, *Cineplex Odeon: An Outline History* (St Paul's Cray: Brantwood Books, 1998).

90 For a background to multiplex developments in North America and beyond see C. R. Acland, *Screen Traffic: Movies, Multiplexes and Global Culture* (Durham, NC and London: Duke University Press, 2003).

91 Gomery, *Shared Pleasures.*

92 D. Puttnam, *The Undeclared War: The Struggle for Control of the World's Film Industry* (London: Harper Collins, 1997), p. 228.

93 *Ibid.*

94 Stones, *America Goes to the Movies.*

95 M. Valentine, *The Show Starts on the Sidewalk: An Architectural History of the Movie Theatre, Starring S. Charles Lee* (New Haven, CT and London: Yale University Press, 1994), p. 182.

96 *Ibid.*, p. 137.

97 W. Paul, 'The K-mart Audience at the Mall Movies', in I. R. Hark (ed.), *Exhibition: The Film Reader*, originally published in *Film History*, 6 (1994), 487–501, p. 82.

98 P. Waldman, 'Silver Screens Lose Some of Their Luster', *Wall Street Journal*, 9 February 1989, cited in Valentine, *The Show Starts on the Sidewalk*, p. 181.

99 See Paul, 'The K-mart Audience at the Mall Movies', p. 81.

100 *Ibid.*

101 Cited in Stones, *America Goes to the Movies*, p. 233.

102 J. Brosnan, '2nd Opinion', *Time Out*, 767 (2–8 May 1985).

6

The multiplex revolution: 1985–present

Our cinemas, like so much in this country, are dirty, decaying, uncomfortable places. (John Boorman, Governor, *bfi*, 1984)[1]

Find a motorway, *any* motorway. Check there are at least one million people who, using that motorway, could get to a field within 35 minutes. Find out the ages and how much they earn. Then build a cinema – call it a multiplex – in the middle of the field. (Lloyd Bradley)[2]

Today, you don't simply watch a film, you experience an adventure. (Warner Village Cinemas)[3]

The period from 1985 marks a decisive shift in the fortunes of the cinema with the introduction and rapid entrenchment of the multiplex cinema. The building of these new cinemas, initially on the edges and latterly in the centre of Britain's towns and cities, was the result of changes in economic, political and cultural policies precipitated by both the apparent triumph of laissez-faire capitalism and the hegemony of the Hollywood film. Moreover, the design of the multiplex and its place within a shifting consumer landscape saw the development of larger and grander buildings often located close to other complementary sites of leisure. As multiplexes proliferated then so audiences increased year-on-year, with the obvious conclusion that they have reversed the previous and seemingly unstoppable decline.

The eve of the multiplex

Since 1985, when Britain's first multiplex cinema called The Point opened in Milton Keynes, we have witnessed a new kind of cinema; new in the sense of being conceived and built recently, and new in that it represents a radical divergence from the ways cinema-going has been seen within the social and cultural sphere. The multiplex is a new generation of picture palace, which has changed the cinema landscape perhaps for ever. Conceived from the outset as a multi-screen cinema, the multiplex has ushered in a cinema-going revival prompting the *bfi*'s Adrian Wootton to claim that: '[w]ithout the capital investment of the multiplexes, the market wouldn't exist as it does today. You can't say that it's been anything but good in sustaining cinema as a mass form'.[4]

By the early 1980s Britain was viewed as a market in which the domestic exhibition sector was in terminal decline, while at the same time being a market in which films from the USA were both popular and dominant. By 1984, in the face of steadily falling audience numbers many Hollywood distributors were on the verge of pulling out of Britain altogether, relegating the country to 'Third World status in cinema terms, with releases handled through local intermediaries from offices in Paris or Los Angeles'.[5] An integral part of the plan to build multiplexes in Britain was an agreement with distributors, some of them part owners of the new cinemas, that patterns of distribution would have to be radically changed. The poor state of the British cinema industry had meant that releases for many Hollywood films were held back for up to six months, since there was little opportunity for distributors to make a good profit on their investment in prints and advertising. Jack Valenti, president of the Motion Picture Association of America (MPAA), was unambiguous in his warning on the state of exhibition in Britain:

> If filmgoing doesn't pick up in Britain, the big Hollywood companies may pull out of distributing all but their surefire hits there – and sell the rest directly to TV or the cassette market. Already it costs £100,000 on average to publicise and launch a feature film in Britain. Except for a *Ghostbusters* or *Beverly Hills Cop* the British box office simply doesn't offer a good enough chance any longer of even getting that sum back plus a profit. Unless British audiences return in numbers to the cinema, American films in Britain are going to get fewer too.[6]

The period from 1985 has been one of strong growth in new cinema building; however, it took a US company (American Multi Cinema or AMC) to introduce the multiplex concept to Britain. The duopoly enjoyed by Rank and ABC with respect to cinema exhibition in Britain stifled new developments, as the two companies failed to invest substantially in new cinemas. Despite the evidence from the suburban USA where the multiplex had bolstered admissions, Rank, ABC and their smaller counterparts increasingly saw rationalisation as the only solution to falling profits. According to Puttnam, Jack Valenti, head of the MPAA, privately approached Rank and other cinema chains with a proposal that they invest in building new cinemas.[7] Neither Rank nor any other chain was interested, though Rank would later be an enthusiastic multiplex operator, riding the wave created by US capital. Of course,

Valenti had good reasons for wanting to stimulate cinema-going in Britain (and Europe); Hollywood dominated cinema screens and he wished that to continue. One industry executive observed that this dominance would lead to a 'soft revolution' in which cinema-goers would be won over by better concessions (drinks and food), better seating, and better auditoria.[8] The introduction of multiplexes in Britain and other parts of the world by exhibitors closely tied to the major studios has been part of a concerted effort to maintain the hegemony of Hollywood. With the arrival of multiplexes the distributors were persuaded to close up release patterns with the USA. As the number of multiplexes grew this delay decreased further as distributors were offered more than one exhibition chain for their releases.[9]

The environment for new cinema development – the laissez-faire approach

The climate in Britain for speculative foreign investment was highly favourable, with a Conservative government that had recast Britain's relationship with the global economy. On the eve of the first multiplex developments in Britain the economy was gearing up for a consumer boom fuelled by tax cuts and falling interest rates. The Conservative government was concerned to stimulate confidence in Britain on the part of domestic and overseas business. In order to encourage inward investment it was prepared to provide assistance with a slew of financial inducements and a relaxed regulatory culture.[10] More importantly, the Conservative government signalled its intentions almost from the outset. During its first year in office it introduced the Local Government, Planning and Land Act 1980 ('the 1980 Act'). The 1980 Act covered the setting up of Urban Development Corporations and Enterprise Zones, and sought to speed up the planning process.[11] During the 1980s planning authorities were instructed to be less rigid when considering applications for planning consent, in line with the government's free enterprise philosophy. Perhaps the most obvious manifestation of this relaxed regulatory environment was the rapid development of out-of-town shopping complexes around many of Britain's major conurbations. One result of this was that from 1981 to 1988 retail sales increased at an average annual rate of 4.8 per cent compared with only 1 per cent between 1971 and 1980.[12]

The steady increase in car ownership throughout the 1980s (the proportion of households with access to a car rose from 59 per cent in 1981 to 68 per cent in 1991 and then to 73 per cent in 2000)[13] and the move by many people to housing developments on the urban fringe, led to greater demands for out-of-town shopping facilities. Moreover, many retailers and particularly the large chains sought to reduce rents and combat the threat to business from city centre congestion by moving outwards. The most common developments were indoor shopping centres and retail warehouses, often called retail parks.[14] They included restaurants and leisure activities such as swimming pools, bowling alleys, bingo halls and, of course, latterly multiplex cinemas.

The provision of new shopping facilities was a key element in the proposed regeneration of regional economies, in particular older industrial areas that had effectively become de-industrialised. The government proposed that the regeneration of these areas would come as a result of providing new jobs and better living conditions. This would not be achieved solely by direct government investment but would require private capital. Amongst a variety of regeneration schemes pursued to this aim the most significant for the development of multiplex cinemas was the Enterprise Zone. This was, according to Secretary of State for the Environment Michael Heseltine, 'a new approach to encouraging the regeneration and expansion of industry and commerce in our urban areas'.[15] The first eleven Enterprise Zones were instigated in 1981, each with an initial ten-year life. They varied from 120 to 1,100 acres and granted existing businesses and prospective developers financial incentives. These included 100 per cent relief from local taxes for ten years and substantial relief against national taxation, a simplified planning policy, streamlined administration, and a reduction in local and central government 'red tape'. There was also no obligation on the part of developers of Enterprise Zones to take into account local plans.[16] The most famous Enterprise Zone was perhaps London Docklands; others included Swansea Valley, Glasgow Clydebank, Newcastle Gateshead, Salford Docks and Trafford Park, and Dudley in the West Midlands. The first eleven Zones were followed by thirteen more in 1983–84, and included Telford, Rotherham, Middlesbrough and North West Kent.

In line with the Government's policy of promoting enterprise, further initiatives were implemented to stimulate commercial and industrial developments in other areas, for example Urban Development Corporations (UDCs). These were charged with the role of 'enabler', 'smoothing the path' for private sector development by reclaiming blighted sites, improving the infrastructure and arranging business grants and loans.[17] UDCs had substantial powers to bypass formal planning procedures and could compulsorily acquire sites for development. Notable UDCs were those of Tyne and Wear, London Docklands, Heartlands in Birmingham, the old dock area around Trafford Park in Manchester and the Don Valley in Sheffield, now home of the Meadowhall shopping centre. Some of these had Enterprise Zones within their areas of remit, such as Docklands, Trafford Park and Tyne and Wear. The imperative was to stimulate the local economy and provide employment. For many of the developers this inevitably meant development of the service sector in the form of retailing and leisure-based industries. US cinema companies saw the parallel between these developments and those that had been so successful in the USA, especially since many catered for the customer arriving by car.

Although the changes in planning regulations provided for in the 1980 Act helped the development of many shopping and mixed-use developments, planning regulations were still perceived as hindering business. In 1984 Prime Minister Margaret Thatcher explicitly identified 'over-regulation', amongst other things, as an obstacle to job creation.[18] The resulting White Paper entitled *Lifting the Burden* (1985) covered a variety of proposals across all areas of government designed to make wealth creation easier and stimulate entrepreneurialism.[19] The key ideological plank for planning, according to Thornley, was that 'there should be a presumption towards allowing development unless a good reason can be presented to oppose it'.[20] In other words the onus was placed upon planning authorities to show why a proposed development should be *refused* (for example on environmental grounds). As Harvey points out, 'the planning authority had to reflect carefully where a refusal to develop would entail economic loss'.[21] Invariably, proposals for major out-of-town shopping centres were approved, usually on the outskirts of major conurbations near to motorway junctions or major orbital roads (such as Lakeside on the M25 in Essex and the MetroCentre in Gateshead). A number of major shopping developments were also completed in new towns such as Telford and Milton Keynes and in older industrial areas within conurbations such as Merry Hill in Dudley, Meadowhall in Sheffield and Salford Quays in Manchester. These centres were the location for the first round of multiplex developments.

The multiplex comes to Britain

American Multi-Cinema (AMC) began to research the British exhibition market in 1979, five years before they became the preferred partner in the development of The Point. The research involved a market survey of a variety of localities. Milton Keynes was ultimately selected. A 'greenfield' site was offered by the Development Corporation in a new town environment, which was near a shopping centre, had good road access and space for parking. The site had been the subject of an earlier proposal by British leisure company Granada for an entertainment complex in 1979. In this plan the largest space was allocated to a bingo hall, seating 1,200 to 1,400 people, with a three-screen, 600-seat cinema taking up half the area of the bingo hall. With the Development Corporation anxious to get the complex started, Granada sent an executive to the USA to look at a particular building technology that might be used. According to Eyles, it was a 'pity that the same executive didn't examine the success that multiplexes were having in the United States by then'.[22]

AMC's opportunity came with the rejection of Granada's bid and the success of Bass Leisure's, which felt that the central attraction of their leisure complex should be a multiplex cinema. Since no British-based exhibitor had any experience in this area they invited AMC to build the cinema. The complex, which cost £7.7m, had two 156-seat auditoriums, two with 169 seats, four with 220 seats and two with 248 seats. In addition to its ten screens, The Point had a restaurant, bar and social club, and was described by one commentator as a 'one-stop entertainment centre'.[23] Taking into account the 2,026 cinema seats the complex could entertain up to 5,000 people. 'For the first time in my life,' said David Puttnam, 'I'm standing in a UK cinema for the 80s and 90s.'[24]

The Point aimed to draw from a catchment area within a fifteen-mile radius inhabited by approximately 1.5 million people, all within a forty-five-minute car drive. Bass Leisure's Peter Sherlock calculated that three-quarters of this population was under 45 years and affluent.[25] The main selling feature of The Point was 'choice', with two or more showings of individual films per evening, at least one screen showing a U certificate film and the promise of a 'flexible' screening programme, which might include foreign-language films. Another dramatic technological feature was the capacity to show one print on up to four screens. Though sceptical about how this might affect the range of choice, Tim Pulleine cited a *Sunday Times* feature, linked to the announcement of the Milton Keynes development, which gave an example of a family from San Diego who 'arrived at the local AMC complex and duly went their several ways, husband taking children to *Care Bears*, wife and her mother selecting *Amadeus*, and grandpa going by himself to *The Killing Fields*'.[26] As for contemporary observers, the reaction was best summed up by the *bfi*'s Director, Wilf Stevenson, who recalled that 'most of us were convinced they were bonkers … People thought that video had killed the cinema off'.[27]

In 1983 Thorn-EMI, the parent company of the cinema chain ABC instigated a re-structuring programme that saw the company amalgamate all of its production, distribution, exhibition and video operations into what was called Thorn-EMI Screen Entertainment (TESE) (though it retained the ABC brand for its cinemas). In charge was Gary Dartnall, originally from the USA, who took the decision to follow AMC's lead. He instigated a multiplex building programme before The Point had opened for business. The site chosen for Thorn-EMI's first multiplex was Salford Quays in Manchester. The estimated cost of the cinema was £3.5m and it consisted of eight screens. For the Thorn-EMI Board the location was the subject of some derision, being as it was a redeveloped former industrial area near the Manchester

Ship Canal, and not a traditional city centre site.[28]

In March 1985 Dartnall outlined his multiplex plans which then consisted of six cinemas, each with six screens, on sites leased in new out-of-town shopping centres in partnership with a US chain. Following the experience of AMC's multiplex in Milton Keynes, and its subsequent developments (such as the MetroCentre Gateshead, Telford and Merry Hill Dudley), TESE were looking for locations adjoining shopping or leisure centres on the edge of cities and towns, with one executive finally admitting that converting existing cinemas was outmoded.[29] More importantly they were looking at areas that had been designated as Enterprise Zones. Dartnall asked the board of Thorn-EMI for £50m to develop multiplexes. At the same time, the company was looking finally to divest itself of the Screen Entertainment division, while retaining its interests in Thames Television and cable television.[30]

However, in 1985, after the collapse of a management buyout proposed by Dartnall, Australia's Alan Bond purchased the entire company. He sold it shortly afterwards for a large profit to the Cannon Group who already owned a considerable number of cinemas. This was a deal in which the Monopolies Commission did not intervene, though they might legitimately have done so. Upon completion of the purchase in 1986 Cannon became the largest cinema exhibitor in Britain, with 201 cinemas and 485 screens. By the time the multiplex at Salford Quays opened in December 1986 it was a Cannon. The ABC brand was consigned to history.[31]

At this point another major exhibitor based in the USA, Cinema International Corporation (CIC) announced plans to develop sites in Britain. Its first multiplex, the Wycombe 6, opened in High Wycombe in 1987. Like AMC, CIC undertook localised research, including surveys of the local population, before building the Wycombe 6. The cinema was located just off the M40 motorway and had a large population of approximately 700,000 within easy travelling distance. Following the experience of AMC at The Point, CIC did not provide its own restaurants. Instead it included space either side of the foyer, which was rented to a national pizza restaurant chain and a company which opened a pub. This would be a model for all subsequent multiplexes that chose to incorporate these sorts of attractions. Adjacent to the multiplex was a large sports centre, a supermarket and a large department store, all additional attractions for visitors. Manager Chris Green felt that the Wycombe 6 was quite unlike any other cinema at that time, '[i]n appearance, it is more like a modern shopping complex than a cinema'.[32] As in the USA, the pattern of multiplex development in Britain was bound up with the shopping centre, in particular the out-of-town shopping centre. By the end of The Point's first year of operation, AMC was well advanced in its plans to build a further six multiplexes within eighteen months, all of which were to be sited in new out-of-town shopping and leisure developments close to major population centres.

One of the observations of the US-based cinema companies was that the nature of the planning process for those new sites which lay outside UDCs and Enterprise Zones was often protracted. In the early 1980s many local authorities were resistant to the development of shopping complexes on sites away from the city centres, as it was the city centres that they were seeking to rejuvenate. Robert Webster, Head of Development at CIC, observed that: '[i]t does take much longer to get projects into action here than in countries such as Australia ... The multiplex concept is already established in Australia and here the working in of cinemas with shopping developments is much slower.'[33] Further, the developers of these new shopping centres felt that there was an economic disadvantage to a cinema on the site. Cinemas were seen as less profitable per square foot than shops and therefore less able to pay high rents.[34] However, the prospect of a cinema was often seen as more attractive to local councils who viewed them as an important additional attraction to local leisure amenities.

The early lesson of Salford Quays and High Wycombe was that a trade-off between developer and cinema operator involving a lower rent for the cinema might secure the necessary planning permission. For their part, developers and local authorities also began to see the potential benefits of having a multiplex cinema in a development. It raised the profile of the development and indeed the area, in turn attracting other investors. For example, the ten-screen multiplex in Telford Town Centre was the eleventh to be built in Britain and was opened in November 1988. Its conception is interesting since the desire for a cinema originated with the new town's Development Corporation. The traditional notion of a 'town centre' results from what a COMEDIA report called 'different historical and cultural trajectories', but Telford's was planned and developed in a relatively short period.[35] Only in the mid-1970s, it was a greenfield site. It has subsequently expanded from a simple indoor shopping centre to a conurbation encompassing office and leisure developments.

The early multiplex developers were keen to minimise potential risks by not owning the building in which the multiplex was housed. AMC, for instance, sold their buildings to outside developers and then leased them back. This meant that capital was not tied up in the building and that if the venture failed, the company would not be responsible for disposing of the property: the building of The Point was a gamble. Nevertheless, after the first year of operation attendances had exceeded one million and the cinema was generating over 20,000 admissions a week. It seemed that the great experiment was set to work. The Head of the Cinematograph

Exhibitors Association (CEA), John Wilkinson, was in no doubt about the impact of the new multiplex operators on attendances. Acknowledging that the indigenous cinema owners had begun to recognise that the problems lay with them and not with audiences he observed that: 'The Point brought together a lot of those ideas in one place, so they were easy to spot and pick up by people who weren't trying them. The multiplexes did stimulate the market, because they made all other exhibitors realize they had to improve.'[36] Notwithstanding the optimism of the CEA, the existing cinema owners continued to view multiplexes as a threat to their business.

During the first few years of operation AMC and CIC had problems in obtaining top Hollywood films due to the system of 'barring' operated by Rank and Thorn-EMI (see Chapter 5). This prevented other cinemas within a fixed distance of their cinemas from getting first-run film prints. Both AMC and CIC lobbied the Office of Fair Trading, the Monopolies and Mergers Commission and the European Commission against this system. However, it was their developing financial muscle in the exhibition market that ultimately forced the break-up of the arrangement, as distributors realised that multiplexes might offer a real regeneration of the market. AMC's Charles Wesoky felt that legislation against Rank/Thorn-EMI's practices was both unnecessary and divisive, stating that he 'took the view that we were competing not against cinema operators, but against that British social institution, the pub … so our ticket price was set to match a couple of pints of beer'.[37]

With Cannon (Thorn-EMI's successor) pledging to build up to ten multiplexes but translating none of these into firm planning proposals, and Rank opening only one new multiplex in 1987, it was left to exhibitors from the USA and Canada to crank up the multiplex building boom that took place in the first five years after The Point opened. In 1988 Boston-based National Amusements opened their first Showcase in Nottingham. Warner Bros. followed with a ten-screen multiplex in Bury in 1989. Canadian multiplex pioneers Cineplex Odeon entered the British market via their Gallery and Maybox chains in 1988.[38] Investment was substantial and, for some companies at least, unsustainable. AMC announced that they were to pull out of the UK market in December 1988. They sold their eight multiplexes to a partnership of CIC and United Artists Communications, which was renamed United Cinemas International (UCI). At around the same time, amidst rumours of financial crisis, Cineplex Odeon sold its interests to Cannon. These ownership changes did not put a brake on developments in any way. Exhibitors continued to identify sites and build new cinemas (see Table 6.1).

Table 6.1 Growth in UK multiplex sites and share of cinema screens 1985–2004

Year	Multiplex sites	Multiplex screens	Non-multiplex screens	Total screens
1985	1	10	1,345	1,355
1986	2	18	1,315	1,333
1987	5	45	1,290	1,335
1988	14	142	1,320	1,462
1989	29	288	1,310	1,598
1990	42	390	1,325	1,715
1991	59	518	1,285	1,803
1992	65	562	1,280	1,842
1993	70	624	1,280	1,904
1994	77	689	1,275	1,964
1995	82	725	1,280	2,005
1996	95	864	1,358	2,222
1997	114	1,089	1,260	2,349
1998	139	1,357	1,224	2,581
1999	166	1,617	1,141	2,758
2000	190	1,875	1,079	2,954
2001	224	2,115	1,049	3,164
2002	222	2,299	959	3,258
2003	234	2,362	956	3,318
2004	238	2,426	916	3,342

Note: a multiplex is defined as a purpose-built cinema of five screens or more.

Sources: Dodona, *Cinemagoing 9* (Leicester: Dodona Research, 2001); UK Film Council, *Statistical Yearbook/Annual Review 2004/05* (London: UK Film Council, 2005); and E. Dyja (ed.), *BFI Film and Television Handbook 2003* (London: British Film Institute, 2002).

From out-of-town to the town centre

All of the multiplex construction that was undertaken in the initial building phase from 1985 to 1990 took place in areas carefully chosen using a range of criteria. First was the multiplex's accessibility to the surrounding population. In the USA multiplex cinemas were built where a surrounding population of 200–300,000 people lived within twenty to twenty-five minutes travelling distance by car. In Britain this figure was revised to 500–600,000 people within a forty-five minute drive, based on an expectation that British people went to the cinema less frequently than those in the USA. Historically, the cinema has been seen as an integral part of the urban landscape and the established geography of the city or town. When the new town of Milton Keynes was selected for The Point, to be followed by greenfield, suburban and new town sites around the country, the mould was cast for the development of the new cinema experience. It would be one orientated towards the cinema-goer who was prepared to travel. This appeal to the mobile traveller was wholly in keeping with contemporary developments in shopping and leisure, and the main appeal was made to the motorist. Many of Showcase's early multiplexes in Britain were sited adjacent to major motorways and were intentionally highly visible from them.[39] This mobile population was one that the multiplex was able to court not only because the sites were convenient, near motorways, with free car parks, but also because many city cinemas had become an unattractive prospect precisely because they could not offer these elements. In 2002 CAVIAR 20 indicated that 74 per cent of people who visited the cinema travelled there by car.[40]

The developments around Britain's cities reflected a phenomenon which commentators such as Soja had observed; that the urban centre was increasingly less of a focus for leisure and entertainment.[41] The plethora of out-of-town multiplex developments that sprang up in Britain throughout the 1980s and 1990s attests to this. Hubbard goes on to raise the issue of why people might prefer these locations, especially given the difficulties of getting to many of them without transport.[42] He concludes that avoiding going to a city centre cinema is part of a 'risk avoidance strategy' based upon a climate of fear that pervades many cities at night.[43] Out-of-town complexes encompassing a range of other attractions, including a multiplex, became more popular because of their increasingly controlled and policed environments. According to Mintel in 2003 there were 200 'multi-leisure parks' (MLPs) in Britain, which are defined as 'a major property development on a single site which is geared principally towards leisure activities' but which is almost always anchored by a multiplex cinema.[44] Though sites adopted a variety of design and spatial approaches a key example was the so-called 'leisure box', such as the LeisureWorld chain, opened by Rank. There a multiplex cinema was located next to an ice rink, tenpin bowling alley and assorted bars and restaurants, all in a 'shed' of around 200,000 sq feet. According to Stephen Yarnold of property consultants Harvey Spack Field, 'people find town centres too threatening in the evenings, and they will travel to find everything under one roof'.[45] Under that one roof or within these retail and leisure parks a relatively small number of retailers and leisure providers tend to populate them. In an article on Warner Bros.' multiplex in Bury, Greater Manchester, Robert Butler observed that: 'On your left there's the Asda superstore, on your right the 32-lane Megabowl. Next to the Megabowl is the Mexican restaurant, Chiquitos, next to Chiquitos is Deep Pan Pizza. Across the 800-space car park rises 55,000 square feet of cinema space.'[46]

In 2000 two trends converged, on the site of a former gas works in Birmingham. The first was a developing trend for ever larger multiplexes with 14–20 screens or more, the second was the development of the 'leisure box' concept. At the forefront of the drive for larger multiplexes was Warner Village, which opened a thirty-screen cinema in Birmingham's Star City in July 2000.[47] It seated 6,500 people and was then Europe's largest cinema. It adjoined a 50,000 sq ft shopping, leisure and restaurant complex in the Heartlands area of the city. Three to four million people lived within a forty-five-minute drive and could take advantage of the 2,750 free parking spaces provided. Described by Carl Wilkinson in the *Observer* newspaper as 'an outpost of America just off Spaghetti Junction',[48] Star City marked another development in cinema design copied from the USA. The complex's US architect Jon Jerde was noted for his flamboyant shopping malls. In Star City the building's aesthetic was described by the architect as a 'new generation of urban entertainment' drawing its inspiration from 'Birmingham's rich tradition as the birthplace of the industrial revolution'.[49]

The development at Star City was not only significant because it signalled the new generation of 'megaplexes'[50] but also because of its location near to Birmingham's city centre. As the 1990s came to a close, many multiplex operators had begun once again to look at the urban centre as a potential site for the cinema. This was a response in large part to changes in the political mood around planning, particularly from 1993 to 1997 under Prime Minister John Major's Conservative government. In a series of Planning Policy Guidance notes (PPGs), which local planning authorities must take into account in preparing their development plans, a new emphasis began to be placed upon regenerating urban centres. In June 1996 *PPG6 Town Centres and Retail Developments* sought to roll back the trend for out-of-town developments, and while not outlawing them completely it sought to encourage edge-of-centre or town centre developments ('town centre' was used generally to cover city, town and suburban district centres). Moreover, *PPG6* was the first to make special mention of multi-screen cinemas.[51] In particular revised PPG6 outlined the Government's objectives thus:

- to sustain and enhance the vitality and viability of town centres;
- to focus development, especially retail development, in locations where the proximity of businesses facilitates competition from which all consumers are able to benefit and maximises the opportunity to use means of transport other than the car;
- to maintain an efficient, competitive and innovative retail sector; and
- to ensure the availability of a wide range of shops, employment, services and facilities to which people have easy access by a choice of means of transport.[52]

Star City was an archetypal 'edge-of-centre' development, though as with many multiplex developments the exhibitors were taking advantage of the fact that the site lay within a part of the city with a designated Economic Development Strategy and under the management of an Urban Development Corporation (UDC). Like the UDCs and Enterprise Zones in the early 1980s, the area of Birmingham in which the Star City complex was built benefited from a mix of public and private investment and relaxed planning regulations. The main difference between developments like Star City and many of those in the 1980s is that the former was built on reclaimed industrial land, known as a 'brownfield' site. Though the site was technically in the inner city it was its proximity to the M6 motorway that was the attraction to the developers.

At the time of its inception there were debates about access to Star City for those without a car, since the prospects of improved public transport links looked, according to the *Birmingham Post*,[53] 'distinctly less promising' particularly since the plans for the Midland Metro Line 2 tram had stalled due to lack of funding. Like many cities, Birmingham was wrestling with demands to regenerate the middle of the city and the desire for more out-of-town and peripheral development. The Council for the Protection of Rural England singled out the Star City site in its booklet entitled *Planning More to Travel Less*, as having poor public transport.[54] Commenting on the pattern for out-of-town activities Terry Grimley observed that the 'West Midlands has a high proportion of non-city centre cinema seats per head of population, and the reason is not hard to find given the motorway box around Birmingham and the strong regional culture of driving everywhere.'[55]

There were some precedents for city centre developments. In 1990 UCI opened an eight-screen cinema in Whiteleys shopping complex, which occupied a former department store in London's Bayswater. This followed a more recent trend in the USA for cinemas to be located in prestigious downtown shopping complexes, such as Chicago's Water Tower complex.[56] Since 2000, there have been many town-centre based multiplex developments and like the 'leisure boxes' on the periphery of the city the multiplex cinema is almost exclusively the anchor tenant to a mixed retail and leisure scheme. The notion of anchorage is important for developers since the multiplex has been successful in encouraging the public into what are termed the 'dead areas' of a shopping and leisure complex, such as upper levels or the dead ends of malls.[57] The multiplex's importance to developers is that they help guarantee visitor numbers (what the industry calls 'footfall') and offset the increased construction and development costs, which are approximately 20 per cent higher than comparable out-of-town sites.[58] The attractions of a mixed use complex extend beyond the possible cost savings to encompass many of the perceived advantages of the out-of-town site, including adjacent car parking, shelter from the elements, proximity of other leisure attractions and personal safety.

AMC, which has re-entered the British multiplex cinema market, has opened two new multiplexes in mixed use developments at Birmingham's Broadway Plaza (a converted children's hospital and adjoining site) and in Manchester's Great Northern development (a converted railway goods warehouse). Another new entrant to the multiplex market, Ster Century have also focused on town centre sites, including The Light in Leeds which incorporates a thirteen-screen cinema and a range of restaurants, bars and shops, as well as a health club. These cinema developments reflect a national trend as the number of screens in city centres or edge-of-centre cinemas has increased by over 20 per cent between 2001 and 2004.[59] According to a report by the London Assembly only two cinemas have been built in out-of-town locations around London since 1998, while during the same period, twelve cinemas have been built in the city centre.[60] Developments in the capital are significant since London's cinemas generate around 30 per cent of total box-office revenue.[61] The changes in planning regulations that have stimulated the growth of cinemas and other leisure sites in urban centres have also seen an increase in the number of residential developments in the city centre and an attempt to encourage, through planning and diversification of land use, an 'urban renaissance'.[62] Implicit within this strategy is a desire to encourage the provision of new housing in the central cores of many of Britain's cities, in line with government policy, as articulated in an Urban White Paper, published in 2002.[63] In Birmingham, according to the city council, the proposal was to build approximately 12,000 apartments and houses in the city centre by the end of 2004, an increase of 50 per cent over the previous ten years.[64]

The design of the multiplex

At a multiplex opening in 1989 two distributors commented, off the record, that they could have well been at an opening for a 'carpet warehouse' rather than a cinema. 'This is *cinema*', they commented. 'This is supposed to be connected in some way to Hollywood, it is supposed to be magic, glamorous ... but you'd never know it.'[65] These comments were rather astute since the design of many early multiplexes was dictated by the possibility of conversion to another use in the event of poor attendance. Essentially metal sheds inexpensively built on level sites; they could easily be converted into a supermarket or DIY warehouse. This flexibility was important in attracting investors, who might otherwise have seen cinemas as a risky venture, particularly given the decline in attendance during the 1960s and 1970s.[66]

If anything signalled a break with previous conceptions of cinemas as 'Picture Palaces' it was this ruthless economising.

Multiplexes are fundamentally similar: they conform to certain styles of design and function in order to deliver as many people as possible to the film.[67] This is particularly true of multiplexes within the same chains (VUE or UCI for example) where the notion of corporate identity is important. Primacy is given to the foyer as the customer's first point of contact, the point at which the identity and ethos of the cinema is firmly established. This houses the box office and the concession counter, and serves as a giant advertising and promotional zone for present and forthcoming films. Evidence suggests that over 70 per cent of visitors to the multiplex spend up to 15 minutes in the foyer.[68] Many multiplexes site video monitors here in order to show film previews though few provide seating for those waiting to enter the auditoria. Function is the prime design imperative; and this is only superficially glossed over with coloured brick, tiles, glass and chrome and other post-modernist adornments which are used to position the multiplex as a contemporary phenomenon.

The necessity of function dictated that The Point's radical pyramid design (described as a 'ziggurat' – 'the Mesopotamian equivalent of the Egyptian pyramid')[69] for instance, was rarely repeated. Nevertheless, multiplexes have sought to present the cinema in a decisively new form in which spacious and bright interiors have replaced the sombre tone of many traditional cinemas. In a letter to the CTA, Fred Windsor begged to disagree, observing that the 'Super Cinemas' of the past were far from sombre in their interiors. While multiplexes were 'cheap and (sometimes) cheerful', he argued, 'they look pretty poor compared with the 1930s Granadas, Gaumonts etc.'[70] Gray was of the view that the design of multiplexes took its cue from 'the interiors of a well-known chain of hamburger restaurants' but that any attempt to re-present the heyday of cinema building would be inappropriate with any kind of 'fake historicism' appearing 'tawdry'.[71]

Given the parlous state of many cinemas in the 1970s and 1980s, it is no surprise that multiplexes sought to mark themselves out as contemporary and futuristic spaces. The only connection between cinemas of old and multiplexes was the feature film, which retained its primacy as a visual and narrative form. No associations needed to be made with the past. These were only desirable when seeking to tap the cinema's previous place as an important institution in the centre of the locality. Indeed, the multiplex is closer to the shopping mall or leisure centre in its design and execution and this has helped to associate it with wider leisure patterns and the changes in demographics. Equally significant is the multiplex's close association with new technologies in projection and sound, and its flexibility with regards to auditoria and film programming. Once again function and commercial efficiency are paramount in the multiplex, as this new technology allows one film to be shown in more than one auditorium in times of high demand.

All this has left traditional cinemas with obvious disadvantages quite apart from those associated with the process of dividing up the building. The paradox of the multiplex development is that it is precisely its multi-screen layout that has been its major selling point, whereas for the 1970s cinema, desperate to boost attendance via greater film choice this was seen as a distinct drawback. Multiplexes have succeeded because they were conceived this way and therefore designed to overcome the fatal combination of lack of room, small screens and bad lines of sight for audiences.

There is one element that is crucial in this whole development and that is the need to make people come to your cinema. All of what we have examined thus far is important, indeed it is perhaps unwise to single out a particular aspect of the multiplex as instrumental in getting people to come back to the cinema, however, multiplexes have had to adopt marketing strategies hitherto unseen in the domestic cinema industry. Multiplexes have attempted to re-articulate the cinema as but one part, albeit the central part, of a total leisure package set around the notion of a 'whole night out' or even a 'whole day out'. The cinema has become not only the best place to see a film but the best place to eat and drink, and even dance, bowl and go to the gym; all of which you can do after doing the weekly shopping nearby. David Fraser, of design company FITCH, advised multiplex operators to increase the amount of 'experience' their customers got from going to the cinema, adding that 'instead of a product-based decision (going to a particular film) the consumer must be invited to make a lifestyle decision (going for an evening out)'.[72]

The multiplex cinema audience

Two distinct trends in the cinema have been manifest since 1984: a) the number of new multiplexes opened has increased annually (see Table 6.1), and b) cinema attendances have increased annually (see Table 6.2). In the period from 1984 to 2004 there was a small net decrease in the number of cinema sites (680 to 646) but a rather more substantial increase in the number of screens (1,355 to 3,342).[73] Although multiplexes account for approximately one third of cinema sites they now account for a majority of screens – 2,426 compared with 916 in other cinemas in 2004.[74]

The effect of multiplex developments on existing cinemas is difficult to gauge and varies with local circumstances. In 1991 UCI estimated that their cinemas had

Table 6.2 Total annual cinema admissions 1984–2005

Calendar year	Admissions (millions)	Calendar year	Admissions (millions)
1984	54.00	1995	114.56
1985	72.00	1996	123.80
1986	75.50	1997	139.30
1987	78.50	1998	135.50
1988	84.00	1999	139.75
1989	94.50	2000	142.50
1990	97.37	2001	155.91
1991	100.29	2002	176.91
1992	103.64	2003	167.30
1993	114.36	2004	171.30
1994	123.53	2005	165.70

Sources: E. Dyja (ed.), *BFI Film and Television Handbook 2004* (London: British Film Institute, 2003); UK Film Council, *Statistical Yearbook 2003*, (London: UK Film Council, 2004); and UK Film Council, *Research and Statistics Bulletin*, 3:2 (March 2006).

taken 10–35 per cent of business away from other cinema operators. Rank insisted that the figure was closer to 50 per cent in the case of many of their Odeon cinemas.[75] In the ten years after the first multiplex opened in 1985, approximately seventy non-multiplex cinemas closed, which meant that for every multiplex opened at least one non-multiplex cinema closed (see Table 6.1). Figures produced by Dodona Research suggested that between 1998 and 2002, as many as 212 cinemas incorporating 504 screens closed, including 62 multiplex screens.[76] In some areas it was competition from multiplexes that resulted in the closure of central sites, and in others companies who had constructed multiplexes nearby closed their old town centre sites. Dodona Research were unambiguous in their assessment of cinema closures, stating that 'cinema closures generally represent a contribution to the process of moving cinemas from where they are not wanted to where they are, most often to somewhere with parking'.[77] It is indisputable that multiplex construction has reversed the overall trend of decline in the cinema infrastructure, for although rates for cinema closures are approximately equal to those of multiplex openings, each new multiplex sees an increase in the total number of screens. The question is whether new custom has been created or whether multiplexes have merely appropriated cinema-goers from traditional and established sites. In 1991 UCI's Managing Director estimated that around 'seventy-five per cent of total admissions to each new cinema was new business'.[78] By 1998 the message from the industry was the same, with Sally Beckett, Director of Publicity at Warner Village, arguing that 'multiplexes don't take audiences away from existing cinemas. They build new audiences instead.'[79]

The general trend therefore is one of increased attendance, but do multiplexes attract a different kind of audience from ordinary cinemas? In 2004 the cinema's core audience was the 39 per cent of 7–14 year olds and 53 per cent of 15–24 year olds who went to the cinema once a month or more.[80] They were followed by the 34 per cent of 25–34 year olds who went to the cinema once a month or more.[81] The significance of these figures is brought into focus if we consider that only 16 per cent of over-35s went to the cinema once a month or more, though this figure increased during the preceding ten years. The core audience for the cinema, namely young people, is the same as that of earlier periods of cinema-going and is particularly evident when one considers the audience for the top twenty films in terms of box-office revenue. To a large extent this reflects Hollywood's predilection for films aimed at a younger audience, and the emphasis on 'blockbusters' (discussed in Chapter 7), which are intimately related to the development and continued success of multiplex.[82]

The initial impact of the multiplex on cinema-going numbers and frequency of visits was dramatic. The 1993 CAVIAR 10 cinema survey concluded that the frequency of visits to multiplexes showed marked changes.[83] In terms of annual trends, the report found that the percentage of people who 'ever go to the cinema' had risen from 38 per cent in 1984 to 62 per cent in 1992. All age groups showed a rise over this period except the 7–14 year olds, with half of frequent visitors (defined as attending two or more times a month) visiting a multiplex cinema.[84] A reason for this was clearly that multiplexes offered more opportunities to visit the cinema by programming eight to twenty films at any one time. Moreover the attraction of the multiplex to car owners meant that the number of 25–34 year-olds visiting the cinema increased and has continued to rise. In the intervening ten-year period the number of people who ever go to the cinema has risen to 82 per cent.[85]

In 1991, the *bfi* reported that multiplexes were successfully appealing to over-35s (who made up 27 per cent of the multiplex audience as opposed to 19 per cent at ordinary cinemas).[86] By 2002 the number of over-35s attending the cinema had shown the most significant growth, with a five-fold increase since 1991. Many multiplex owners recognise that the over–35 age group is a significant growth sector. Given that the multiplex is twenty years old in 2005, this group would have been cinema's most enthusiastic attendees in the pre-multiplex era. Moreover, the numbers and popularity of many high-profile children's films suggests that many over-35s are taking children to the cinema. It seems clear that, at least from 2004, filmmakers and distributors have been able to tailor their output to appeal to this group.[87]

In 2002, a new cinema promotions agency, Mellow Marketing, was commissioned to help distributors to market cinema to over-40s. They have promoted films such as *Nicholas Nickleby* (2002), *Evelyn* (2002) and *I Capture the Castle* (2003), in some cases offering preview tickets through *Saga Magazine*, *Reader's Digest*, the radio station Classic FM and Channel 4's *Richard & Judy*.[88] According to Mellow Marketing, 'The over-40's are an important cinema-going audience. They are a discerning, educated audience with a high disposable income and a high propensity to spend on a range of branded goods and services.'[89]

At the time Britain's first multiplex was being planned by AMC in 1984, the average Briton was going to the cinema once a year, while in the USA that year the comparable figure was four times. As multiplexes were being built in Britain the industry was looking to increase yearly admissions to the level in the USA. In 1996 the number reached two, a direct result of the new multiplex concept. By 2003, Britons went to the cinema 2.8 times a year on average, while in the USA the figure had risen to five times a year.

The impact of the multiplex on cinema-going

In statistical terms the cinema audience has more than tripled in the period since 1984 and cinema building is taking place on a scale unprecedented since the 1930s. Multiplexes have radically altered our perceptions and experiences of the cinema. From the 1960s cinemas came to be seen as unattractive and moribund places which people were gradually less inspired to visit, notwithstanding the periodic blockbuster which has lured even the diehard non-cinema-goer back for a temporary flirtation. However, since the cinema-going nadir in the mid-1980s there has been a revival, prompting the question: 'Why has cinema-going become more popular and to what extent has the multiplex been instrumental in this trend?'

First, one qualification should be made. Even the 2005 figure of 165.7 million admissions a year is a small figure (equivalent to the total for 1971). Despite this, cinema-going is becoming more popular and the influence of the multiplex cinema cannot be denied. The attraction of the multiplex is based upon the reality that compared to many existing cinema; they offer greater comfort, convenience, facilities, flexibility and film choice. The accepted wisdom is that the room for cinema expansion is there and that it is the multiplex that will fill it.

It is difficult to ascertain whether the rise in admissions has benefited independent cinemas (overwhelmingly found in town and city centre sites) and non-multiplexes. This is due to the propensity to measure screens rather than sites. Expressed as a market share, the proportion of the cinema audience accounted for by independents is contracting year-on-year, so that by 2002 only 19 per cent of screens were accounted for by independent cinemas.[90] Their share of the overall audience fell correspondingly (though the over-35s attend independent cinemas in proportionately greater numbers according to research by Mintel).[91] A further reason for the decline in numbers attending independent cinemas is that multiplexes have been increasing the number of specialist films shown. This in turn has reflected a wider number of such films picked up by major distributors for a discussion of distribution (see Chapter 7).[92]

In 1996 the National Campaign for Local Cinemas was formed in response to what it identified as at least one hundred cinema closures in the last twenty years. Although not 'overtly anti-multiplex', the group was opposed to out-of-town developments, which they saw as deleterious to town centres.[93] Les Bull was unambiguous in his reading of the multiplex boom, arguing that 'there seems nothing the older cinemas can do to attract the audiences once a multiplex opens in the same area'.[94] Bull was offering an anecdotal view of the relationship between the multiplex and the traditional cinema, which reflected a popular idea that given the choice, cinema-goers would flock automatically to the multiplex. In many ways the statistics for the multiplex's share of the audience support this view, although in 2002 there were still over 400 traditional cinemas in Britain, many of which were thriving.[95]

There are a number of small chains operating successfully, often filling gaps in existing multiplex provision, for example Apollo, Reeltime and City Screen.[96] All are interesting case studies and offer a sense of a more diversified cinema landscape than might immediately be apparent from the broader statistical picture. City Screen's Picturehouse chain began in 1989 and now operates eighteen sites across Britain. It shows both mainstream and arthouse films, concentrating on town centre sites and encouraging customer loyalty with membership and mailing schemes. The company has also been imaginative in terms of funding, since their cinemas in Stratford East (in London) and Stratford-upon-Avon both drew on contributory grant aid from the Arts Council of England (ACE). City Screen sees its audience as 'upmarket' and not necessarily that of the multiplex.[97] Indeed the company website states that City Screen 'prides itself on an offer which is the antithesis of the multiplex'.[98] Nevertheless, as the only cinema in the surrounding area one is often likely to find Hollywood films showing on both screens at the Picture House in Stratford-upon-Avon.

In many cases the reality is that traditional cinemas have little choice but to imitate the multiplex in their attempts to survive. There seems little doubt that the hegemony of the multiplex in the exhibition of films is now virtually complete. Multiplexes take over three-quarters of the total UK box-office and account for three-quarters of admissions. There you have it: the domination of the multiplex is surely indisputable. Those non-multiplex cinemas that continue to attract audiences do so overwhelmingly because they either have no multiplex competitor nearby (unlikely in the main population areas of Britain) or they have had to offer a comparable service in terms of comfort, concessions and picture and sound quality. For many this has meant refurbishment. For example, Northern Morris Associated Cinemas, which operates five cinemas in the north of England, have refurbished a range of traditional cinemas including the recently rescued former ABC cinema in Lancaster.

In the USA multiplexes, or increasingly megaplexes,[99] have sought to widen their appeal to audiences via a relentless drive for innovation and new ways of marketing cinema-going.[100] The most dramatic, is the development of what are variously called New Entertainment Concepts, which are often part of an increasing trend towards joint ventures with other media-based and electronics companies. They involve the development of new film formats such as IMAX and 3D IMAX, and cinema-sites that offer associated video games and virtual reality technology.

Many companies, including Sony Cinemas and Cineplex Odeon, have invested heavily in IMAX – a film format 10 times larger than a 35mm frame which requires gigantic screens of around 20 metres high and 26 metres wide, encompassing the entire range of vision.[101] Britain has also seen an increase in the number of IMAX cinemas. Unlike the USA however, the IMAX has not commonly been integrated into complexes shared with multiplex cinemas. The National Museum of Photography, Film & Television in Bradford incorporated an IMAX cinema when it opened in 1983, but the burgeoning number of sites is a recent phenomenon. In 1999 the British Film Institute (*bfi*)[102] opened a 477-seat IMAX cinema (with the help of National Lottery funding) at the Bull Ring near London's Waterloo Bridge. The *bfi* believed that IMAX would be 'a popular cultural experience' and 'a unique new attraction'.[103] The development of some nine IMAX cinemas across Britain followed, in cities and towns including Glasgow, Bristol, Manchester, Birmingham and Bournemouth.

Central to the appeal of IMAX is the notion of spectacle, in which audiences are invited to thrill at the scale and clarity of image and sound. The lack of any Hollywood films or other feature films made in the IMAX format has meant that for the most part the films have been documentaries and other short films. In 2004 the *Independent* reported that the IMAX cinema was struggling to attract audiences across Britain and cited Birmingham's IMAX cinema, which 'went out of business after losing £600,000 in a year and playing to audiences as small as four'.[103] In the same article, the IMAX Corporation admitted to being disappointed with the format's performance in the UK, especially since the evidence of other countries, particularly the USA, was that it had a viable future. A spokesperson suggested that location was an issue in Britain, with many complexes 'not ideally placed in the city', though the cinemas' high cost of admission seemed more likely to be the issue.[105] One irony is that many IMAX cinemas have been able to show 70mm prints of older films, such as *2001: A Space Odyssey* (1968) to audiences now unable to find screens large enough in even the biggest multiplexes.

The future of the multiplex

From 1998 to 2001 multiplex building enjoyed a boom, with over 100 sites opened and approximately 1,000 screens added (see Table 6.1). Since this peak in 2001, there is evidence that multiplex building and operation is beginning to decline. This may be partly due to the broader economic cycle; especially given the complex funding arrangements for multiplexes in Britain. Construction mirrors the boom and bust pattern of the British and global economy, with periodic upturns and downturns.[106] Many industry analysts speculate on the extent to which Britain may be 'over-screened', though the number of screens is not the only deciding factor in assessing the health of the multiplex industry. The cost of a cinema ticket has been rising faster than admissions, meaning that the amount of money taken at the box office has increased disproportionately; total exhibition revenue more than doubled between 1996 and 2002 from £484m to £901m.[106]

The industry is now increasingly characterised by competition, however, the multiplex operators in the first years of the building boom endeavoured to avoid competing with each other. The market-research driven opening programme and the scope for developments to take place many miles apart allowed this. Where multiplexes were opened in the catchment areas of others, such as in Derby, the consequences were obviously reduced admissions figures for both operators. Avoidance of direct competition is difficult to maintain. The future will increasingly be one of head-to-head competition. For example, in 2004 Sheffield had 55 screens and over 11,000 seats; Birmingham and the West Midlands had approximately 160 screens, with over 38,000 seats. It is unlikely that competition between multiplexes will rest on the films being shown. More significant will be 'customer care', 'value for money' and quality assurances with regard to facilities. When it opened in 1997 visitors to Virgin's multiplex in Birmingham's Great Park were able to take part in Premier Screen, described as the 'the cinema equivalent of flying 'upper class' with its own private bar and waitress service'.[108] The VUE megaplex in Star City (formerly owned by Warner Village) gives over three screens to what it calls Gold Class, in which cinema-goers sit in reclining leather armchairs, consume complimentary popcorn and are able to purchase alcohol. Some of UCI's Filmworks complexes incorporate screens called The Gallery, offering the same services and facilities as VUE's Gold Class. UGC (now part of the Cineworld chain) offer a loyalty card scheme in which cinema-goers pay a flat monthly fee for unlimited visits. This form of marketing has become characteristic of the multiplex experience and of the competition between operators.

Although the multiplex industry in Britain has always seen the majority of sites and screens concentrated in the hands of a few companies, its history has witnessed a regular cycle of takeovers and mergers. In 1990 Metro Goldwyn Mayer cinemas assumed control of the Cannon chain, before it was itself subject to a takeover by Virgin cinemas in 1995. In 1999 Virgin was subsequently sold to the French company UGC. Warner Bros. cinemas merged with the Australian company Village Roadshow to form Warner Village in 1998, only to announce in 2003 that it was selling its cinema interests to SBC Cinemas who rebranded the chain as VUE cinemas. The volatility of the industry was demonstrated in 2003, when The Point in Milton Keynes –the cinema which had kick-started the development of the multiplex in Britain – was leased by UCI to Stelios Haji-Ioannou, owner of easyJet and re-branded as easyCinema. The radical approach of easyCinema was to vary the price of seats depending upon demand so that at times of least demand they might cost as little as 20p.[109]

By the end of 2004 the industry entered a period of consolidation as companies began to increase their chains via a process of acquisition and takeover. In August 2004 it was reported that equity firm Terra Firma had bid successfully for both the Odeon and UCI cinema chains, giving the company approximately 40 per cent of the UK cinema market. In December 2004 a private-equity group called Blackstone, which purchased the Cine-UK chain in September 2004, purchased all of UGC's British-based cinemas and began to re-brand their entire chain as Cineworld. The resultant company owned over 800 screens and became the second largest chain in Britain. Both of these major takeovers demonstrate the renewed interest in the cinema sector by private equity companies, drawn perhaps by the possible real estate values of many cinemas, particularly those located in city centres. According to Dodona Research, in the two years prior to March 2005 some two-thirds of cinema screens in the UK had been traded.[110]

At the start of 2005 the multiplex industry was dominated by four companies

– Cine-UK (including UGC), Terra Firma (UCI and Odeon), National Amusements (Showcase) and Vue (including Ster Century). They owned approximately 73 per cent of screens in Britain.[111] Having diversified considerably after the duopoly of the post-war period this new spate of mergers and takeovers sees the exhibition sector once again consolidated to a significant degree. It is unclear whether the Office of Fair Trading (OFT) will recommend examining the situation, though any attempt to sell off cinema sites would almost certainly attract the OFT's attention. In 1994 the Monopolies and Mergers Commission report into the supply of films for exhibition had concluded that despite some issues with alignments (offering films to particular cinema circuits with which the distributor has an agreement) and minimum exhibition periods for films, '[t]he transformation of the industry over the last decade has worked well for consumers … Today, apart from the practices we have criticized, competition in the markets under investigation is effective'.[112] At that time the industry was becoming more pluralised, though one might also reflect on the finding of the 1966 and 1983 Commission reports (see Chapter 5) which concluded that the duopolistic practices that prevailed then were most certainly not in the public interest.[113]

In the period since 1991 there has been a parallel development of smaller multiplex cinemas (5–6 screens), often operated by newer and smaller domestic exhibitors such as Apollo. They have looked to build in areas not previously seen as viable for the large chains, with smaller catchment areas. In 2002 a joint *bfi* and UK Film Council study into local cinemas revealed that only 1 per cent of multiplex developments were in areas with a population of less than 55,000 people.[114] These developments have often taken place in Britain's smaller towns and cities such as Lincoln, Leamington Spa, Mansfield, Exeter and Kettering. This has been perceived as an essentially good development as it often signals a return of the cinema to many towns that have previously seen them close.

In the main population areas, such as the West Midlands, West Yorkshire, Greater Manchester, Strathclyde, Lothian and London, the four major companies are cementing their control. Moreover, they are reinforcing their dominant position with regards to box-office revenues through their control of the larger multiplexes. Although the areas with the highest concentration of multiplexes are predictably London and the major conurbations, it is finally possible to see the development of the multiplex as a national phenomenon. It was in 1998 that the number of multiplex screens exceeded the number of screens in traditional cinemas for the first time. Indeed, with a little over 1,000 screens left in these traditional cinemas (see Table 6.1) Dodona Research argue whether the term multiplex 'any longer possesses much meaning over and above what is conveyed by the word cinema'.[115]

Notes

1 Cited in B. Slater, 'Getting it On: Examining Film Exhibition in the UK', *Vertigo*, 2:4 (Spring 2003), p. 22.

2 L. Bradley, 'The Appliance of Science', *Empire*, 5 (November 1989), pp. 50–5.

3 Publicity material for Warner Village Cinemas (1998).

4 Cited in S. Caulkin, 'Invasion of the Multiplex Monsters', *Observer*, 18 August 1998.

5 *The Hollywood Reporter*, May 1991, p. S-4.

6 Cited by Alexander Walker, *Evening Standard*, 25 July 1985.

7 D. Puttnam, *The Undeclared War: The Struggle for Control of the World's Film Industry* (London: Harper Collins, 1997), p. 317.

8 *The Hollywood Reporter*, May 1991, p. S-3.

9 *Ibid.*

10 A. Gamble, *Britain in Decline: Economic Policy, Political Strategy and the British State*, fourth edition (Basingstoke: Macmillan, 1994).

11 See A. Thornley, *Urban Planning under Thatcherism: The Challenge of the Market*, second edition (London: Routledge, 1993).

12 J. Harvey, *Urban Land Economics,* fourth edition (Basingstoke: Macmillan, 1996), p. 207.

13 Office of National Statistics, *Living in Britain: Results from the 2000/01 General Household Survey* (London: HMSO, 2001), p. 6.

14 For a brief overview of developments see J. Fernie, 'The Coming of the Fourth Wave: New Forms of Retail Out-of-town Development', *International Journal of Retail & Distribution Management*, 23:1 (1995) 4–11.

15 Foreword to D. Rodrigues and P. Bruinvels, *Zoning in on Enterprise: A Businessman's Guide to the Enterprise Zones* (London: Kogan Page, 1982).

16 See S. V. Ward, *Planning and Urban Change* (London: Paul Chapman Publishing, 1994).

17 Harvey, *Urban Land Economics*, p. 328.

18 See Ward, *Planning and Urban Change*.

19 *Lifting the Burden*, Cmnd 9571, (London: HMSO, 1985).

20 Thornley, *Urban Planning under Thatcherism*, p. 137.

21 Harvey, *Urban Land Economics*, p. 207.

22 A. Eyles, *The Granada Theatres* (London: Cinema Theatre Association/British Film Institute, 1998), p. 221.

23 N. Floyd, 'View to a Screen Killing', *Stills* 19 (May 1985), p. 23.

24 *Screen International*, 30 November 1985, p. 2.

25 I. McAsh, 'Take 5: People in Camera', *Films on Screen and Video*, 5:1 (June 1985), pp. 14–15.

26 'Multiplex and Metro', *Sight and Sound*, 54:3 (Summer 1985), p. 154.

27 Cited in the *Independent on Sunday*, 4 December 1994.

28 See A. Eyles, *ABC: The First Name in Entertainment* (London: Cinema Theatre Association/British Film Institute, 1993).

29 Cited in Floyd, 'View to a Screen Killing', p. 23.

30 *Ibid.*
31 The ABC brand was resurrected in 1996 with the sale of the majority of Virgin's non-multiplex cinemas to a company called Cinven. The Odeon chain was subsequently purchased by Cinven in 2000 whereupon all of the ABC cinemas were renamed Odeon, thus ending Rank's long established role in the British cinema industry.
32 *Screen International,* 25 July 1987, p. 16.
33 *Ibid.*, p. 20.
34 *AIP & Co,* 78 (October 1986).
35 COMEDIA in association with the Calouste Gulbenkian Foundation, *Out of Hours: A Study of Economic, Social and Cultural Life in 12 Town Centres in the British Isles: Summary Report,* COMEDIA: London, 1991, p. 5.
36 *The Hollywood Reporter,* May 1991, p. S-19.
37 *Ibid.*
38 See P. Turner, *Cineplex Odeon: An Outline History* (St. Paul's Cray: Brantwood Books 1998).
39 See P. Turner, *Showcase Cinemas: An Outline History* (St. Paul's Cray: Brantwood Books, 1999).
40 Cinema Advertisers Association (CAA), *Cinema and Video Industry Audience Research (CAVIAR) Number 20* (2003).
41 For example, see E. Soja, *Postmodern Geographies* (New York: Verso, 1989) and *Thirdspace* (Oxford: Oxford University Press, 1996). See also J. Hannigan (ed.), *Fantasy City: Pleasure and Profit in the Postmodern Metropolis* (London: Routledge, 1998).
42 P. Hubbard, 'Fear and Loathing at the Multiplex: Everyday Anxiety in the Post-industrial City', *Capital and Class,* 80 (2003), 51–76.
43 *Ibid.*, p. 58.
44 Mintel Reports 'Multi-leisure Parks – UK', *Leisure Intelligence Pursuits,* March 2004.
45 Cited in the *Guardian,* 8 October 1995.
46 R. Butler, 'A Night at the Pictures in 1994', *Independent on Sunday,* 16 October 1994.
47 See P. Turner, *Warner Cinemas: An Outline History* (St Paul's Cray: Brantwood Books, 1997) for discussion of the company's development of the 'megaplex'. In 2002 Warner Village undertook a rationalisation of the Star City site and closed nine of the thirty screens, removing all fixtures and equipment. The site is now operated by VUE cinemas.
48 'Welcome to Cinema Paradiso', *Observer,* 17 August 2003.
49 Jon Verde cited in G. Younge, 'The Big Picture', *Guardian,* 26 July 2000.
50 According to the Union Internationales des Cinémas (a trade body representing exhibitors across Europe) a 'megaplex' is defined as a cinema with at least 16 screens.
51 See J. Pal and P. Jones, 'Multiplexes – What's the Picture?', *Town and Country Planning,* 65:12 (December 1996), 344–5.

52 Planning Policy Guidance Note 6 (PPG6), *Town Centres and Retail Developments* (revised June 1996), Ministry of the Environment, para. 1.1, p. 5.

53 *Birmingham Post*, 2 May 1997.

54 Council for the Protection of Rural England (CPRE), *Planning More to Travel Less*, (London, 1997), cited in the *Birmingham Post*, 2 May 1997.

55 *Birmingham Post*, 2 May 1997.

56 See A. Eyles, 'Cinema 1989–90 – Exhibition', in BFI, *Film and Television Handbook 1991* (London: British Film Institute, 1990).

57 *Building*, 5 May 2000.

58 *Ibid.*

59 UK Film Council, *Statistical Yearbook/Annual Review 2004/05* (London: UK Film Council, 2005), p. 40.

60 London Assembly, *Picture Perfect? A London Assembly Report into the Capital's Cinemas*, Culture, Sport and Tourism Committee, Greater London Authority 100032379 (2003).

61 J. Oliver, 'The Battle for London's West End: Is it Now Over?', *Screentrade*, February 2004.

62 For example see *Making it Happen: Urban Renaissance and Prosperity in our Core Cities: A Tale of Eight Cities*, Office of the Deputy Prime Minister (April 2004), which examines Birmingham, Bristol, Leeds, Liverpool, Manchester, Newcastle, Nottingham and Sheffield.

63 Department of Environment, Transport and the Regions (DETR) Urban White Paper, *Our Towns and Cities: The Future: Delivering an Urban Renaissance*, Cm 4911, (London: The Stationary Office, 2000).

64 *Birmingham Post*, 8 October 2003.

65 Cited in *Producer*, 12 (Summer 1990), p. 21.

66 *Stills*, 21 (October 1985).

67 See E. Heathcote, *Cinema Builders* (Chichester: Wiley-Academy, 2001) for some examples of contemporary cinema design and architecture.

68 *CAVIAR 20* (2003).

69 McAsh, 'Take 5: People in Camera', p. 15.

70 *CTA Bulletin*, 32:4, (July/August 1996), Cinema Theatre Association, p. 16.

71 R. Gray, *Cinemas in Britain: 100 Years of Cinema Architecture* (London: Cinema Theatre Association/British Film Institute, 1996), p. 131.

72 Cited by L. Felperin, 'Multiplexity' in: *The PACT Magazine*, 56 (September 1996), p. 19.

73 *Screen Finance*, 2 March 2000 and 26 March 2003.

74 UK Film Council, *Statistical Yearbook/Annual Review 2004/05*, p. 42.

75 *Screen Digest*, July 1991.

76 Dodona, *Cinemagoing 11*, (Leicester: Dodona Research, 2003) p. 16.

77 *Ibid.*, p. 17.

78 *Moving Pictures International*, 17 January 1991, p. 12.

79 Cited in the *Observer*, 27 September 1998.

80 UK Film Council, *Statistical Yearbook 2004/05*, p. 53.

81 *Ibid.*

82 See M. Jancovich and L. Faire, 'The Best Place to See a Film: The Blockbuster, the Multiplex, and the Contexts of Consumption', in J. Stringer (ed.), *Movie Blockbusters* (London: Routledge, 2003).

83 Cinema Advertisers Association (CAA), *Cinema and Video Industry Audience Research (CAVIAR) Number 10* (1993).

84 *Ibid.*

85 CAA, *CAVIAR 20.*

86 Eyles, 'Cinema 1989–90 – Exhibition', p. 39.

87 UK Film Council, *Statistical Yearbook 2004/05.*

88 Mintel Reports, 'Cinemas – UK', *Leisure Intelligence Reports,* May 2004.

89 See company website at www.mellowonline.com/about/index.htm (accessed September 2004).

90 Mintel Reports, 'Cinemas – UK'.

91 *Ibid.*

92 See UK Film Council, *Statistical Yearbook 2004/05* and Dodona, *Cinemagoing 11.*

93 See *CTA Bulletin,* 30:6 (September/October 1996), Cinema Theatre Association.

94 *CTA Bulletin,* 32:2 (March/April 1996), Cinema Theatre Association, p. 3.

95 In 2003, the *bfi* and the UK Film Council commissioned a study to 'measure and assess the impact of local cinemas on the social, cultural and economic life of their communities'. The report, entitled *The Impact of Local Cinema,* was published in November 2005. See: www.ukfilmcouncil.org.uk/statistics/localcinemaproject/ (accessed January 2005).

96 See Dodona, *Cinemagoing 11* and Mintel Reports 'Cinemas – UK' for details of individual chains and their cinema holdings.

97 See *Picture House,* 23 (Summer 1998), Cinema Theatre Association, p. 35.

98 www.picturehouses.co.uk/site/city-screen.htm (accessed September 2004).

99 Term coined by *Variety* in 1994 – see P. Noglows, 'Here Come the Megaplexes: Exhibs Usher in 24-Screen "Destinations"', *Variety,* 356 (22–28 August 1994), 65–6.

100 For a discussion of this and similar developments in Canada and the USA see C. Acland, 'Cinemagoing and the Rise of the Megaplex', *Television & New Media,* 1:4 (2000), 375–402.

101 For a brief overview of IMAX developments see C. Acland, 'IMAX Technology and the Tourist Gaze', *Cultural Studies,* 12:3 (1998) 429–45.

102 In 1998 as part of a review of the British Film Institute called 'A Time of Change' the organisation was 'rebranded' and the *bfi* acronym changed to italic and lower case.

103 *IMAX: A Bigger Vision,* publicity brochure published by British Film Institute, 1996.

104 S. Bloomfield, 'Credits roll on the huge-screen revolution as Imax cinema closes', *Independent,* 4 January 2004. The IMAX cinema in Birmingham's Millennium Point complex has since re-opened.

105 *Ibid.*

106 See Dodona, *Cinemagoing 11.*

107 *Ibid.,* p. 28.

108 *Screen International*, 24 January 1997, p. 33

109 Initially, easyCinema incurred problems obtaining first-run films from distributors who were reluctant to accept the pricing structure, particularly since easyCinema wanted to negotiate a fixed fee for film rentals. After negotiations with the major distributors easyCinema now has access to first-run features but has had to increase its minimum price for seats. See www.easycinema.com.

110 Dodona, *Cinemagoing 14* (Leicester: Dodona Research, 2005).

111 UK Film Council, *Statistical Yearbook 2004/05.*

112 Monopolies and Mergers Commission, *Films: A Report on the Supply of Films for Exhibition in Cinemas in the UK*, Cmnd 2673, 1994, para. 1.17., p. 5. The Commission found that a 'complex monopoly situation' existed involving the five leading distributors, the four independent distributors and the five leading exhibitors, with several uncompetitive practices in the cinema industry. The Commission highlighted the system of 'alignments' in which distributors favour one particular exhibition chain with which it has an agreement to the exclusion of another. In addition, minimum exhibition periods were often stipulated of four weeks or longer as a condition of getting films to show. This was seen as disadvantaging single-screen cinemas and smaller, independent distributors.

113 Monopolies Commission, *Films: A Report on the Supply of Films for Exhibition in Cinemas*, HC 206, 1966 and Monopolies and Mergers Commission, *Films: A Report on the Supply of Films for Exhibition in Cinemas*, Cmnd 8858, 1983.

114 *The Impact of Local Cinema: Overview* (*bfi*/UK Film Council, 2005) .

115 Dodona, *Cinemagoing 11*, p. 17.

7

The future for cinema exhibition in the digital age

Woman on train: 'Fancy coming to the cinema tonight?'
Man on train (looking at his iPod): 'The what?' (Cartoon in *Sight and Sound*)[1]

The cinema and the home

Part of this book has been concerned with interrogating the simple view that the case for cinema as a site of public enjoyment was to be preferred to that of the television, and its position within a site of private enjoyment. When the first multiplex opened it was easy to make a distinction, technologically speaking at least, between television and cinema. At its best television could offer a square screen size of some 29 inches, with NICAM stereo sound (developed by BBC engineers in the early 1980s) and the ability to show pre-recorded feature films via a video recorder; cinema however, could offer a high definition large-scale image projected onto a 40–50 foot screen, with multi-channel surround sound.

By the end of the 1980s many of the features of the cinema were beginning to find their way into the domestic sphere. The traditional television screen format of 4:3 ratio began to be supplemented by the 16:9 widescreen format, which was able to show many feature films without the need for cropping (known as 'pan and scan'). Many manufacturers are now offering back-projection, plasma and LCD (liquid crystal display) television sets with screen sizes of up to 60 inches, which offer substantially improved picture quality and clarity. Two-channel stereo has given way to five, six and seven-channel surround sound, such as Dolby Digital and Dynamic Theater Sound (DTS). These developments, coupled with the advent of digital broadcast technology, as typified by Sky Digital, cable and Freeview digital services, offer the possibility of High Definition Television (HDTV) in the near future.[2] Finally, the VCR, for so long the stalwart of domestic pre-recording and playback, has been supplanted by digital technology in the shape of DVD (Digital Versatile Disc), which offers superior picture and sound quality, as well as the ability to record. Following its launch in 1997 in the USA and in 1998 in Europe, DVD has become the fastest growing new film entertainment format in history, with sales rising over 400 per cent in the year after they were introduced in Western Europe.[3] In Britain around 61 per cent of homes had a DVD player in 2004.[4]

The importance of other film outlets for the Hollywood studios cannot be underestimated, since the proportion of foreign revenues derived from cinema rentals, which used to be almost the total, now accounts for approximately a quarter.[5] Since 1985 the major source of foreign revenue has become home video, followed by cinema exhibition and television, in that order.[6] Speaking in 2004 Daniel Battsek, Executive Vice President of Buena Vista International, argued that if 'the VCR was the saviour of cinema – the DVD is perhaps the saviour of the entire film industry', citing the fact that in Britain six out of every seven DVDs sold was a feature film.[7] In 2003 consumers in Britain spent more than four times as much renting or buying videos and DVDs (£3.13 billion) than they did at the cinema box-office (£770 million).[8] The attraction of DVD to the film industry lies not only in the studios' ability to market films in different ways (films can be released with different endings and with deleted scenes, or in 'Directors' Cuts'), but also in the potential re-release titles.

The implication for the cinema generally, and multiplexes in particular, is that domestic viewing technologies will continue to be the mediums through which most film viewing takes place. In 2004 there were 2,237 films shown on terrestrial network television.[9] Video and DVD rentals account for 156 million transactions, an average of six per household.[10] By the end of 2005 44 per cent of homes in Britain subscribed to cable or satellite television, with more homes now subscribing to BSkyB services than there are using any other television platform in Britain.[11]

With video recorders and DVD players in so many homes, it looks likely that film rental will continue to be an important factor in people's film viewing, particularly as films released on video and DVD are available some twelve months before they are broadcast on satellite. In their research in 1985, Docherty, Morrison and Tracey pointed out that 'cinema and film are not inseparable, one can love film separately from the cinema'.[12] For most people, they argued, watching a film on video or on satellite television was about enjoying the film itself, with little intention of recreating the experience that is cinema. In many ways the evidence suggests that this is still the case; domestic film viewing is still subject to the conditions of domestic life and the clear importance of home-based leisure. Nevertheless, the developments in home cinema technologies outlined above are beginning to blur the distinctions with the cinema, technologically at least. Launching their new digital service in

1998, BSkyB's Chief Executive, Mark Booth, proposed that it would 'revolutionise the way we look at television' with the film channel promising to 'bring the equivalent of a multiplex cinema into our living rooms'.[13]

Herein rests a tension between the attractions of watching films in the home and at the multiplex. New domestic viewing technologies have sought to reproduce, in part, the experience of the multiplex, while the multiplex has attempted to recast cinema's relationship with the audience and the domestic family audience in particular. In the same way that film viewing in the home developed as a result of changes in the private sphere, so multiplexes have attempted to develop in relation to changes in the leisure patterns in the public sphere. Part of their success has been the way in which they have been able to overcome the concerns of an increasingly privatised society by stressing comfort, familiarity, safety and convenience. The development of the multiplex is symptomatic of great faith in the public consumption of the image and the notion of public entertainment. The key to attracting potential cinema-goers lay in recognising the importance of controlling public space and averting people's fears about the city.[14] Indeed, in 1987 Sumner Redstone, the chairman of US cinema chain National Amusements, argued that exhibitors had to compete not only with domestic entertainments but also the safety of the home; a place 'free from the hazards of the city streets'.[15]

Attracting audiences to the cinema

We arrive at this point having established a series of 'truths': a) the number of people going to the cinema has increased annually since 1984; b) the percentage of multiplex visits is significantly higher than the percentage of multiplex screens and c) the multiplex sector accounts for a disproportionately large percentage of total industry revenues. It does not take a dramatic leap of faith to conclude that the annual increases in attendance are accounted for by the advent of the multiplex.[16] So, the rather obvious question is why are multiplexes so popular with audiences when cinema had been declining prior to their inception?

The main attraction identified by exhibitors was the fact that the multiplex offered considerably greater choice of films and more comfort. As traditional cinemas shrank in size during the 1960s and 1970s, twinning, tripling and quadrupling screens, the amount of room for the patrons of these cinemas also appeared to shrink. Multiplexes have been designed from the outset as multi-screen venues and along with new materials and the benefit of space; have successfully appealed to people's sense of desire for comfort. In his study of cinemagoing in Leicester, Hubbard found that respondents placed great emphasis upon comfort, particularly when comparing and contrasting the multiplex with other venues.[17] Moreover, the general *ambiance* of the multiplex was made more attractive by the spatial features of the buildings and in particular the amount of space (imagined or otherwise) that cinema-goers felt they had. In particular, the design of the foyer necessitated less interaction with others, the streamlined process of ticket sales meant less queuing and generally lower occupancy rates in auditoria meant the possibility of sitting away from others.[18]

The visitor to almost any multiplex cinema cannot fail to be aware of how radically different it is from its forerunner both spatially and architecturally. The illuminated display of current films showing is given a large and privileged place above the entrance and is visible from some distance. The Showcase cinema, just off the M6 motorway near Walsall, has a large display at the entrance to the car park, visible from the motorway itself. This strategy is deliberate since research early on in the development of the multiplex suggested that many multiplex-goers made up their minds about what film to see as little as fifteen minutes beforehand.[19] Many multiplex cinemas, by virtue of their position in an open space fronted or surrounded by a car park, are approached and viewed from a distance. Resplendent with logo, glitzy designs of steel, glass and coloured brick, and brightly lit, the multiplex promises a place of entertainment that is in tune with its contents – namely the glamour and excitement of the feature film and specifically, the Hollywood feature film.

In design and construction the multiplex resembles many leisure facilities, especially those originating in the USA. Their features have come to connote pleasure and importantly consumption, in line with other leisure developments, for example the shopping mall. Multiplex cinemas, both in terms of their exterior appearance and initially the foyer, communicate in specific ways with their potential users, who in turn attribute specific meanings to them. An analogy can be made between the multiplex and the fast-food restaurant since both sites determine spatially the relationship between consumer and provider, and the ways consumers perceive the site of exchange. In emphasising the importance of consumption and a wider leisure imperative, in which cinema is seen as but one part, multiplexes have historically featured bars and restaurants attached to foyers or in adjacent complexes. Bruno Frydman, then AMC Europe President, was explicit about the company's intentions:

> The reasons which lay behind our desire to build multiplexes in Europe had to do principally with the synergies which they can generate, especially in the area of catering. We thus tried to position ourselves in the leisure industry, with plans to open big cinema theatres that would create major audience flows: all these people would be customers not only inside, but also outside theatres, in complexes with many bars and restaurants offering a range of after-show attractions.[20]

Historically, the cinema has derived the lion's share of its profits from the sale of confectionery, drinks and food. This is still true of the multiplex which uses the concession counter and its array of new food lines as another key selling point for the cinema experience. Multiplex cinema chains have made strong profits from concessions and associated products. According to Peter Dobson, then managing Director of Warner Bros. Theatres in Britain, 25 per cent of revenues come from concessions with profit figures as high as 80 per cent.[21] All of the major cinema chains have concentrated heavily on the sale of concessions, not only because they are highly profitable but also because the profits do not have to be shared with the distributor, unlike box-office receipts.

If we accept that the prime motivating factor in multiplex construction is function, we must also accept that multiplex cinemas were developed to attract people back to the cinema, as well as those who were already cinema-goers. They had to achieve two aims which are common to the cinema generally and which Ellis identified as marketing two distinct aspects: 'the single film in its uniqueness and its similarity to other films; and the experience of cinema itself'.[22] If the TV and home cinema have operated to reinforce the cultural importance of the film via a notion of the cinema, multiplexes have tried to reassert the experience of the cinema above mere references to it in conceptions of the film. An attempt has been made to redefine that experience along the lines of the wider concept of 'leisure' while retaining the notion that the cinema is the best place to see a film, and further reassert that those films are made *for* the cinema. In a study taken from a range of different cinema provision Wilkinson interviewed cinema-goers. Sites used included Star City megaplex in Birmingham, the easyCinema at the former Point multiplex in Milton Keynes, the 22-seat Screen Room in Nottingham and the Electric cinema in London's Notting Hill. A Star City interviewee clearly articulated this leisure imperative:

> I think it's expensive, but then it is a posh kind of place, isn't it? We usually come with the kids but tonight we escaped to see *X-Men 2* and now we're going for a meal here in the complex. Star City's got everything: restaurants, cinema, free parking. It's good that they show new Indian films, too. It brings in more people, especially considering how multicultural Birmingham is. The only thing it lacks is someone to bring you drinks and popcorn at your seat. We used to go to the Odeon and UGC in the city before we were married but now we'd choose Star City over anywhere else.[23]

The myth of 'choice' – the *product* or what used to be called movies

Unlike fast-food restaurants that offer a broadly standardised product, cinemas rely on a product that that is less predictable and less standardised – the feature film (or *product* as it is known in the production, distribution and exhibition industries). Crucial to the continued success and growth of cinemas are films, and more particularly a steady supply of films that audiences want to see. During 2004 there were 451 films were exhibited in Britain (and the Republic of Ireland), of which 178 were US solo or co-productions with other countries, 20 were US/UK joint productions, 73 were UK productions or co-productions with other countries, with the remainder from Europe and the rest of the world.[24] The distribution of the bulk of these films, namely those made in Hollywood, was undertaken by the five major distribution companies operating in Britain (20th Century Fox, Buena Vista International, Warner, United International Pictures (UIP) and Columbia) all of which are US-owned. The rest of the distribution sector is made up of independents that promote the bulk of British films and all foreign films, including many independent US films. The product sold at multiplexes is overwhelmingly that produced by the major Hollywood studios, themselves owners of many of the distributors. In general this monopolisation of British screens by the US film industry follows a developing trend over the period since the end of the First World War (see Chapter 2).

Speaking in 1997 at Cambridge University, Karsten-Peter Grummitt, Managing Director of Dodona Research, confidently assured delegates that cinema admissions would grow by 50 per cent over the next few years,[25] for the following reasons:

> first because a multiplex just opened five minutes down the road from where I live, cutting 15 or 20 minutes off my former journey time to a multiplex. And, because there are two of them, they play more films. More convenient access and more choice will play a large part in encouraging that one extra visit a year.[26]

Grummitt was echoing a popular version of the multiplex attraction, that of 'choice', which all multiplex companies use as a potent selling point. It is difficult to argue against this position when a multiplex with ten screens either replaces a traditional twinned or tripled cinema or is built in an area that previously lacked a cinema. All of the technical developments of the multiplex have left traditional cinemas with obvious disadvantages. The paradox of the multiplex development is that its multi-screen layout has been the main selling point, while for the 1970s cinema desperate to boost attendance via greater film choice, it was seen as a distinct drawback. Multiplexes were conceived this way and were designed to overcome the fatal combination of lack of room, small screens and bad lines of sight for audiences. Herein lies the revolution that is the multiplex cinema. On any day of the week a ten-screen multiplex can offer ten to fourteen films at a variety of times and at a variety of prices. Research makes it clear that this is the single biggest appeal of the multiplex cinema,[27] though here again we must be cautious, since the notion of 'choice' needs to be qualified.

Despite an increase in screens there are still not enough for all of the films made. This is the case for both English language and foreign films. This is exacerbated by the tendency for multiplexes to hold over some films for successive weeks. This is in large part because the decisions on which films to programme, made by the large multiplex chains' central buyers, are based on a judgement as to whether they are able to play profitably for a month or more. So, the fact that many more films are made than can be physically shown is incidental since only a finite amount are truly profitable. These are often major releases such as Hollywood-made starring vehicles and mainstream US-produced films. Inevitably, distributors and cinema owners select only those films that they judge will be successful, which for the distributors and producers are the films that have been publicised at enormous cost.

The British Screen Advisory Council, in its submission to the UK Film Council on the future of cinema in the UK, identified what it saw as two major reasons why there were not enough available screens:

> There would appear to be a glut of films targeted at mainstream audiences, which dominate the programmes in the multiplexes. Even in areas which are regarded as being over-screened, the evidence suggests that market forces tend to encourage rival local multiplexes to show the same selection of titles as each other rather than to target niche audiences.
>
> It seems that the expected return on investment in two- or three-screen cinemas dedicated to non-mainstream movies is rarely sufficiently high for commercial operators to justify building independent circuits around the country.[28]

Initially, it was believed that the advent of multiplexes would break up the previous distribution and exhibition duopoly and enable greater access to screens for independent and art films. In the early days multiplex operators like AMC indicated that the provision of ten screens meant that they would be prepared to show non-mainstream films. This had been a popular claim when chains were tripling cinemas in the 1970s.[29] However, like then, many multiplexes have not carried through this idea. In the early stages of multiplex development some sites, notably The Point, clearly anxious to counter criticism from independent companies such as Artificial Eye that space was not being made available, tentatively programmed foreign and arthouse films. Robert Beeson of the independent distribution company Artificial Eye wryly recalled in 1989 that The Point did programme *Subway* (1985) in its early days, 'only to report droves leaving the cinema aghast at having to read subtitles'.[30] He went on to say that 'rather than try to build an audience for such material, it seems that the company used this one experience as proof that foreign films are box-office death'.[31]

As we have seen, the upswing in the cinema attendance in 1984 corresponded not only with multiplexes but also with a series of well-hyped Hollywood blockbuster films (see Chapter 5). Corrigan identified these blockbuster films as having a particular mode of address that was aimed at an 'impossibly large and undefined audience', rather than a particular sector.[32] This notion was taken up by Buckland who saw this address based on a 'mix of genres – often combining action-adventure with comedy, drama, romance, science-fiction and the like – and by means of a remodelling of character and plot'.[33] The emphasis here is on the ways in which the Hollywood studios are able to offer a steady supply of blockbusters, which are, according to the box-office receipts for both the USA and Britain, consistently the most popular films amongst the viewing public. In his analysis of 'McDonaldization' Ritzer considered the number of sequels and derivative films being produced and argued that in Hollywood, 'predictable products, particularly sequels to successful movies – at the expense of movies based on new concepts, ideas, and characters – abound'.[34] Clearly, the decision to make a sequel is based on a series of economic and creative decisions. They allow studios to predict box-office success to a greater degree. Cinema audiences, we are told, like sequels because they offer familiar characters in familiar settings, together with the certainty that the filmmakers will offer us even more spectacular action sequences in an effort to outdo the previous films. As Jancovich and Faire argue, the multiplex 'has not only transformed the meaning of the blockbuster but was itself a response to developments in the blockbuster'.[35]

Since the other prerequisite of a blockbuster is a high budget, the major studios have spent the last twenty to thirty years reducing the number of films they make in favour of a smaller number of higher cost films that are marketed more widely and more intensely. The theory is that these big-budget films will take large amounts at the box-office, provided they are suitably hyped in the press and released at the right time. Increasingly the right time is the summer since Hollywood takes around one third of its annual box-office during July, August and September.[36] Despite the number of blockbusters consistently appearing and constantly increasing in production costs (the average combined production and marketing budget for a Hollywood film surpassed $100 million in 2003)[37] many believe that the market is not healthy and is being limited by too many films of this kind. Although this is a perennial source of angst in Hollywood, it does not seem to translate into a significant shift in the kinds of films being released by the major studios. Rather, the response is often to cut down the number of films being made, thus limiting still further the variety of films on offer.

The problem for cinema audiences in Britain is that, despite smaller numbers of films being made every year by the major Hollywood studios, those that are made receive a disproportionate amount of resources in terms of marketing and screen time. This is clearly a function not only of the cultural power of Hollywood in contemporary cinema but also of the organisation of distribution and exhibition. This power and organisation is increasingly related to the steady process of vertical integration in the film industry. Rather than seeing this as problematic, the National Heritage Committee explicitly argued *for* vertical integration in 1995, amongst both British and overseas film companies, on the grounds that:

> Such a development would have numerous benefits. These include giving producers a better understanding of the marketplace for films through closer ties with their colleagues in distribution and exhibition, which would translate into more successful pictures.[38]

Yet, at the same time the report admitted that the new films attracted to Britain would 'primarily include … films funded ultimately by the US majors with money they would otherwise choose to send back to America'.[39] In 2003 the successor to this committee, the Culture Media and Sport Committee, concluded that the 'UK had tried to mimic the US system without success' and that '[a]ttempts to play the Hollywood game had largely failed'.[40]

The result of this with regard to choice (which is cited as the core appeal of the multiplex concept) is that multiplexes may not be offering as great a range of 'product' as we imagine. Independent producers and distributors find themselves in the paradoxical position of witnessing an increase in screens at the same time as outlets for their films are diminishing. In this context it is worth noting that the number of films exhibited at any one time is a fraction of those on offer, many of which are destined for the swift journey straight to video/DVD. Nigel Andrew felt that the blame could be placed solely at the feet of the multiplex companies and their concentration on mainstream Hollywood films. He observed that 'a multiplex's command of 20 different screens doesn't mean it will devote a single one to anything risky. So the beleaguered army of the world's arthouses bids for these blighted films.'[41]

Many multiplexes, for example UCI, did start to programme arthouse films one night a week. The films chosen were generally 'critically acclaimed' foreign and English language films, non-mainstream films, and older films not seen in the cinema for some years. Selected by House Managers and via suggestions from the audience, UCI's 'Director's Chair' has proved enduring and popular. Nevertheless, the overwhelming rationale is that 'non-mainstream product' is not good box-office. Many circumstances conspire to make this so, including the fact that independent distributors are only able to make a limited number of prints, and the enormous cost of marketing films.[42]

An exception to this might be the growth of films distributed in Britain from the Indian sub-continent, 55 in 2004 compared to 71 from all of Europe.[43] Though there are independent cinemas (such as Piccadilly Cinemas, which operates cinemas in Birmingham and Leicester) dedicated to showing Indian films (so called 'Bollywood') many of the multiplex chains have also begun to recognise this large potential market.[44] At its Star site in Birmingham VUE (formally Warner Village) dedicates three or four screens a week to films from the Indian sub-continent. As Gary Younge observed:

> Star City complex was not just significant architecturally, since its programming policy was to dedicate six screens to films from South-Asia, notably India and so-called 'Bollywood' films. In an interesting departure from the imperative of having a large mobile population within a forty five minute drive, Warner Village looked to the large British-Asian population in Birmingham and beyond, in Wolverhampton, Leicester or Derby.[45]

UGC (a relative newcomer to the UK multiplex industry and now part of the Cineworld chain – see Chapter 6) claims to make a consistent effort to promote independent and foreign language films at many of their multiplexes. Its website asserts that the company 'lead the field in terms of the range of films we screen at our cinemas, giving smaller independent films equal billing alongside large Hollywood releases'.[46] Of course, for those cinemas that have carved out niches as arthouses the prospect of a multiplex competing with them for non-mainstream films is alarming, not least since many smaller distributors will relish the prospect of a large chain, with multiple screens, selecting films from its roster. A problem arises, according to Slater, when the multiplex is unable to market the film in an appropriate way to attract an audience.[47] In what he described as this 'post *Crouching Tiger ... Amelie* world' Slater (who worked for some years in the independent exhibition sector) observed that the changes in programming signified 'an attempt to abandon the notion of a specialist cinema: just lump it all in together and let the audience figure it out'.[48]

Arthouse or 'specialised cinema'

This situation and the whole issue of minority interest and 'arthouse' films may nevertheless have acted to the benefit of some small specialised commercial and grant-aided cinemas. These cinemas might potentially benefit from the failure of multiplexes to establish large audiences and provide space for these types of films.

The arthouse or specialised cinema represents an alternative site of consumption to the multiplex, both spatially and in terms of capital, though the relationship is, in Harbord's terms, characterised by a dynamic interplay in which their identities are specified in relation to each other.[49] Put simply, the notion of an 'independent' cinema requires a cinema that it is independent *of.* Independent cinemas, according to Slater, offer a stark contrast to the multiplex with the two spaces 'crudely delineated by class and age'.[50] The contrast was echoed by a spokesperson from cinema company Ster-Kinekor, who observed that '[i]f you look at your consumer, it's your popcorn-and-chips brigade that goes to the commercial cinema, the coffee and cake brigade that goes to the arthouse. They are different markets.'[51] Despite the use of popular stereotypes, the idea of different markets is reinforced in Wilkinson's interview with a visitor to the Electric Cinema, Notting Hill:

> It's my first time at the Electric – Stan brought me. I live in Clapham, so I tend to go to the Picture House or come into town to the Arts Club in central London. If I'm going out to see an arts film, I'd come to a cinema like this, but if I'm watching something like Spider-Man I'd go to the local Odeon. We came tonight because the tickets are cheaper on a Monday and the place is really out of the norm. The bar is cool and the chocolate brownies are fantastic.[52]

As Harbord observed, arthouse cinema 'attempts a heterogeneous programme of films made outside the studio system, embracing at least three forms of filmic classification: the formally innovative film, the social realist text and foreign films (mainly including American films that fall outside the former two descriptions)'.[53] According to the *Guardian* film critic Derek Malcolm, 'the arthouse is really just a non-Hollywood house which represents 80% of the world's film-making output'.[54]

The specialised cinema sector in Britain is difficult to quantify accurately, though the UK Film Council commissioned a major study into the specialised exhibition and distribution in 2002.[55] The report's authors identified some key characteristics of specialised cinema including: 'a film whose language, form or subject matter tends to result in it obtaining only a limited release'; 'a film which is initially targeted and/or marketed at a niche market'; 'a film which is released with less than 50 prints'; 'films which normally reach a more limited market than mainstream releases (e.g. classics)'; or 'films which may not have a wide or global appeal or may address a specific section of the community'.[56] The list implies that specialised films constitute a small proportion of the total films released in any one year; however the reality is that films viewed as 'non-mainstream' make up half of the total.[57] Their distribution is restricted primarily by the small numbers of prints struck, while venues showing them are limited and cinema runs are short. Conversely, many independent cinemas have been unable to compete with the multiplexes and other large cinemas when showing mainstream films; a situation made worse by the attitude of many large distributors who place restrictive conditions upon the showing of their product.

In practice these restrictions have included limiting the ability of exhibitors to set their own admission prices and promotional activities, and the use made of their screens (showing different films on the same screen or moving a film from one screen to another).[58] The difficult position faced particularly by independent cinemas with four screens or less was highlighted in the 1994 Monopolies and Mergers Commission (MMC) report into exhibition.[59] In this report the MMC was critical of the distributors' practice of imposing minimum exhibition periods on smaller cinemas with not more than four screens. The Films (Exhibition Periods) Order 1996, produced in response to the MMC report, made it unlawful for a distributor to make it a condition of supply that an exhibitor show a film for more than two weeks.[60] In 2004 the Office of Fair Trading (OFT) looked at film exhibition and distribution and re-examined The Films (Exhibition Periods) Order 1996.[61] The OFT concluded that while there was broad agreement that the order was still relevant, there was also evidence that some distributors were attempting to evade it. Independent cinemas reported that when they proposed to show a film for two weeks or less then all too often the 'distributors find other reasons for refusing to supply the film, for example that no print is available'.[62]

Specialised cinema exhibition can be distinguished from a broader commercial independent sector not just by content but through a complex system of financial support and charitable status. There are many subsidised arts cinemas, such as the *bfi*'s Regional Film Theatres (RFTs). The majority of the cinemas operate as independent charitable trusts, while others are controlled by local authorities or educational establishments. RFTs do not constitute a circuit, though in the past many have benefited from a centralised booking service provided by the *bfi*. There is also a network of independently-owned cinemas, some of which are supported financially by the *bfi* through grants, with others supported through film booking and publicity services. The largest chains are City Screen, Zoo Cinema Exhibition and Mainline, which between them control over 30 cinemas. Finally, there is a plethora of part-time facilities in arts and community centres, including mobile touring cinemas and in excess of 320 film societies.[63] With multiplex cinemas operating on admissions of approximately 50,000 per screen per annum (and up to 80,000 depending upon location) the commercial independent sector often operates on the basis of 20–30,000 admissions per screen with consequently narrowed profit margins.[64]

In 2003 the *bfi* closed its regional programme unit, which meant that small exhibitors had to deal directly with distributors, and could therefore no longer rely on collective buying power. At the time that the cuts were announced there was considerable reaction from RFTs and other small exhibitors, with twenty-six cinema managers writing a letter to the then *bfi* Chairman Anthony Minghella, calling for a re-think. Alan Alderson-Smith, head of cinema at Phoenix Arts in Leicester, argued that it was a 'tragedy for cultural cinema that the *bfi* are even contemplating abolishing this last true link with the rest of the UK', while it would 'erode yet further the opportunities for UK audiences to see something other than the increasing number of Hollywood movies permeating British cinema screens'.[65] In a memorandum submitted to the Select Committee on Culture, Media and Sport, the Association of Independent Film Exhibitors also sought to stress the problems which would be brought about by the closure of the unit by arguing that the decision 'brings into question how the *bfi* will continue to have any regional impact'.[66]

Digital cinema

Technology doesn't matter. Nobody pays to see it, nobody cares. Any discussion of where cinema goes must remember this. There is a danger that those promoting technology see it as an attraction in itself, and those ignorant of it are overawed by the enthusiasm.[67]

Cinema's saviour, in particular that of the specialised sector, is currently claimed to be the development of electronic cinema (e-cinema) and digital cinema (d-cinema). Broadly speaking, e-cinema is concerned with the development of digital technologies across the levels of film production, distribution and exhibition, while d-cinema is concerned with distribution and exhibition. According to Watson and Morris, d-cinema can be defined as 'the projection of full-length feature films to audiences in a purpose-built cinema where the quality of projection is not less than that provided by current 35mm technology'.[68] Though the film is currently contained on a series of disks delivered to cinemas, d-cinema might also entail the delivery of the film over satellite or via broadband Internet in the future. The film is projected onto the cinema screen by a digital light processor (DLP) which generates an image by bouncing light off three chips, each covered with over a million tiny, individually moveable mirrors. The technology was based upon the work of the US-based company Texas Instruments, though rival systems are being developed by other large multinational electronics corporations.[69] At the moment however, DLP is the most popular technology and is currently installed in some of Britain's most prestigious cinemas, including the Odeon Leicester Square in London. In all by 2004 there were eighteen screens in Britain equipped with digital projection facilities, a doubling in number over the previous year.[70]

The development of technologies to project digital images onto a screen follows in the wake of the steady adoption of Digital Video as a replacement for 16mm celluloid in the production of low-budget films. In recent years digital cameras have been developed that are seen as rivalling 35mm for picture quality. These so-called 24P cameras include the CineAlto HDCAM, developed by Sony Corp. in conjunction with Panavision.

The implications for cinemas and independent and arthouse cinemas in particular are popularly expressed as an opportunity to diversify programming and reduce the costs of distribution. According to the Department for Culture, Media and Sport (DCMS) 'd-cinemas' schedules can be changed much more frequently, responding both to market conditions, different audience groups, and varying deals with distributors'.[71] In part this flexibility rests upon the costs of duplication relative to those of celluloid since the existence of a digitalised master means that making copies is substantially cheaper. However, the current high cost of DLPs is a severe restriction to their widespread adoption, particularly in smaller, independent cinemas and small chains. This has led to the development of a series of initiatives designed to promote d-cinema as a way of delivering a broader range of films to new audiences. At the forefront of these moves has been the UK Film Council which launched its Digital Screen Network (DSN) in 2005. The initiative, costing some £11.5m, will involve the equipping of over 200 cinemas across Britain with DLPs over a period of 18 months. Participating cinemas will guarantee to show a specified number of specialised films a week including foreign language films, in return for the installation and maintenance of the equipment.

The curtains close, the lights go on

It is very easy to posit the notion that there is something implicitly 'good' about cinema: that it needs preserving, rather like working industrial museums. Like notions of heritage that extend to other versions of culture and cultural institutions, there are dominant versions of what cinema is, or should, be about. The days in which cinema assumed a position of primacy as both a mass-leisure activity and the 'best place to see a film' are gone. Many of us will continue to love older cinemas; however the future of film exhibition, at least in the immediate future, looks increasingly tied up with that of the multiplex. This study has tried to explain why criticism can be levelled at the multiplex cinema; however, one is bound to conclude that in many important ways multiplexes are to be welcomed with reservations. The future of the cinema is still unclear in many respects. Projections on audience trends are that annual admissions will continue to increase – 200 million by 2008 according to Dodona research[72] – but what then? The multiplex cinema market has proved to be both cyclical and occasionally volatile over its first twenty years, with the numbers of multiplexes reaching possible saturation point by 2010.

In the meantime, however, multiplex construction continues with the size of complex progressively increasing. Films themselves, however, are still derived from the narrow economically orientated US industry in which film production is fast becoming but a small part of giant multinational concerns. In its study of the capital's cinemas, the London Assembly noted that of the sixty-eight films shown outside the West End during one week in August 2003 more than 75 per cent of all screenings were for just six films.[73] This testifies not only to the homogeneity of film exhibition but also to the power of the distributors. It is difficult not to be cynical when one considers that many multiplex owners are intimately connected to the distribution of films via their position as either distributors themselves or part of corporations who own distribution networks. The old 'duopoly' system in which certain chains obtained exclusive rights to certain distributor's films may have been broken, but what we have seen is greater standardisation across the board. According to film director Terry Gilliam, the combination of Hollywood and the multiplex is a 'huge disaster' which 'limits what we see and what we choose to see. It limits our expectations. Somehow it's all wrong.'[74]

Nevertheless, multiplexes are to be congratulated for re-establishing the notion that new cinemas can be built and can attract people; the challenge is to engender a more diverse film culture in which the film is seen in more internationalist terms. The responsibility for a more diverse market may continue to fall to the independent sector, though this will be increasingly difficult if the independent distribution sector is not strengthened accordingly. The advent of d-cinema might be the saviour for specialist film in the short term but one wonders if the corollary of these developments will be the end of celluloid itself, surely the most enduring 'standard' of them all.

Notes

1   *Sight and Sound*, May 2006, p.3.
2   BSkyB launched its HDTV service in 2006, though subscribers need to upgrade to a new plasma or LCD television set in order to receive the service. Similarly, the BBC intends that most programme production will be in High Definition by 2010. See A. Oliphant (ed.), *BBC R & D Annual Review April 2004–March 2005*, www.bbc.co.uk/rd/pubs/annual-review/index.shtml (accessed July 2005).
3   *Screen Digest*, May 2000.

4 British Video Council, *2005 BVA Yearbook* (London: British Video Council, 2005).

5 T. Balio, 'Adjusting to the New Global Economy: Hollywood in the 1990s', in A. Moran (ed.), *Film Policy: International, National and Regional Perspectives* (London: Routledge, 1996).

6 T. Balio, '"A Major Presence in all of the World's Important Markets': The Globalization of Hollywood in the 1990s', in S. Neale and M. Smith (eds), *Contemporary Hollywood Cinema* (London: Routledge, 1998).

7 *The Film Industry: Changing Times, Changing Business Models*, a seminar organised by the British Screen Advisory Council, March 2004, available at www.bsac.uk.com/reports/onlineconference.htm (accessed August 2004).

8 UK Film Council, *Statistical Yearbook/Annual Review 2004/05* (London: UK Film Council, 2005), pp. 8 and 62.

9 *Ibid.*, p. 69.

10 *Ibid.*, p. 61.

11 Ofcom, *The Communications Market: Digital Progress Report Digital TV*, Q4 March 2006.

12 D. Docherty, D. Morrison and M. Tracey, 'Who Goes to the Cinema?', *Sight and Sound*, 55:2 (Spring 1986), 81–5, pp. 84–5.

13 Quoted in the *Independent*, 4 February 1998.

14 C. R. Acland, *Screen Traffic: Movies, Multiplexes and Global Culture* (Durham, NC and London: Duke University Press, 2003).

15 *Variety*, 25 November 1987, p. 32, cited in *ibid.*, p. 146.

16 See D. Puttnam, *The Undeclared War: The Struggle for Control of the World's Film Industry* (London: Harper Collins, 1997).

17 See P. Hubbard, 'A Good Night Out? Multiplex Cinemas as Sites of Embodied Leisure', *Leisure Studies*, 22 (July 2003), 255–72.

18 *Ibid.*

19 *Screen International*, 22 August 1991, p. 16.

20 Speech by Bruno Frydman, 'Exporting the Multiplex Model to Europe: Th Experience of AMC', at the MEDIA Salles round table, *The Impact of Multiplexes on the Cinema Market and on their Environment*, Amsterdam – Cinema Expo International, 15 June 1998. Available at www.mediasalles.it/expo98fr.htm#ing (accessed August 2005).

21 Cited in the *Independent on Sunday*, 4 December 1994.

22 J. Ellis, *Visible Fictions: Cinema, Television, Video*, revised edition (London: Routledge, 1992), p. 25.

23 C. Wilkinson, 'Welcome to Cinema Paradise', *Observer*, 17 August 2003.

24 UK Film Council, *Statistical Yearbook 2004/05*, p. 12.

25 In 1997 annual admissions stood at 137 million. By 2005 the number was 165 million, an increase of approximately 20 per cent.

26 Dodona Research, 'Coming Soon - A Cinema Near You?', presentation given by Karsten-Peter Grummitt at Jesus College, Cambridge, September 1997, www.dodona.co.uk/somethingtoread.html (accessed December 1997).

27 See Cinema Advertisers Association (CAA), *Cinema and Video Industry Audience*

Research (CAVIAR) Number 20, (2003).

28   British Screen Advisory Council, *A Brighter Picture: A Submission to the Chairman of the Film Council by BSAC*, 15 February 2000, p. 8.

29   For a contemporary analysis see B. Edson, 'Commercial Film Distribution and Exhibition in the UK', *Screen*, 21:3 (1980), 36–44.

30   *Sight and Sound*, 57:4 (Autumn 1990), p. 4.

31   *Ibid.*, p. 4.

32   T. Corrigan, *A Cinema without Walls: Movies and Culture after Vietnam* (London: Routledge, 1991), p. 24.

33   W. Buckland, 'A Close Encounter with Raiders of the Lost Ark: Notes on Narrative Aspects of the New Hollywood Blockbuster', in S. Neale and M. Smith (eds), *Contemporary Hollywood Cinema* (London: Routledge, 1998), p. 167.

34   G. Ritzer, *The McDonaldization of Society*, revised edition (Thousand Oaks, CA: Pine Forge Press, 1996), p. 91.

35   M. Jancovich and L. Faire, 'The Best Place to See a Film: The Blockbuster, the Multiplex, and the Contexts of Consumption', in J. Stringer (ed.), *Movie Blockbusters* (London: Routledge, 2003), p. 190.

36   E. Helmore, 'Monsters that are Eating up Hollywood', *Observer*, 28 June 1998. See also T. Shone, *Blockbuster: How Hollywood Learned to Stop Worrying and Love the Summer* (London: Simon & Schuster, 2004).

37   N. Hopkins, 'Movie Budgets Reach for the Sky', *The Times*, 5 March 2005.

38   Department of National Heritage, *A Policy Document, Incorporating the Government's Response to the House of Commons National Heritage Select Committee, The British Film Industry* (London: HMSO, 1995), p. 282.

39   *Ibid.*

40   House of Commons Culture, Media and Sport Committee, *The British Film Industry Sixth Report of Session 2002–03 Volume I Report, together with formal minutes* HC 667-I, 18 September 2003, p. 65.

41   N. Andrew, 'Goodbye to the Big Thrill', *Financial Times Weekend*, 3–4 May 2003.

42   According to The UK Film Council a film like one of the *Harry Potter* series is released in the UK with more than 1,000 film prints. Some larger films might be released with approximately 70 prints, while the average number of prints of a foreign language specialist film available to cinemas at any one time is 8. See 'UK Film Council Announces Million Pound Move to Increase Choice of Films at UK Cinemas', 19 March 2003, at www.ukfilmcouncil.org.uk/news/?p=1048024636125 &skip=150 (accessed July 2005).

43   UK Film Council, *Statistical Yearbook 2004/05*, p. 12.

44   In its report for the UK Film Council KPMG identified 47 cinemas which showed 'Bollywood' films, with 58 screens devoted to these films. See UK Film Council, *Specialised Film Exhibition and Distribution Strategy – Main Report*, KPMG, (January 2002), p. 12. Available at www.ukfilmcouncil.org.uk/filmindustry/specdistexhib.

45   G. Younge, 'The Big Picture', *Guardian*, 26 July 2000.

46   See www.ugccinemas.co.uk/AffichePage.jgi?ALIAS=groupeugc/11a (accessed July 2005).

47   B. Slater, 'Getting it On: Examining Film exhibition in the UK', *Vertigo*, 2:4 (Spring 2003).

48   *Ibid.*, p. 22.

49   J. Harbord, *Film Cultures* (London: Sage, 2002).

50   Slater, 'Getting it On', p. 22.

51   Quoted in M. Clulow, 'A Tear-jerker at the Movies', *Independent on Sunday*, 5 April 1998.

52   Wilkinson, 'Welcome to Cinema Paradise', *Observer*, 17 August 2003.

53   Harbord, *Film Cultures*, p. 43.

54   *Guardian*, 26 September 1998.

55   UK Film Council, *Specialised Film Exhibition and Distribution Strategy*.

56   *Ibid.* p. 8.

57   *Ibid.*

58   See Office of Fair Trading, Decision of the Director General of Fair Trading pursuant to section 14(2) No. CA/98/10/2002 'Notification by the Film Distributors' Association Ltd (formerly the Society of Film Distributors) of its standard conditions for licensing the commercial exhibition of films', 1 February 2002 (Case CP/1321-00/S).

59   Monopolies and Mergers Commission, *Films: A Report on the Supply of Films for Exhibition in Cinemas in the UK*, Cmnd 2673, 1994.

60   *The Films (Exhibition Periods) Order 1996* (SI 1996 No 3140). Made: 12 December 1996. In force: 1 March 1997.

61   Office of Fair Trading, *Review of Orders Following 1983 and 1994 MMC Monopoly Reports on the Supply of Films for Exhibition in Cinemas*, 26 July 2004.

62   *Ibid.*, para. 5.20, p. 27.

63   See UK Film Council, *Film Society Survey 2004: UK Film Council Distribution and Exhibition* (London: UK Film Council, 2005), p. 16.

64   See R. Baker, J. Ron Inglis and J. Voss, *At a Cinema Near You: Strategies for Sustainable Local Cinema Development* (London: British Film Institute, 2002).

65   Quoted in S. Morris, 'Funding Cut could Hit Art Cinemas', *Guardian*, 22 March 2003.

66   Memorandum submitted by the Association of Independent Film Exhibitors, 'Is there a British Film Industry?', House of Commons Culture, Media and Sport Committee, *The British Film Industry Sixth Report of Session 2002-0, Minutes Of Evidence - Volume II* (HC 667-II), 20 May 2003.

67   Owen Thomas, producer Elemental Films, quoted in Department for Culture, Media and Sport (DCMS), *Screen Digest Report on the Implications of Digital Technology for the Film Industry*, 2002, p. 32.

68   N. Watson and R. Morris, *Specialised Exhibition and Distribution: E-Cinema: A Study for the Film Council*, Para, 4.2, p. 5. Available at www.ukfilmcouncil.org.uk/filmindustry/specdistexhib/ (accessed August 2005).

69   For an explanation of the technology see www.dlp.com/dlp_cinema/dlp_cinema_digital_cinema_101.asp (accessed June 2005).

70   UK Film Council, *Statistical Yearbook/Annual Review 2004/05*, p. 43.

71 DCMS, *Screen Digest Report on the Implications of Digital Technology for the Film Industry*, p. 43.

72 Dodona, *Cinemagoing 12* (Dodona Research, Leicester, 2004).

73 London Assembly, *Picture Perfect? A London Assembly Report into the Capital's Cinemas*, Culture, Sport and Tourism Committee, Greater London Authority (October 2003), p. 6.

74 Quoted in the *Guardian*, 10 February 1998.

Select bibliography

Acland, C. R. 'Cinemagoing and the Rise of the Megaplex', *Television & New Media*, 1:4 (2000), 375–402

Acland, C. R. *Screen Traffic: Movies, Multiplexes and Global Culture* (Durham, NC and London: Duke University Press, 2003)

Agajanian, R. '"Just for Kids": Saturday Morning Cinema and Britain's Children's Film Foundation in the 1960s', *Historical Journal of Film, Radio and Television*, 18:3 (1998), 395–409

Aldgate, A. and Richards, J. *Britain Can Take It: The British Cinema in the Second World War*, second edition (Edinburgh: Edinburgh University Press, 1994)

Armes, R. *A Critical History of the British Cinema* (London: Secker and Warburg, 1978)

Atwell, D. *Cathedrals of the Movies: A History of British Cinemas* (London: Architectural Press, 1981)

Auty, M. and Roddick, N. (eds) *British Cinema Now* (London: British Film Institute, 1985)

Baillieu, B. and Goodchild, J. *The British Film Business* (London: John Wiley & Sons, 2002)

Balio, T. (ed.) *The American Film Industry*, revised edition (Madison, WI: The University of Wisconsin Press, 1985)

Bamford, K. *Distorted Images: British National Identity and Film in the 1920s* (London: I. B. Tauris, 1999)

Barnes, J. *The Beginnings of the Cinema in England 1894–1901, Volume One: 1894–1896*, revised and enlarged edition, ed. R. Maltby (Exeter: University of Exeter Press, 1998)

Barnes, J. *The Rise of Cinema in Great Britain, Volume Two: Jubilee Year 1897* (London: Bishopgate Press, 1983)

Barr, C. (ed.) *All Our Yesterdays: 90 Years of British Cinema* (London: British Film Institute, 1986)

Belton, J. *Widescreen Cinema* (Cambridge, MA: Harvard University Press, 1982)

Betts, E. *The Film Business: A History of British Cinema 1896–1972* (London: George Allen & Unwin, 1973)

Blanchard, S. 'Cinemagoing, Going, Gone?', *Screen*, 24:4–5 (July–October 1983), 109–13

Bottomore, S. 'The Panicking Audience?: Early Cinema and the "Train Effect"', *Historical*

Journal of Film, Radio and Television, 19:2 (1999), 177–210

Bottomore, S. '"Nine Days' Wonder": Early Cinema and its Sceptics', in C. Williams (ed.), *Cinema: the Beginnings and the Future* (London: University of Westminster Press, 1996)

Box, K. *The Cinema and the Public* (An Inquiry into Cinema Going Habits and Expenditure Made in 1946), New Series 106 (London: Ministry of Information, 1946)

Browning, H. E. and Sorrell, A. A. 'Cinemas and Cinema–going in Great Britain', *Journal of the Royal Statistical Society*, 117:2 (1954), 133–70

Burrows, J. 'Penny Pleasures: Film Exhibition in London during the Nickelodeon Era, 1906–1914', *Film History*, 16 (2004), 60–91

Butler, I. *'To Encourage the Art of the Film': The Story of the British Film Institute* (London: Robert Hale, 1971)

Cargin, P. (ed.) *An Introduction to Film Societies and the BFFS* (London, British Federation of Film Societies, 1998)

Chanan, M. *The Dream that Kicks: The Prehistory and Early Years of Cinema in Britain*, second edition (London: Routledge, 1996)

Clegg, R. (ed.) *Odeon* (Birmingham: Mercia Cinema Society, 1985)

Commission on Educational and Cultural Films (CECF), *The Film in National Life* (London: George Allen and Unwin, 1932)

Culkin, N. and Randle, K. 'Digital Cinema: Opportunities and Challenges', *Convergence*, 9:4 (Winter 2003), 79–98

Curran, J. and Porter, V. (eds) *British Cinema History* (London: Weidenfeld and Nicolson, 1983)

Denzin, N. *The Cinematic Society: The Voyeur's Gaze* (London, Thousand Oaks, CA and New Delhi: Sage, 1995)

Dickinson, M. and Street, S. *Cinema and State: The Film Industry and the Government 1927–1984* (London: British Film Institute, 1985)

Docherty, D., Morrison, D. and Tracey, M. *The Last Picture Show: Britain's Changing Film Audience* (London: British Film Institute, 1987)

Donald, J., Friedberg, A. and Marcus, L. (eds) *Close up, 1927–1933: Cinema and Modernism* (London: Cassell, 1998)

Doyle, B. 'The Geography of Cinemagoing in Great Britain, 1934–1994: A Comment', *Historical Journal of Film, Radio and Television*, 23:1 (2003), 59–71

Durgnat, R. *A Mirror for England: British Movies from Austerity to Affluence* (London: Faber and Faber, 1970)

Ellis, J. *Visible Fictions: Cinema, Television, Video*, revised edition (London: Routledge, 1992)

Elsaesser, T. (ed.) *Early Cinema: Space, Frame, Narrative* (London: British Film Institute, 1990)

Eyles, A. *ABC: The First Name in Entertainment* (London: Cinema Theatre Association/ British Film Institute, 1993)

Eyles, A. *Gaumont British Cinemas* (London: Cinema Theatre Association/British Film Institute, 1996)

Eyles, A. *The Granada Theatres* (London: Cinema Theatre Association/British Film Institute, 1998)

Eyles, A. *Odeon Cinemas 1: Oscar Deutsch Entertains Our Nation* (London: Cinema Theatre Association/British Film Institute, 2002)

Eyles, A. *Odeon Cinemas 2: From J. Arthur Rank to the Multiplex* (London: Cinema Theatre Association/British Film Institute, 2005)

Fullerton, J. (ed.) *Celebrating 1895: The Centenary of Cinema* (Sydney, Australia: John Libbey and the National Museum of Photography, Film and Television, Bradford, 1998)

Geraghty, C. *British Cinema in the Fifties: Gender, Genre and the 'New Look'* (London: Routledge, 2000)

Glancy, H. M. *When Hollywood Loved Britain: The Hollywood 'British' film 1939–45* (Manchester: Manchester University Press, 1999)

Gledhill, C. *Reframing British Cinema 1918–1928: Between Restraint and Passion* (London: British Film Institute, 2003)

Gomery, D. *Shared Pleasures: A History of Movie Presentation in the United States* (London: British Film Institute, 1992)

Gray, R. *Cinemas in Britain: 100 Years of Cinema Architecture* (London: Cinema Theatre Association/British Film Institute, 1996)

Gunning, T. 'The Cinema of Attractions: Early Film, its Spectator and the Avant–Garde', in T. Elsaesser (ed.), *Early Cinema: Space, Frame, Narrative* (London: British Film Institute, 1990), first published in *Wide Angle*, 8:3/4 (1986), 63–70

Hall, S. and Whannel, P. *The Popular Arts* (London: Hutchinson Educational, 1964)

Hanson, S. 'Spoilt for Choice? Multiplexes in the 90s', in R. Murphy (ed.), *British Cinema of the 90s* (London: British Film Institute, 2000)

Harbord, J. *Film Cultures* (London: Sage, 2002)

Harding, C. and Lewis, B. (eds) *Talking Pictures: The Popular Experience of the Cinema* (Castleford: Yorkshire Arts Circus/Bradford: National Museum of Photography, Film and Television

Harding, C. and Popple, S. *In the Kingdom of Shadows: A Companion to Early Cinema* (London: Cygnus Arts, 1996)

Hark, R. (ed.) *Exhibition: The Film Reader* (London: Routledge, 2002)

Harper, S. 'A Lower Middle-Class Taste-Community in the 1930s: Admissions Figures at the Regent Cinema, Portsmouth, UK', *Historical Journal of Film, Radio and Television*, 24:4 (2004), 565–87

Harper, S. and Porter, V. *British Cinema of the 1950s: The Decline of Deference* (Oxford: Oxford University Press, 2003)

Hartog, S. 'State Protection of a Beleaguered Industry', in J. Curran and V. Porter (eds), *British Cinema History* (London: Weidenfeld and Nicolson, 1983)

Hayward, P. and Wollen, T. (eds) *Future Visions: New Technologies of the Screen* (London: British Film Institute, 1993)

Herbert, S. *A History of Early Film: Volumes 1–3* (London: Routledge, 2000)

Herbert, S. *A History of Pre-Cinema: Volumes 1–3* (London: Routledge, 2000)

Herbert, S. and McKernan, L. (eds) *Who's Who of Victorian Cinema: A Worldwide Survey*

(London: British Film Institute, 1996)

Higson, A. 'The Discourses of British Film Year', *Screen*, 27:1 (January–February 1986), 86–109

Higson, A. (ed.) *Young and Innocent?: The Cinema in Britain 1896–1930* (Exeter: University of Exeter Press, 2002)

Higson, A. and Maltby, R. (eds) *'Film Europe' and 'Film America': Cinema, Commerce and Cultural Exchange 1920–1939* (Exeter: Exeter University Press, 1999)

Hiley, N. '"At the Picture Palace": The British Cinema Audience, 1895–1920', in J. Fullerton (ed.), *Celebrating 1895: The Centenary of Cinema* (Sydney, Australia: John Libbey and the National Museum of Photography, Film and Television, Bradford, 1998)

Hiley, N. '"Let's Go to the Pictures": The British Cinema Audience in the 1920s and 1930s', *Journal of Popular British Cinema*, 2 (1999), 39–53

Hiley, N. '"No Mixed Bathing": The Creation of the British Board of Film Censors in 1913', *Journal of Popular British Cinema*, 3 (2000), 5–19

Hiley, N. 'Nothing More than a "Craze": Cinema Building in Britain from 1909 to 1914', in A. Higson, *Young and Innocent?: The Cinema in Britain 1896–1930* (Exeter: University of Exeter Press, 2002)

Hill, J. *Sex, Class and Realism: British Cinema 1956–1963* (London: British Film Institute, 1986)

Hill, J. 'Government Policy and the British Film Industry 1979–90', *European Journal of Communication*, 8:2 (1993), 203–24

Hill, J. *British Cinema in the 1980s* (Oxford: Oxford University Press, 1999)

Hill, J. 'Contemporary British Cinema: Industry, Policy, Identity', *Cineaste*, 26:4 (2001), 30–3

Hill, J. and McLoone, M. (eds) *Big Picture Small Screen: The Relations Between Film and Television* (Luton: University of Luton Press, 1996)

Hogenkamp, B. *Deadly Parallels: Film and the Left in Britain 1929–39* (London: Lawrence and Wishart, 1986)

Holmes, S. 'A Night in at the Cinema: The Film Premiere on 1950s British Television', *Journal of British Film and Television*, 2:2 (2005), 208–26

Houston, P. *The Contemporary Cinema* (Harmondsworth, Penguin, 1963)

Hubbard, P. 'Screen-shifting: Consumption, "Riskless Risks" and the Changing Geographies of Cinema', *Environment and Planning A*, 34:7 (July 2002), 1239–58

Hubbard, P. 'A Good Night Out? Multiplex Cinemas as Sites of Embodied Leisure', *Leisure Studies* 22 (July 2003) 255–72

Hunnings, N. M. *Film Censors and the Law* (London: Allen and Unwin, 1967)

Jackson, A. *Semi-Detached London: Suburban Development, Life and Transport, 1900–39*, second edition (Didcot: Wild Swan Publications, 1991)

Jancovich, M. and Faire, L. with Stubbings, S. *The Place of the Audience: Cultural Geographies of Film Consumption* (London: British Film Institute, 2003)

Jarvie, I. 'British Trade Policy versus Hollywood, 1947–1948: "Food before flicks"?', *Historical Journal of Film, Radio and Television*, 6:1 (1986), 19–41

Kuhn, A. 'Cinema-going in Britain in the 1930s: Report of a Questionnaire Survey',

Historical Journal of Film, Radio and Television, 19:4 (1999), 531–43

Kuhn, A. *An Everyday Magic: Cinema and Cultural Memory* (London: I. B. Tauris, 2002)

Laing, S. *Representations of Working Class Life 1957–1964* (London: Macmillan, 1986)

Lewis, S. 'Local Authorities and the Control of Film Exhibition in Britain in the Interwar Period', *Journal of Popular British Cinema*, 3 (2000), 113–20

Low, R. *The History of the British Film 1918–1929* (London: George Allen & Unwin, 1971)

Low, R. *The History of the British Film 1906–1914* (London: George Allen & Unwin, [1949] 1973)

Low, R. *The History of the British Film 1914–1918* (London: George Allen & Unwin, [1950] 1973)

Low, R. *The History of the British Film 1929–1939: Film Making in 1930s Britain* (London: Allen & Unwin, 1985)

Low, R. and Manvell, R. *The History of British Film 1896–1906* (London: George Allen & Unwin [1948] 1973)

McKibbin, R. *Classes and Cultures in England 1918–1951* (Oxford: Oxford University Press, 1998)

Macnab, G. *J. Arthur Rank and the British Film Industry* (London: Routledge, 1994)

Maltby, R. '"D" for Disgusting: American Culture and English Criticism', in G. Nowell-Smith and S. Ricci (eds), *Hollywood and Europe: Economics, Culture and National Identity 1945–95* (London: British Film Institute, 1998)

Mannoni, L. *The Great Art of Light and Shadow: Archaeology of the Cinema*, trans. and ed. Crangle, R. (Exeter: University of Exeter Press, 2000)

Manvell, R. *The Film and the Public* (Harmondsworth: Penguin, 1955)

Mayer, J. P. *Sociology of Film* (London: Faber and Faber, 1946)

Mayer, J. P. *British Cinemas and Their Audience* (London: Dobson, 1948)

Miles, P. and Smith, M. *Cinema, Literature & Society: Elite and Mass Culture in Interwar Britain* (London: Croom Helm, 1987)

Miller, T., Govil, N., McMurrin, J., Maxwell, R. and Wang, T. *Global Hollywood 2* (London: British Film Institute, 2005)

Moran, A. (ed.) *Film Policy: International, National and Regional Perspectives* (London: Routledge, 1996)

Moss, L. and Box, K. *The Cinema Audience* (An enquiry made by the Wartime Social Survey for The Ministry of Information), New Series, No. 37b, June–July, 1943

Murphy, R. 'Coming of Sound to the Cinema in Britain', *Historical Journal of Film, Radio and Television*, 4:2 (1984), 143–60

Murphy, R. *Realism and Tinsel: Cinema and Society in Britain, 1939–48* (London: Routledge, 1989)

Murphy, R. (ed.), *British Cinema of the 90s* (London: British Film Institute, 2000)

Murphy, R. (ed.) *The British Cinema Book*, second edition (London: British Film Institute, 2001)

National Council of Public Morals, Cinema Commission, *The Cinema: Its Present Position and Future Possibilities* (London: Williams and Norgate, 1917) reprinted in full in S. Herbert, *A History of Early Film: Volume 3* (London: Routledge, 2000)

Olins, W. 'The best place to see a film?', *Sight and Sound*, 54:4 (Autumn 1985), 241–4

PEP (Political and Economic Planning) *The Factual Film: A Survey by The Arts Enquiry* (London: Oxford University Press, 1947)

PEP *The British Film Industry* (London: Political and Economic Planning Office, 1952)

PEP *The British Film Industry 1958* (London: Political and Economic Planning Office, 1958)

Poole, J. 'British Cinema Attendance in Wartime: Audience Preference at the Majestic, Macclesfield, 1939–1946', *Historical Journal of Film, Radio and Television*, 7:1 (1987) 15–34

Puttnam, D. *The Undeclared War: The Struggle for Control of the World's Film Industry* (London: Harper Collins, 1997)

Richards, H. 'Memory Reclamation of Cinema Going in Bridgend, South Wales, 1930–1960', *Historical Journal of Film, Radio and Television*, 23:4 (2003), 341–55

Richards, J. 'The British Board of Film Censors and Content Control in the 1930s: Images of Britain', *Historical Journal of Film, Radio and Television*, 1:2 (1981), 95–116

Richards, J. 'The British Board of Film Censors and Content Control in the 1930s: Foreign Affairs', *Historical Journal of Film, Radio and Television*, 2:1 (1982), 39–48

Richards, J. *The Age of the Dream Palace: Cinema and Society in Britain 1930–1939* (London: Routledge & Kegan Paul, 1984)

Richards, J. 'Cinema-going in Worktown: Regional Film Audiences in 1930s Britain', *Historical Journal of Film, Radio and Television*, 14:2 (1994), 147–66

Richards, J. *Films and British National Identity* (Manchester: Manchester University Press, 1997)

Richards, J. 'British Film Censorship', in R. Murphy (ed.), *The British Cinema Book*, second edition (London: British Film Institute, 2001)

Richards, J. (ed.) *The Unknown 1930s: An Alternative History of the British Cinema, 1929–39* (London: I. B. Tauris, 1998)

Richards, J. and Sheridan, D. *Mass-Observation at the Movies* (London: Routledge & Kegan Paul, 1987)

Robertson, J. C. *The British Board of Film Censors: Film Censorship in Britain, 1896–1950* (London: Croom Helm, 1985)

Rossell, D. 'A Chronology of Cinema 1889–1896', *Film History*, 7:2 (1995), 115–236

Rowson, S. 'A Statistical Survey of the Cinema Industry in Great Britain in 1934', *Journal of the Royal Statistical Society*, XCIX (1936), 67–129

Ryall, T. *Britain and the American Cinema* (London, Thousand Oaks, CA and New Delhi: Sage, 2001)

Sedgwick, J. 'The Market for Feature Films in Britain, 1934: A Viable National Cinema', *Historical Journal of Film, Radio and Television*, 14:1 (1994), 15–36

Sedgwick, J. *Popular Filmgoing in 1930s Britain: A Choice of Pleasure* (Exeter: University of Exeter Press, 2000)

Shafer, S. *British Popular Films 1929–1939: the Cinema of Reassurance* (London: Routledge, 1997)

Shand, P. M. *Modern Theatres and Cinemas: The Architecture of Pleasure* (London: B. T. Batsford, 1930)

Shapiro Sanders, L. '"Indecent Incentives to Vice": Regulating Films and Audience Behaviour from the 1890s to the 1910s', in A. Higson, *Young and Innocent? The Cinema in Britain 1896–1930* (Exeter: University of Exeter Press, 2002)

Sharp, D. *The Picture Palace and Other Buildings of the Movies* (London: Hugh Evelyn, 1969)

Sinfield, A. *Literature, Politics and Culture in Postwar Britain* (London and Atlantic Highlands, NJ: The Athlone Press, 1997)

Smith, J. 'Cinema for Sale: The Impact of the Multiplex on Cinema-Going in Britain, 1985–2000', *Journal of British Film and Television*, 2:2 (2005), 242–55

Smith, S. J. *Children, Cinema and Censorship: From Dracula to the Dead End Kids* (London: I. B. Tauris, 2005)

Smith, S. J. 'A Riot at the Palace: Children's Cinema-going in 1930s Britain', *Journal of British Film and Television*, 2:2 (2005), 275–89

Spraos, J. *The Decline of the Cinema: An Economist's Report* (London: George Allen & Unwin, 1962)

Staples, T. *All Pals Together: The Story of Children's Cinema* (Edinburgh: Edinbury University Press, 1997)

Stead, P. *Film and the Working Class: The Feature Film in British and American Society* (London: Routledge, 1989)

Stokes, M. and Maltby, R. (eds) *Identifying Hollywood's Audiences: Cultural Identity and the Movies* (London: British Film Institute, 1999)

Stokes, M. and Maltby, R. (eds) *Hollywood Spectatorship: Changing Perceptions of Cinema Audiences* (London: British Film Institute, 2001)

Stones, B. *America Goes to the Movies: 100 Years of Motion Picture Exhibition* (Hollywood: National Association of Theater Owners, 1993)

Street, S. *British National Cinema* (London: Routledge, 1997)

Strinati, D. and Wagg, S. (eds) *Come on Down? Popular Media Culture in Post-war Britain* (London: Routledge, 1992)

Swann, P. *The Hollywood Feature Film in Postwar Britain* (London: Croom Helm, 1987)

Toulmin, V. 'Telling the Tale: The Story of the Fairground Bioscope Shows and the Showmen who Operated Them', *Film History*, 6 (1994), 219–37

Valentine, M. *The Show Starts on the Sidewalk: An architectural History of the Movie Theatre, Starring S. Charles Lee* (New Haven, CT and London: Yale University Press, 1994)

Wasko, J. *How Hollywood Works* (London: Sage 2003)

Williams, C. (ed.) *Cinema: The Beginnings and the Future* (London: University of Westminster Press, 1996)

Williams, D. 'The Cinematograph Act of 1909: An Introduction to the Impetus Behind the Legislation and Some Early Effects', *Film History*, 9 (1997), 341–50

Williams, D. 'Never on Sunday: The Early Operation of the Cinematograph Act of 1909 in regard to Sunday Opening', *Film History*, 14 (2002), 186–94

Williams, R. 'Cinema and Socialism', in Tony Pinkney (ed.), *The Politics of Modernism* (London: Verso, 1996)

Index

Note: 'n.' after a page reference indicates the number of a note on that page